"As the British Constitution is the most subtle organism which has proceeded from progressive history, so the American Constitution is the most wonderful work ever struck off at a given time by the brain and purpose of man."
WILLIAM E. GLADSTONE.

"The example of changing a constitution, by assembling the wise men of the State, instead of assembling armies, will be worth as much to the world as the former examples we had given them. The Constitution, too, which was the result of our deliberations, is unquestionably the wisest ever presented to men."
THOMAS JEFFERSON.

OUR UNKNOWN CONSTITUTION

(Understandably Written for the Layman)

By

WILLIAM HARMAN BLACK

JUSTICE OF THE SUPREME COURT OF THE STATE OF NEW YORK;
AUTHOR OF "NEW YORK AND NEW JERSEY CORPORATIONS,"
"A REAL CRIMINAL CASE," AND "HOW TO CONDUCT
A CRIMINAL CASE."

REAL BOOK COMPANY
Woolworth Building
NEW   YORK   CITY

PHILADELPHIA
DAVID McKAY COMPANY
WASHINGTON SQUARE

Copyright, 1933, by
WILLIAM HARMAN BLACK

MANUFACTURED COMPLETE BY
KINGSPORT PRESS, Inc.
KINGSPORT, TENNESSEE
United States of America

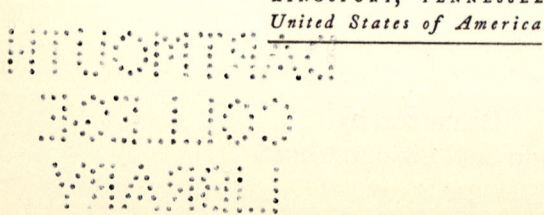

*With his permission, this volume is inscribed
to that profound statesman, devoted
defender of the Constitution and
progressive American,*

HOMER S. CUMMINGS,

*Attorney General of the
United States*

TO THE READER

OUR ignorance of our own Constitution is a national crime.

When you have heard the words "Constitution" or "Constitutional," your first shuddery reaction was that you were about to listen to something very profound about a very mysterious document adopted sometime in the early days of the Republic. With this vague picture in your mind, you at once decided that as it was far too deep for you, you had better go to another subject. As a matter of fact, the Constitution is the briefest and simplest instrument ever penned by earnest and sincere statesmen.

You may be surprised to learn that this Constitution, which embodies mankind's loftiest purposes, was conceived in a patriotic subterfuge on the part of the leaders who wrote it. The story of this episode and others like it, make the subject as fascinating as a romance.

You have probably never realized that the people of the *United States* live under forty-nine Constitutions. They all live under the *Federal* or *United States* Constitution, and every one of them also lives under one of the forty-eight *State* Constitutions. These *State* Constitutions and all Federal or national laws must conform to the *United States* Constitution, and all the laws of the *States* must not only conform to the Constitution of the *United States* but to the Constitution of the particular *State* that passes them. James Madison said that "a law violative of a constitution established by the people themselves would be considered by the judges null and void."

The several *States* have the right to construe their own constitution and laws as they see fit, so long as they do not infringe upon the Federal Constitution and the laws of the *United States,* or upon the rights of citizens of other *States*.

As you go deeper into the Constitution, you will find that hair-splitters have tried to complicate it, and that sectional, industrial, or financial groups have sought under it the very advantages which its framers determined they should never have. You will find, too, that tinkerers, with no fundamental knowledge of its purposes, have sought to bend it to their desires, and that *State* leaders have sought sometimes to hold the *national* Government to too strict compliance with its provisions, and that *national* leaders have sought to encroach upon the rights of the *States*.

You will find, too, that the views of men are constantly veering with regard to the Constitution, because political points of view are in constant flux, and because some of the present generation consider it only in the light of changed financial, agricultural, mechanical, and transportation conditions.

Our country is in the midst of vital changes, and in these days of new laws and cinematic public sentiment it is imperatively necessary to know upon what foundation our *national* Government was built by the *States*. But in order to form just conclusions, you must know definitely of the times that were the setting for the adoption by Congress of our Declaration of Independence in 1776, the Articles of Confederation which followed it through the action of Congress in March, 1781, and the Constitution that was recommended by the Constitutional Convention in September, 1787, and adopted by conventions of the people of the *States* during the period from December, 1787, to May, 1790.

As you have probably not read the *United States* Constitution, and none of the forty-eight *State* Constitutions, when a new law is passed you are, of course, unable to form any opinion as to whether or not such a law is or is not constitutional. The same is also true of old laws whose constitutionality is frequently not attacked until many years after they are passed.

However well intentioned you may be as to obeying the Constitution of the *United States* or the Constitution of the *State* you live in, proper respect for and obedience to these Constitutions are not easy for you. You feel that you cannot understand them unless you are a "profound Constitutional lawyer."

The Constitution of the *United States* is a contract entered into between the *United States* Government, the *people* of the *United States* as citizens of the *United States*, the *States* as *States*, and the citizens of the *States*, and nothing short of the statesmanship of our forefathers could possibly have steered it through the storms that beset every effort to enact it.

The Declaration of Independence, adopted by the "representatives of the *United States* of America in Congress assembled," was signed by the *States*, followed by the names of their representatives.

The Constitution of the *United States* covers seven articles with twenty-six sections in the Constitution itself, and twenty articles with thirty-six sections in the amendments. It was also signed by the *States* when adopted at the Constitutional Convention, before being submitted through Congress to each separate *State* for ratification or rejection by *State* conventions.

You will bear in mind that both the Articles of Confederation and the Constitution were enacted as Federal[1] charters of government for the united *Colonies* or *States* after they had announced their separation from England by the passage by Congress of the Declaration of Independence, July 4th, 1776.

The Articles of Confederation, which were adopted by Congress in 1781, were faulty in that they dealt with *States*. They did not properly reach the individual citizen. The Confederation was merely a so-called "League of Friendship," and could take no effective action without nine *States,* or two-thirds of the thirteen. Five *States* could block anything. Every *State* had to vote for amendments before they could be adopted. This made it practically an unchangeable instrument. One fatal weakness was the lack of a Federal judiciary; another, that it had no power to prescribe a national monetary system; another, that it did not regulate interstate commerce, and another, that it could not enforce the collection of taxes. These defects were recognized, and in the wisdom of the fathers of the Republic there resulted the Annapolis Convention in 1786, where "commissioners" represented the various *States*. At this Convention there were not enough *States* represented to adopt a Constitution. So the Convention adjourned to Philadelphia,

---

[1] "Federal" means "pertaining to or derived from a compact between the *States*," which by the terms of the compact surrender their general *sovereignty* and consolidate into a new *State,* as a "federal *union*."

where finally all the *States* were represented. The representatives of these *States* in the Convention agreed on a form of Constitution, which on September 17th, 1787, was signed by all the *States* except Rhode Island, and transmitted to Congress on that day; on September 28th, 1787, Congress submitted the Constitution to the thirteen *States* for ratification or rejection. It became effective June 21st, 1788, after ratification by nine *States*—Virginia and New Hampshire sharing the honor on the same day. On the 29th day of May, 1790, Rhode Island, holding the last of the thirteen *State* conventions, ratified the Constitution. There were no more *State* conventions of the *people* to pass on any part of the Constitution until the Twenty-first or Prohibition Repeal Amendment was submitted to the *States* by Congress in 1933.

If and when the *people* repeal the Eighteenth Amendment, it will be the first amendment ever repealed. Even when there has been an amendment adopted, the original section still appears in the Constitution as it was before amendment.

As soon as the *national* Constitution was ratified by the *States* it became in respect to the powers ceded to the *United States* greater than the *States* which ceded these powers. From the moment of its adoption the Constitution of the *United States* prohibited any provision in any of the *State* Constitutions as then adopted, or thereafter to be adopted, which would violate the provisions of this *national* Constitution to which all the *States* had agreed. So that our *national* Constitution is the very base upon which rest not only the material rights of our citizens as citizens of the *United States,* but also the rights of the citizens of the

States continued or organized under the Constitution of the *United States*.

James Bryce says in his *Studies in History and Jurisprudence* that:

> Not one of the forecasts of the opponents of the Constitution has proved true. The *States* are still strong, the President is not a despot, though for a time during the Civil War he came near being one, nor has he ever fallen under the influence of any European power. The House does not consist of the "wealthy and well-born." The larger *States* do not combine against nor press hardly on the smaller. No great country has had so few wars or indeed so few foreign complications of any kind. The Senate is still often called "an oligarchy," but this means only that it consists of comparatively few persons, most of them wealthy, and that it has a strong corporate feeling in favor of the personal interests of each of its members. It is really as dependent on public opinion as the House, perhaps even more afraid of public opinion, and as directly the creature of party machinery, though less directly of popular election.
>
> One is surprised to find that of the many arrows of accusation levelled at the Constitution, all should have flown wide of the mark.

and on page 431 he says:

> Differences upon questions of legislation are always liable to produce deadlocks. There is no remedy for such a situation. The only recourse in case of difference is to try to get the two Houses to agree through the mediation of conferees appointed by both Houses. If they can compromise the differences, their agreement is confirmed by both Houses. If they fail, there is nothing more to be done at the time.

I have discussed the rights of the Federal Government, the rights of the *States,* the rights of the citizens, the rights of civil litigants, and of men accused of crimes, and political rights.

I have given particular attention to the relationship

between Congress and the Supreme Court, between Congress and the *people* of the *United States,* between the Supreme Court and the *people* of the *United States,* between the Supreme Court and the Government of the *United States,* and between the Supreme Court and the *States.*

I have given short descriptions of the personality of the men who wrote the Constitution and pen portraits of the more important figures who took part. The notes at the bottom of each page give the authorities for the statements of fact.

The best of the old books on the Constitution are by the historian Bancroft and by the great Supreme Court Justice Story. Professor Willoughby of Johns Hopkins University has written the most comprehensive modern treatise on it. The first two were published before the selfishness of sections or interests or classes had sought to rend it, and they reflect the enduring view of the great purposes for which the Constitution was written. I make no apology for so frequently quoting from Professor Lee's *The Story of the American Constitution.* It is the latest and best popular volume on the subject.

But the total pages of the early monumental books alone are well over twenty thousand. So this volume is written for the man or woman who has not the time nor the inclination to wade through these weighty tomes to find out what the Constitution is.

The Constitutional Convention kept very imperfect records of its sessions, which were held in secret. But Madison kept a wonderful diary, which was published fifty years later, after he had died. Later, there came to light the notes of Hamilton, Yates, Pierce, McHenry, and Paterson.

This book tells how and when the Constitution was amended in the first ten amendments, known as the "Bill of Rights," and why and how and when it was amended ten more times after the adoption of the "Bill of Rights." I have also briefly shown some of the results of the adoption of the Constitution, how workable it is, and whether or not certain parts of it should be amended or repealed, and how this may be accomplished.

The notes have been inserted for those readers who care to go more fully into any point discussed.

A later volume will discuss the more technical points involved.

WILLIAM HARMAN BLACK.

New York, October, 1933.

CONTENTS

CHAPTER		PAGE
	FOREWORD	V
I	THE SPIRIT OF THE CONSTITUTION	1
II	THE PEOPLE OF THE DIFFERENT AMERICAN COLONIES WERE OF DIFFERENT NATIONAL STOCKS	6
III	AMERICA'S EARLIEST IMPULSES TO COLLECTIVE ACTION—THE BOSTON TEA PARTY	12
IV	THE DECLARATION OF INDEPENDENCE—PREPARATION FOR WAR—ARTICLES OF CONFEDERATION	19
V	THE ARTICLES OF CONFEDERATION ARE REFERRED TO STATES	27
VI	ARTICLES OF CONFEDERATION ADOPTED BY THE STATES—THEIR AMENDMENT DISCUSSED	35
VII	A PATRIOTIC SUBTERFUGE TO REORGANIZE THE UNITED STATES	43
VIII	THE PEOPLE AND THE STATES	54
IX	ARE WE A NATION OF PEOPLE, OR A UNION OF STATES, OR BOTH?	59
X	TROUBLES WITH THE ARMY—HELPLESSNESS OF THE GOVERNMENT	64
XI	THE DELEGATES TO THE CONSTITUTIONAL CONVENTION	72
XII	PROCEEDINGS IN THE CONSTITUTIONAL CONVENTION AND IN CONGRESS	79
XIII	RATIFYING THE CONSTITUTION	148
XIV	A BRIEF ANALYSIS OF THE CONSTITUTION AND ITS AMENDMENTS	162
XV	AMENDING THE CONSTITUTION	203
XVI	SHALL CONGRESS REFER AMENDMENTS TO THE CONSTITUTION FOR ADOPTION OR REJECTION BY THE STATES, TO STATE LEGISLATURES, OR TO CONVENTIONS CHOSEN BY THE PEOPLE OF EACH STATE?	218

CHAPTER		PAGE
XVII	THE NINTH AND TENTH AMENDMENTS	228
	SUMMARY	250
	APPENDIX A: PARALLEL COMPARISON OF ARTICLES OF CONFEDERATION AND THE CONSTITUTION	251
	APPENDIX B: PARALLEL COMPARISON OF THE "VIRGINIA" AND THE "NEW JERSEY" PLANS CONSIDERED IN THE CONSTITUTIONAL CONVENTION	261
	APPENDIX C: SUMPTUARY LAWS	281
	APPENDIX D: HOW RHODE ISLAND RATIFIED THE CONSTITUTION	283

AUTHORITIES MOST FREQUENTLY QUOTED IN THIS VOLUME

Bancroft, George, *History of the Formation of the Constitution of the United States of America;* 2 vols. D. Appleton & Co., New York, 1882.

Beard, Charles A. and Mary R., *The Rise of American Civilization;* 2 vols. The Macmillan Co., New York, 1928.

Beck, James M., *The Constitution of the United States.* Doubleday, Doran & Co., New York, 1928.

Burdick, Charles K., *The Law of the American Constitution.* G. P. Putnam's Sons, New York, 1923.

Elliot, Jonathan, *Debates on the Federal Constitution;* 5 vols. J. B. Lippincott, Philadelphia, 1836.

Encyclopædia Britannica, fourteenth edition. The Encyclopædia Britannica Co., Ltd., London and New York, 1929.

Farrand, Max, *The Records of the Federal Convention of 1787;* 3 vols. Yale University Press, New Haven, 1911.

Federalist, The; edited by Henry Cabot Lodge. G. P. Putnam's Sons, New York, 1888.

Fiske, John, *The Critical Period of American History, 1773–1789.* Houghton, Mifflin Co., Boston and New York, 1888, 1916.

Lee, Howard B., *The Story of the Constitution.* The Michie Co., Charlottesville, Va., 1932.

Madison, James, Papers of (Diary of the Proceedings of the Constitutional Convention); edited by H. D. Gilpin. Langtree & O'Sullivan, Washington, 1840.

Story, Joseph, *Commentaries on the Constitution of the United States;* 2 vols. Little, Brown & Co., Boston, 1891.

Warren, Charles, *The Making of the Constitution.* Little, Brown & Co., Boston, 1928.

Willoughby, Westel Woodbury, *The Constitutional Law of the United States;* 3 vols., second edition. Baker, Voorhis & Co., New York, 1929.

Wilson, Woodrow, *Constitutional Government in the United States.* Columbia University Press, New York, 1908.

OUR UNKNOWN CONSTITUTION

CHAPTER I

THE SPIRIT OF THE CONSTITUTION [1]

THE spirit of the Constitution does not mean the spirit of the men who framed the Constitution. It means only so much of their spirit as they specifically embodied in the Constitution itself. Unfortunately, since the Supreme Court of the *United States* decided, in United States *vs*. Trans-Missouri Freight Association,[2] that the legislative history of a statute is not controlling in construing a statute, the spirit of the framers of the Constitution really makes very little difference, except to the extent that it was crystallized in the written provisions of the Constitution itself. The only instances in which we can consider the spirit

---

[1] On April 6th, 1796, James Madison said: "After all, whatever veneration might be entertained for the body of men who formed our Constitution, the sense of that body could never be regarded as the oracular guide in expounding the Constitution. As the instrument came from them, it was nothing more than a draft of the plan, nothing but a dead letter, until life and validity were breathed into it by the voice of the *people,* speaking through the *State* Conventions. If we were to look, therefore, for the meaning of that instrument beyond the face of the instrument, we must look for it, not in the General Convention which proposed, but in the *State* Conventions which accepted and ratified it." (Warren's *The Making of the Constitution*, p. 794.)

[2] 166 United States Reports, p. 318.

of the framers of the Constitution are those instances where one particular proposition, or two alternative propositions, were voted upon. In a particular case, the vote that carried a proposal would specifically show that it embodied the sentiment of the members of the Constitutional Convention. A vote against it would show that it did not contain sentiments that the Convention favored. Where two alternative propositions were presented, a vote for one would show that the sentiment of the members of the Convention was for it, and that it was a vote against the views embodied in the alternative or opposite proposal.

"There is, too, a general acquiescence in the doctrine that debates in Congress are not appropriate sources from which to discover the meaning of this language of a statute passed by that body. . . ." "The reason is that it is impossible to determine with certainty what construction was put upon an act by the members of a legislative body that passed it by resorting to the speeches of individual members thereof. Those who did not speak may not have agreed with those who did; and those who spoke might differ from each other, the result being that the only proper way to construe a legislative act is from the language used in the United States *vs.* Trans-Missouri Freight Association, 166 U. S. p. 318.

"Closely allied to the assertion that the Constitution is to be interpreted in the light of the 'natural law,' is the doctrine that the fundamental purpose of the Constitutional Fathers was the erection of a free republican government, and that, therefore, the Constitution should, whatever its express terms may provide, never be so construed as to violate the abstract principles deducible from this fundamental fact. Generally speaking, whereas the so-called natural laws have reference to the private rights of the citizen, the protection of his person and property, these principles claimed to be deducible from the spirit of the Constitution as the framework of a free government have reference to the public and political rights of the individual.

"Stated in this abstract, philosophical form, the doctrine that the 'spirit' of the Constitution is to prevail over its language has no more legal validity than has the doctrine of natural law." [3]

"The courts in considering the constitutionality of a statute hold themselves bound by the words of the statute, that is, they determine the intent of the legislature by the words it has employed." [4]

The Government of the *United States* is a unique piece of machinery where the gears of the big wheel, representing the *national* or *Federal* Government, seldom mesh with the gears of the forty-eight small wheels representing the *States* that make up the *Union*. One of the few times the teeth of the two sets of wheels do mesh is when there is an appeal from the *State* courts to the Supreme Court of the *United States*. When there is a conflict between the *State* courts and the lower *United States* courts, the gears do not mesh, but they do strike and grind. The *State* courts seldom seek to interfere with the *United States* courts, but the *United States* courts do frequently intervene in cases where the *State* courts claim jurisdiction. These conflicts of jurisdiction have usually resulted in the retention of the controversy by the *United States* courts.

[3] Willoughby's *The Constitutional Law of the United States,* Vol. I, pp. 67, 68.
[4] *Ibid.,* p. 55.

This causes bitter charges of usurpation against the *United States* courts. Recently the Supreme Court of the *United States* has sent back to a *State* court a case involving the enforcement of a *State* law.[5] This has greatly increased the popularity of the Supreme Court of the *United States*.

The Constitution which was adopted by the Constitutional Convention began in a patriotic subterfuge and ended in a nonsectional and unselfish compromise.[6] It did not entirely please any element, but it represented an accommodation of the views of divergent groups, separated by sharp lines of self-interest. It was primarily a compromise between the men who represented the interests of the small *States* and those who represented the interests of the big *States*. The small *States* had small populations. The big *States* had comparatively big populations. The leaders of the small *States* were afraid that if the Government was to be conducted entirely by popular vote, the large population of the big *States* would overwhelm the sparse populations of the small *States*. So the small *States* refused to agree to the Constitution that the Constitutional Convention finally adopted unless the big *States* agreed in the Constitution to give each of them the same representation in the Senate that the big *States* were to have. The little *States* also made the big *States* agree that the article in the Constitution

[5] The case I refer to was the five cents fare controversy, where the District Court of the *United States* temporarily enjoined the Transit Commission and the city of New York from enforcing the five cents fare that the subway company had by written contract agreed to. The reason for this injunction was that the subway company claimed that to cause it to carry out its contract to transport passengers for five cents would confiscate its property or revenue. (Gilchrist *vs.* Interborough Rapid Transit Co., 279 U. S. 159.)

[6] See chapter 7, page 43.

stating how the Constitution should be amended should provide that no amendment could be adopted without the approval of three-fourths of the *States* acting as *States*. The *States* with small populations believed they would always be able to muster, in their defense against unfair amendments, more than one-fourth of the whole number of the *States* of the *Union*. This would, under Article V of the Constitution (which provides how it shall be amended), enable the small *States* to block any proposed Constitutional provision that they should consider unjust to them.

As an additional protection to the rights of the small *States*, Article V provides "that no *State*, without its consent, shall be deprived of its equal suffrage in the Senate." [7]

[7] That is, two Senators from each *State*.

CHAPTER II

THE PEOPLE OF THE DIFFERENT AMERICAN COLONIES WERE OF DIFFERENT NATIONAL STOCKS

ONE of the most striking features about the organization of the *United States* is that the Colonies which made it up were founded by rival powers."[1]

The Venetian, John Cabot, was sent on a voyage of discovery by Henry VII of England. He found Newfoundland and the St. John Islands in 1495, then he went from the 56th[2] to the 38th[3] degree of north latitude. For England he claimed all the land from the 38th degree to the Gulf of Mexico.

The first conflict in America[4] was between England and the Indians, who refused to recognize the right of any other country to their lands.

The first charter granted by England to any American territory was that by James I to Sir Thomas Gates and others, between the 34th[5] and 45th[6] degrees of north latitude. An "enlarged" charter was granted to the Treasurer and Company of Adventurers of London, for the first colony in Virginia.[7]

[1] Bancroft's *History of the Constitution of the United States*, Vol. I, p. 6.
[2] Cape Harrigan, Labrador.
[3] Mouth of Chesapeake Bay.
[4] Black's *Lincoln the Democrat*, p. 4.
[5] Wilmington, N. C.
[6] Cape Hatteras.
[7] Story's *Commentaries on the Constitution of the United States*, p. 11.

The Colonists in the Colonies granted by the English Crown were not wholly of the English race . . . there were Swedes, Germans, and Swiss.[8]

Sir Walter Raleigh, whose services earned his knighthood at the hands of Queen Elizabeth, secured from her a wine monopoly covering a princely grant of land in what is now Virginia. There he found, however, that tobacco would yield them larger revenue. The grants to Raleigh were "a kind of autonomous state." His corporation was practically perpetual. They had constitutions under which citizens and officials lived. The corporations had the duty to "propagate the Christian religion to such people as live in darkness and miserable ignorance of the true knowledge and worship of God." So in Virginia the creed of the Anglican Church was made the law of the plantations. James I in 1606 authorized the London Company to found Virginia. Other charters were granted in 1609 and 1612. The King, after a quarrel with the company in 1619, established the House of Burgesses, to give the Colony local government. As a result of quarrels between the middle class and the aristocratic element, proceedings were started to forfeit the charter, which was annulled in 1624, when the Colony became a royal province.[9]

The Separatists, flying from an encounter with the Church of England, landed in Holland, where the Dutch guilds kept them out of the most profitable callings. They decided, as they were unable to endure their great labors and the oppression of their children, with the consequent danger of "falling into ungodly ways through contact with those of other faith," to

---

[8] Beck's *The Constitution of the United States*, p. 34.
[9] Beard's *Rise of American Civilization*, p. 34.

seek another country. So they secured the backing of a coterie of merchants in London and obtained permission to settle in Virginia. They left Delftshoven in 1620 in the *Speedwell*, and after they had been joined by others at Southampton in the *Mayflower*, they set sail for America. When they found the *Speedwell* unseaworthy, the stouter-hearted among them boarded the already crowded *Mayflower*, which sailed in September. Before disembarking, forty-one Pilgrim Fathers entered into a compact for the common good. Blown far from their original destination, they finally landed at Plymouth in December. The new Colony grew so slowly that at the end of seventy-one years it only had 7000 people.[10]

In 1629 a mercantile corporation was chartered as the Massachusetts Bay Company. The Plymouth settlers had no charter of incorporation from the British Crown. The Massachusetts Company had the right to an actual self-governing state. In New England the town instead of the county became the unit of social and political life.

The severe religious life of Massachusetts caused some of the inhabitants to form Rhode Island, Connecticut, and New Hampshire. With five others, Roger Williams founded Providence in 1636 on Narragansett Bay. His colleague, Anne Hutchinson, in 1638 founded the Colony at Portsmouth, New Hampshire. Charles II of England in 1663 granted a royal charter to a union of towns now composing Rhode Island. At the beginning of the Revolution their Governor and Company said, "Distillery is the main

[10] *Ibid.*, p. 48.

OUR UNKNOWN CONSTITUTION

hinge upon which the trade of the Colony turns."[11]

In the years 1635 and 1636 pioneers from the Massachusetts Colony went to the valley, where they inaugurated the towns of Hartford, Windsor, and Wethersfeld. Other Puritans started New Haven and other places along the Long Island Sound. These were continued under a formal constitution, and in 1662 they all combined under a royal charter as "The Governor and Company of the English Colony of Connecticut in New England." Finally other Massachusetts communities beyond the Merrimac River became in 1679 "The Royal Province of New Hampshire."[12]

In 1664 Lord Berkeley and Sir George Carteret got from the Duke of York a grant of land between the Delaware and the Hudson Rivers. They called it New Jersey. Into this new territory came Connecticut Puritans, Presbyterians, and English Quakers. Philip Carteret, the first Governor, established the City of Newark. But these grantees, "weary of a very expensive feather," relinquished the Colony to the Crown of England in 1702, and for a while it was united with New York. New Jersey was finally given a separate royal Governor.[13]

In 1670 William Penn held a claim against Charles II of England for £16,000, in payment of which he got a grant to what afterwards became Pennsylvania. Seeing the necessity for a coast line, Penn secured from the Duke of York "the Delaware region to the south, which had been wrested from the Swedes by the Dutch,

[11] *Ibid.*, p. 56.
[12] *Ibid.*, p. 59.
[13] *Ibid.*, p. 68.

and from the Dutch by the English." This territory remained under the Penns, as the separate Colony of Delaware, until the Revolution.[14]

Lord Baltimore secured from Charles I a great area of land which he called Maryland, after the French Queen Henrietta Maria. His charterers were made absolute lords and proprietaries on payment annually to the English Crown of two Indian arrowheads and one-fifth of the gold and silver found there. Lord Baltimore became Captain General, head of the Church, and the source of all civil and Church offices. When the Catholic James II lost his kingdom in 1688, the Baltimores lost Maryland, but twenty years later it was regained by them.[15]

Charles II of England granted a great body of land known as Carolina, but the owners in 1729 sold out to the Crown.

The opening up of Georgia, the last English settlement in the Colonies, came about through the sympathy of one of the world's great philanthropists for imprisoned debtors in England. On the suggestion of James Oglethorpe, George II in 1736 granted a large territory south of South Carolina to a board of trustees. Slavery was forbidden, because the trustees did not want a province "void of white tenants, filled with blacks, the precarious property of a few." But the Colonists there soon demanded slaves, like the other Colonies had.[16]

The land of the corporation managed by the trustees became a royal province in 1752.

By the Treaty of 1763 England got from France the

[14] *Ibid.*, p. 70.
[15] *Ibid.*, p. 59.
[16] *Ibid.*, p. 77.

territory from the Allegheny Mountains to the Mississippi River, and from the border of west Florida to the Great Lakes.[17]

By the Quebec Act in 1774 England had declared that the Ohio River was to be the southern boundary of Canada.

France likewise claimed certain American territory by the same right of discovery, as also did Holland.

Strangely enough, Spain, from whose shores voyaged forth America's discoverer, had but scant footing in the new continent, and at the beginning claimed only Florida.

With these varied bloods and diverse traditions, the subsequent solidarity of the Colonies is more than noteworthy. Nothing except the flame of liberty could have fused them into the cohesive union that finally won them freedom.

[17] Fiske's *The Critical Period of American History*, p. 18.

CHAPTER III

AMERICA'S EARLIEST IMPULSES TO COLLECTIVE ACTION.
THE BOSTON TEA PARTY

EACH of the thirteen American Colonies had been permitted by England to make its own laws applying solely within its own Colony. Therefore "Colonial history was marked by a spirit of individualism, a natural partiality for local rule, and a tenacious adherence to their special privileges." [1]

"In 1643 three [2] New England Colonies joined in a short-lived *'Confederacy'* for mutual protection, especially against the Dutch. Each member reserved its peculiar jurisdiction and government, and an equal vote in the general council." [3]

"Common danger gave the next impulse to collective action. Rivers, which were the convenient warpaths of the natives (Indians), flowed in every direction over the land of the Five Nations,[4] against whom in 1684 measures of defense, extending from North Carolina to the northern boundary of New England, were concerted. Later, in 1751, South Carolina joined the

[1] Beck's *The Constitution of the United States,* p. 32.
[2] Beck says four: Massachusetts, Plymouth, Connecticut, and New Haven.
[3] Bancroft's *History of the Constitution of the United States,* Vol. I, p. 6.
[4] Five Nations was the Iroquois League, comprising the following tribes of Indians in the central and western part of what is New York State: Mohawk, Oneida, Cayuga, Onondaga, and Seneca. Afterwards, in 1712, the Tuscaroras joined the League.

Northern Colonies in a truce with the same tribes." [3]

From 1685 to 1688 James II of England began to suppress the American Colonial Legislatures, and to consolidate his Colonies under the rule of a single Governor.

In 1696 John Locke,[5] in the lately created Board of Trade,[6] suggested that a captain general of all the forces on the Continent of North America be employed, "with such power as could be exercised through the prerogative of a constitutional king." [7]

In 1697 William Penn [8] appeared before this Board. He advised that there be an annual congress of two delegates from *each American province* "to determine by plurality of voices the ways and means for supporting *their union,* providing for *their* safety, and regulating *their* commerce."

In 1721, in order to secure the necessary co-operation for England in its rivalry with France for North American territory, Lord Stairs suggested a lord lieutenant over all of them, and for a general council of two delegates from *each province,* one of the two being elected every other year.[7]

In order to raise money to pay ten thousand troops which he intended to send to America to protect the American Colonies against the Indians and French,

[3] *Loc. cit.*
[5] John Locke was an English philosopher, 1632–1704.
[6] Board of Trade in Great Britain was a department of the Government. After the dissolution of several earlier bodies, it has existed in its present form since 1786. It has control over patents, weights and measures, copyright, companies in bankruptcy, and merchant shipping.
[7] Bancroft's *History of the Constitution of the United States,* p. 7.
[8] William Penn, 1644–1718, English Quaker and founder of Pennsylvania.
[7] *Loc. cit.*

King George III proposed to levy a direct tax on the people. The Colonists objected to taxation because they had no proper representation in Parliament. The English statesmen Pitt and Fox took the side of the Americans. But the King persevered, and Parliament in 1765 made ready to pass the Stamp Act, which required the Colonists to use stamps in law, business papers, pamphlets, and newspapers.

Benjamin Franklin, who was Colonial agent in London, fought this legislation, but Parliament passed it. Finally delegates from nine of the American Colonies in the so-called Stamp Act Congress in 1765 drew up the Declaration of Rights, announcing that the Colonists possessed the same rights as all other British subjects in England. They complained that as they were not represented in Parliament, it had no power to tax them. After numerous public protests, when General Gage brought to Boston two British regiments from New York, the Boston massacre occurred and several Americans were killed.

The Stamp Act was repealed in 1766, but was followed by the Townshend Act, which taxed tea, window glass, paper, and paints, to pay the King's soldiers sent to America, and the governors, judges, and other officers of the Crown in the Colonies. The duties under the Townshend Act were finally removed, except a small tax on every pound of tea. Notwithstanding the declaration of the Colonists that they would not buy the tea, cargoes of it were sent to Charleston, New York, Boston, Philadelphia, and Annapolis in 1773. The only cargo allowed to land was at Charleston. When the tea ships came into Boston Harbor, the people refused to let them unload. The Governor would not permit them to return unless unloaded, and the people under Samuel Adams held an immense meeting, but they took no formal action. On the night of December 16th, 1773, citizens disguised as Indians emptied the chests of $100,000 worth of tea, which they threw into the water. The King then closed the port of Boston and installed a military governor.

This was followed in May, 1774, by the invitation of the Virginia House of Burgesses to meet in Philadelphia, September 5th, 1774.[9]

On September 5th, 1774, the First Continental Congress [10] of Delegates, appointed and chosen by the several Colonies and provinces of North America to consider their actual situation and the differences between them and Great Britain, was held at Carpenters Hall, Philadelphia, when delegates from New Hampshire, Massachusetts Bay, Rhode Island and Providence Plantations, Connecticut, City and County of New York, and other counties in the Province of New York, New Jersey, Pennsylvania, Newcastle, Kent, and Sussex, in Delaware, Maryland, Virginia, and South Carolina, met. Georgia alone was unrepresented.[11] Peyton Randolph was chosen president.

September 6th, 1774, the Congress rules gave each Colony one vote. A Commission was appointed to state the rights and grievances of the Colonies and the proper means to redress them.

On September 24th, 1774, the Congress resolved to consider only rights infringed by the British Parliament after 1763.

On September 27th, 1774, the Congress resolved that after December 1st, 1774, there should be no im-

[9] Beck's *The Constitution of the United States*, p. 36.
[10] "The Old Congress."
[11] Burdick's *The Law of the American Constitution*, p. 7.

portation of goods into British America from Great Britain or Ireland, or any goods exported therefrom.

On September 30th, 1774, the Congress resolved that all exportation to Great Britain and Ireland or West Indies should cease, unless America's grievances should be redressed.

On October 7th, 1774, on receipt of a letter from the Committee of Correspondence at Boston, the Congress of Delegates resolved to appoint a Committee to write General Gage that Boston was suffering in the common cause of America, and that it approved her resistance to the obnoxious acts of Parliament, and that all America ought to support Massachusetts.

On October 11th, 1774, the Congress of Delegates unanimously resolved to memorialize the people of British America, stating the necessity of adhering to the measures of Congress, and sent an address to Great Britain.

On October 14th, 1774, Congress made a declaration and framed resolves relative to the rights and grievances of the Colonies.

On October 14th, 1774, the Congress unanimously resolved "that the respective Colonies are entitled to the common law of England, and more especially to the great and inestimable privilege of being tried by their peers of the vicinage according to the course of that law, . . . and to the English statutes as existed at the time of their colonization . . ." [12]

When the news of the fate of Boston reached the other Colonies, Colonial Conventions were held, and the plan of a General Congress, as proposed by Massachusetts and Virginia, was adopted.

[12] Elliott's *Debates on the Federal Constitution*, Vol. I, p. 44.

October 22nd, 1774, Congress dissolved, recommending the reconvening of the delegates at Philadelphia, May 10th, 1775.

In 1774, when the British Parliament sought to punish Boston by armed coercion, delegates of the inhabitants of twelve of the *Colonies* in a *Continental* Congress petitioned the King, but the petition was not received.[13]

October 26th, 1774, the address to the inhabitants of Quebec set forth the spirit of sympathy and invited union with them to resist.

On May 10th, 1775, as recommended by the preceding Congress,[14] the delegates of the United Colonies of New Hampshire, Massachusetts Bay, Rhode Island and Providence Plantations, Connecticut, New York, New Jersey, Pennsylvania, Newcastle, Kent and Sussex in Delaware, Maryland, Virginia, North Carolina, and South Carolina, assembled in Congress in Philadelphia, and resolved to recommend to the respective Assemblies and Conventions of the United Colonies where no government sufficient to the exigencies of their affairs had been established, to adopt such a government as should, in the opinion of the representatives of the *people,* best conduce to the happiness and safety of their constituents in particular, and of America in general.

On May 5th, 1775, a preamble to this resolution was agreed to, which stated the intention to totally suppress the exercise of every kind of authority under the British Crown.

[13] Bancroft's *History of the Constitution of the United States,* Vol. I, p. 10.
[14] Elliott's *Debates on the Federal Constitution,* Vol. I, p. 45.

On May 15th, 1775, a Rhode Island delegate took his seat. That Colony had not up to that time been represented.

There was no voting by the Colonies, but occasional listening to utterances which implied that Americans were now thrown into a single mass, and this body sent addresses to the King, to the people of the Colonies, of Quebec, and of Great Britain, and prepared a declaration of rights.

These rights, which had been infringed since 1763, they described as innovations, and claimed themselves to be the true conservatives, who only desired peace on the basis of the former Constitution. The opposition which Massachusetts was making to the recent acts of Parliament was approved, and it was decided to stand by her.

"Before the second Continental Congress in 1775, the accidental clash at Lexington and Concord (April 19th, 1775) had taken place . . . and the Congress became a provisional government. . . . Each Colony had a vote, and every measure required unanimous consent." [15]

On May 16th, 1775, the Congress went into the Committee of the Whole, on the State of America.

On May 26th, 1775, the Congress resolved to put the Colonies immediately in a state of defense, that a fresh petition be sent to the King, and that a letter to the people of Canada be reported.

[15] Beck's *The Constitution of the United States*, p. 36.

CHAPTER IV

THE DECLARATION OF INDEPENDENCE—PREPARATION FOR WAR—ARTICLES OF CONFEDERATION

ON MAY 31st, 1775, the first North American Declaration of Independence was adopted at Charlotte, Mecklenburg County, North Carolina.[1]

Many of the phrases are word for word as they appear in the Declaration of Independence. The Minutes of the Meeting were destroyed by fire in 1800. Whether the Declaration of Independence followed the words of the Mecklenburg Declaration, or whether the latter, having been probably replaced from memory, was tinctured with the former, is a disputed question.

On June 3rd, 1775, a Commission was appointed by Congress to draw a petition to the King.

June 14th, 1775, the Congress resolved to enlist companies of riflemen for a year's service in the Continental Army.

On June 19th, 1775, George Washington received his commission as Commander-in-chief.

July 6th, 1775, a previously appointed committee brought in a declaration by representatives of the United Colonies of North America, setting forth the causes and necessity of arming, to be published by General Washington before his arrival at the camp before Boston. Washington, on taking command of

[1] *American Encyclopædia*, Vol. X, "Mecklenburg." *Encyclopædia Britannica*, Vol. XV, p. 170.

the Army in Massachusetts, discriminated between the proper functions of the *individual Colonies* and "that power and weight which ought of right to belong only to the *whole.*" [2]

July 26th, 1775, Benjamin Franklin was appointed Postmaster General, for posts from Falmouth to Savannah, Georgia, with such additions as he saw fit.

When the Revolution began, all countries, including the American Colonies, had a state religion, except Rhode Island, and even it denied Catholics the right to vote, but in 1776 Virginia adopted a Bill of Rights, and in 1785 enacted Jefferson's statute of religious liberty. In 1787, in the Philadelphia Constitutional Convention, Charles Pinckney introduced a clause, "but no religious test shall ever be required as a qualification to any office or public trust under the *United States,*" and at the suggestion of Patrick Henry it was resolved that "Congress shall make no law respecting an establishment of religion, or prohibiting the free exercise thereof." Afterwards, the *States* adopted similar guaranties in their *State* Constitutions.[3]

On July 28th, 1775, an address to the people of Ireland was adopted.

On July 31st, 1775, Congress declared that a resolution of the British House of Commons of February 20th, 1775, known as "Lord North's motion," was "inadmissible as the basis of reconciliation, because it did not renounce the pretended right to tax the Colonies." This resolution proposed to transfer the right of taxing the Colonies to Colonial Assemblies.

---

[2] Bancroft's *History of the Constitution of the United States,* Vol. I, p. 18. Washington to Richard Henry Lee, August 29, 1775. Sparks, iii, 68, 69.

[3] Lee's *The Story of the American Constitution,* p. 128.

On August 1st, 1775, Congress adjourned to September 5th, 1775.

On October 13th, 1775, after reconvening, Congress ordered two armed vessels fitted out.

Thomas Paine, in his *Common Sense,* half a year before the Declaration of Independence, said: "Nothing but a Continental form of government can keep the peace of the continent. Let a Continental Conference be held, to frame a Continental charter. . . . The bodies chosen conformably to such charter shall be the *legislators and governors* of this continent. We have every opportunity and every encouragement to form the noblest, purest constitution on the face of the earth."

On October 30th, 1775, Congress ordered two more vessels fitted out. Congress proceeded to carry out other preparations for war.

On June 7th, 1776, Richard Henry Lee introduced a resolution into Congress, declaring "That the United Colonies are and ought to be free and independent *States,* and that their political connection with Great Britain is and ought to be dissolved."

On June 10th, 1776, it was resolved that a Committee should be appointed to prepare a declaration to the following effect: "That the United Colonies are, and of right ought to be, free and independent *States;* that they are absolved from all allegiance to the British Crown; and that all political connection between them and the State of Great Britain is, and ought to be, totally dissolved." On the preceding day it was determined that the Committee for preparing the declaration should consist of five, and they were chosen accordingly, in the following order: Mr. Jefferson, Mr. J. Adams, Mr. Franklin, Mr. Sherman, Mr. R. R. Livingston.

On June 11th, 1776, a resolution was passed to appoint a Committee to prepare and digest the form of a *confederation* to be entered into between the *Colonies*, and another Committee to prepare a plan of treaties to be proposed to foreign powers.

On June 12th, 1776, it was resolved that a Committee of Congress should be appointed, by the name of a Board of War and Ordnance, to consist of five members.

On June 15th, 1776, George Washington was unanimously chosen General. These measures resulted from the British military proceedings at Lexington, Massachusetts, on the 19th of the preceding April, and the burning of Charlestown, near Boston, indicating Great Britain's intention of compelling the *Colonies'* submission by arms.

"Liberty" is defined by Webster's New International Dictionary, at page 1243, as follows:

1. State or fact of being a free person; exemption from subjection to the will of another claiming ownership of the person or services; freedom;—opposed to slavery, serfdom, bondage, subjection, etc.

2. The state, or the sum of the rights and immunities of those whose rights and privileges are protected by an organized civil community (civil liberty), or of those who are invested with the right effectually to share in framing and conducting the government under which they are politically organized (political liberty), or those who are free from external restraint in the exercise of the rights that are considered without the province of a government to control (individual liberty). Individual liberty under modern constitutional governments in general involves freedom of the person in going and coming (personal liberty), equality before the courts, security of private capital, freedom of opinion and its expression, and freedom of conscience.

The same dictionary at page 1999 defines "sovereignty" as "the quality or state of being a sovereign; also the power, right, authority, or status of a sovereign."

A "sovereign" is defined as:

1. A person who is chief or supreme over others; as: (A) formerly, a chieftain or lord, a husband, a mayor, or provost (this sense being still locally retained in Ireland), the head of a monastery or convent, etc.

(B) The person or body in which is vested the supreme or highest power in a state; the person or body having independent and supreme authority; as (1) in a monarchy, a king, queen, emperor, or the like. (2) In an oligarchy, limited monarchy, republic, democracy, or the like, the body of men (sometimes called the collective sovereignty) in whom the supreme power is vested, or whom the people generally, habitually obey. (3) In an empire embracing one or more subordinate countries, the state vested with sovereignty.

June 22, 1775, Congress resolved to issue 2,000,000 Spanish milled dollars, to be redeemed by twelve Confederated Colonies, which had so pledged.

On June 25th, 1776, a declaration of the deputies of Pennsylvania met in provincial conference, expressing their willingness to concur in a vote declaring the *United States* free and independent *States,* was laid before the Congress and read.

On June 28th, 1776, the Committee appointed to prepare a Declaration of Independence brought in a draft, which was read, and ordered to lie on the table.

"From the facile and brilliant pen of Thomas Jefferson there poured forth (in the Declaration of Independence) with extraordinary charm and lucidity an avowal of wrongs endured, and rights proclaimed, which fired the minds of all men with a new conception of liberty and nationalistic aim. . . . Into the Constitution were written positive guarantees against a repetition of those wrongs and usurpations of government which had been decried and 'submitted to a candid world' in the Declaration." [4]

On July 1st, 1776, a resolution of the Convention of Maryland, passed the 28th of June, 1776, authorizing the deputies of that Colony to concur in declaring the United Colonies free and independent *States*, was laid before the Congress and read. On the same day the Congress resolved itself into a Committee of the Whole, to take into consideration the resolution respecting independency.[5]

"The Congress which adopted the Declaration of Independence, July 4, 1776, sat in Philadelphia in the same room in which the Constitution was drafted eleven years later, and eight of its members signed the latter instrument. It was composed of fifty-six members, one more than participated in the Constitutional Convention, and all of the Colonies were represented. . . . On August 2, 1776, the document was signed by all members, except Matthew Thornton, of New Hampshire, who was absent, but his signature was added early in November." [6]

On July 2nd, 1776, a resolution declaring the Colonies free and independent *States*, was adopted by the Congress of the Colonies. A declaration to that effect was, on the same and the following days, taken into further consideration. It referred to "these *United Colonies.*"

"The Revolution had left them as thirteen sovereign nations, and in the Articles of Confederation they had refused to surrender their sovereignty, but had entered into a mere treaty which they styled 'a league of

---

[4] Lee's *The Story of the American Constitution*, p. 50.
[5] Elliott's *Debates on the Federal Constitution*, Vol. I, p. 55.
[6] Lee's *The Story of the American Constitution*, p. 51.

friendship,' each *State* retaining 'its sovereignty, freedom, and independence.' "[7]

On July 4th, 1776, the Declaration of Independence was finally agreed to, engrossed on paper, signed by John Hancock as President, and directed to be sent to the several Assemblies, Conventions, and Committees, or Councils of Safety, and to the several commanding officers of the Continental troops, and to be proclaimed in each of the *United Colonies,* and at the head of the Army.

July 12th, 1776, the Committee on the Form of the Confederation between the Colonies made its report. This Committee had been appointed June 11th, 1776.

On August 2nd, 1776, a copy of the Declaration of Independence was engrossed on parchment and signed by all except one of the fifty-six signers whose names now appear upon it.

Benjamin Franklin submitted Articles of Confederation to the Continental Congress, but at first no action was taken. His sketch became the basis, however, of the scheme of July 12th, 1776, by the Committee appointed for that purpose. This was amended and debated until November, 1777, when it was agreed to by Congress and submitted to the *States.*[8]

November 15th, 1777, Congress directed that the Articles of Confederation,[9] which it had adopted in the fall of 1777, should be proposed to the Legislatures of all the *States,* with a circular letter recommending them as containing the only plan of union at all likely to be adopted,[10] so that if approved, they could au-

[7] *Ibid.,* p. 60.
[8] See parallel column comparison of the Articles of Confederation and the Constitution in Appendix B, p. 261.
[9] Burdick's *The Law of the American Constitution,* p. 9.
[10] Fiske's *The Critical Period of American History,* p. 93.

thorize their delegates to ratify them in Congress, in which event they should become conclusive.

On November 17th, 1777, the Committee brought in a circular letter to accompany the Articles, and thirteen copies were signed by the President, and forwarded to the several *States*.

CHAPTER V

THE ARTICLES OF CONFEDERATION ARE REFERRED TO THE STATES

THE official letter to the *State* Legislatures, accompanying the Act of Confederation, was as follows:

In Congress, Yorktown, November 17, 1777.

Congress having agreed upon a plan of confederacy for securing the freedom, sovereignty, and independence of the *United States,* authentic copies are now transmitted for the consideration of the respective Legislatures.

This business, equally intricate and important, has, in its progress, been attended with uncommon embarrassment and delay, which the most anxious solicitude and persevering diligence could not prevent. To form a permanent union, accommodated to the opinion and wishes of the delegates of so many *States,* differing in habits, produce, commerce, and internal police, was found to be a work which nothing but time and reflection, conspiring with a disposition to conciliate, could mature and accomplish.

Hardly is it to be expected that any plan, in the variety of provisions essential to our union, should exactly correspond with the maxims and political views of every political state. Let it be remarked, that, after the most careful inquiry, and the fullest information, this is proposed as the best which could be adapted to the circumstances of all, and as that alone which affords any tolerable prospect of general ratification.

Permit us, then, earnestly to recommend these Articles to the immediate and dispassionate attention of the Legislatures of the respective *States.* Let them be candidly reviewed under a sense of the difficulty of combining in one general system the various sentiments and interests of a continent divided into so many sovereign and independent communities; under a conviction of the absolute necessity of uniting all our councils, and all our strength, to maintain and defend our common liberties; let them be examined with a liberality becoming brethren and fellow-citizens surrounded by the same imminent dangers, contending for the same illustrious prize, and deeply interested in being forever bound and connected together by ties the most intimate and indissoluble; and, finally, let them be adjusted with the temper and magnanimity of wise and patriotic legislators, who, while they are concerned for the prosperity of their own more immediate circle, are capable of rising superior to local attachments, when they may be incompatible with the safety, happiness, and glory of the general confederacy.

We have reason to regret the time which has elapsed in preparing this plan for consideration; with additional solicitude we look forward to that which must be necessarily spent before it can be ratified. Every motive loudly calls upon us to hasten its conclusion.

More than any other consideration, it will confound our foreign enemies, defeat the flagitious practices of the disaffected, strengthen and confirm our friends, support our public credit, restore the value of our money, enable us to maintain our fleets and armies, and add weight and respect to our councils at home and to our treaties abroad.

In short, this salutary measure can no longer be deferred; it seems essential to our very existence as a free *people;* and, without it, we may soon be constrained to bid adieu to independence, to liberty, and safety—blessings which, from the justice of our cause, and the favor of our Almighty Creator, visibly manifested in our protection, we have reason to expect, if, in an humble dependence on His divine providence, we strenuously exert the means which are placed in our power.

To conclude: If the Legislature of any *State* shall not be assembled, Congress recommend to the executive authority to convene it without delay; and to each respective Legislature it is recommended to invest its delegates with competent powers, ultimately, in the name and behalf of the *State,* to subscribe Articles of Confederation and Perpetual Union of the *United States,* and to attend Congress for that purpose on or before the 10th day of March next.[1]

[1] Elliott's *Debates on the Federal Constitution,* Vol. I, pp. 69, 70.

Under these Articles of Confederation no measures could be carried without the assent of a *majority* of all the *States*, and no important measures without the consent of nine *States*, and no amendment to the Articles without *unanimous consent*.[2] Each *State* had one vote.

There was a President of Congress, but he had no more power than any delegate. There was no provision for a supreme executive with authority to enforce the laws.

During a Congressional recess the country was run by an Executive Committee of one member from each *State*, known as the Committee of the *States*.

No *State* could engage in war except by way of defense against sudden Indian attack.

The Articles show that political action was at no time based on the view of the *States* as absolutely sovereign, but they also show that the share of *sovereignty* accorded to Congress was very inadequate, even to the purposes of an effective *Confederation*.[3]

The most fundamental attribute of *sovereignty*, the power of tax, was not given to Congress. It could only make requisitions upon the thirteen members in proportion to the assessed value of their real estate, and it was not provided with any means of enforcing these requirements. The Articles contained nothing

---

[2] "The necessity of the consent of every one of the thirteen *States* to any amendment of the *Confederacy* gave Rhode Island a terrible control over the destinies of America. Against its obstinacy the *Confederation* was helpless." (Bancroft's *History of the Constitution of the United States*, Vol. I, p. 43.) Fiske's *The Critical Period of American History*, p. 99. See Appendix D, p. 283.

[3] Fiske's *The Critical Period of American History*, pp. 97, 98.

except a vague promise on the part of the *States* to obey.[4]

Article 2 of the Articles of Confederation provided that "each *State*[5] retain its sovereignty, freedom, and independence, and every power, jurisdiction, and right, which is not by this *Confederation* expressly delegated to the United States, in Congress assembled."

Article 3: "Said *States* enter into a firm league of friendship between the *States* . . . for their common defense, the security of their liberties, and their mutual and general welfare. . . ."

Article 4: ". . . inhabitants . . . shall be entitled to all the privileges and immunities of free citizens; . . . and shall enjoy therein all the privileges of trade and commerce, subject to the same duties, impositions, and restrictions as the inhabitants thereof respectively, provided that such restrictions shall not extend so far as to prevent the removal of property imported into any *State*,[6] to any other *State* of which the owner is an inhabitant; provided also, that no impositions, duties, or restrictions shall be laid by any *State* on the property of the *United States* or either of them."

The Articles of Confederation provided that the Congress was to be continued, and was to consist of

[4] "These Articles (of Confederation) dealt with the *States* only, and made no attempt at reaching the individual citizen. Each *State* retained 'its *sovereignty,* freedom and independence.' . . . No affirmative action could be taken except upon the vote of nine *States;* thus any five *States* could, and often did, block the most needed legislation. Moreover, the Articles themselves prevented any correction of their own defects, for they could be amended only by the consent of the Legislature of each of the thirteen *States*." (Lee's *The Story of the American Constitution*, p. 11.)

[5] The *State's sovereignty,* not the individual's, nor the *people's sovereignty.*

[6] Slaves were property.

delegates annually appointed by the Legislature of each *State*, and paid by their *States*.

On April 26th, 1778, the Congress adopted the report of the Committee appointed to prepare a letter to the *States* that "had not authorized their delegates to ratify the *Confederation*." That letter read:

Sir: Congress, intent upon the present and future security of these *United States*, has never ceased to consider a confederacy as the great principle of union, which can alone establish the liberty of America, and exclude forever the hopes of its enemies. Influenced by considerations so powerful, and duly weighing the difficulties which oppose the expectation of any plan being formed that can exactly meet the wishes and obtain the approbation of so many *States*, differing essentially in various points, Congress have, after mature deliberation, agreed to adopt, without amendments, the *Confederation* transmitted to the several *States* for their approbation. The *States* of New Hampshire, Massachusetts Bay, Rhode Island and Providence Plantations, Connecticut, New York, Pennsylvania, Virginia, North Carolina, and South Carolina have ratified the same, and it remains only for your *State*, with those of ———, to conclude the glorious compact, which, by uniting the wealth, strength, and councils of the whole, may bid defiance to external violence and internal dissensions, whilst it secures the public credit both at home and abroad. Congress is willing to hope that the patriotism and good sense of your *State* will be influenced by motives so important; and they request, sir, that you will be pleased to lay this letter before the Legislature of ———, in order that, if they judge it proper, their delegates may be instructed to ratify the *Confederation* with all convenient despatch; trusting to future deliberations to make such alterations and amendments as experience may show to be expedient and just.[7]

"The four fatal defects in the Articles of Confederation were the omission of a federal judiciary with power to enforce, the powerlessness of Congress to enforce treaties, the failure to provide proper supreme

[7] Elliott's *Debates on the Federal Constitution*, Vol. I, p. 68.

executive power, and the lack of Congressional power over commerce between the *States* and with foreign countries. Each *State* collected its own tariff against foreign countries and against other *States*." [8]

The submission of the Articles of Confederation for ratification brought on an avalanche of discussion by correspondence, on the hustings, and in the press of the day.

Washington urged Benjamin Harrison, Mason, Wythe, Jefferson, Nicholas, Pendleton, and Nelson "not to be satisfied with places *in their own State* while the common interests of America were mouldering and sinking into irretrievable ruin, but to attend to the momentous concerns of an empire." [9]

Washington advised Virginia to forego "the liberty to reject or alter any act of Congress which in a full representation of *States* has been solemnly debated and decided on," otherwise he believed there was no hope of consolidating the *Union*.[10]

June 26th, 1778, the form of a ratification of the Articles of Confederation by the *States* was adopted by Congress, and ordered engrossed on parchment, so that it should be signed by the delegates under the authority of the several *States*. New York, New Hampshire, Virginia, and North Carolina only accepted them provided all the other *States* did.

In May, 1780, two days after Burgoyne's surrender, Maryland resolved that "the *United States* in Congress assembled should have the sole and exclusive

---

[8] Lee's *The Story of the American Constitution*, p. 16.
[9] Bancroft's *History of the Constitution of the United States*, Vol. I, p. 19. Sparks, vi, 150.
[10] Bancroft's *History of the Constitution of the United States*, Vol. I, p. 20. Washington to James Duane, December 26, 1780. MS.

right to ascertain and fix the northwestern boundary of such *States* as claim to the Mississippi River . . . and lay out the land beyond the boundary so ascertained into separate and independent *States* from time to time, as the numbers and circumstances of the people may require." Maryland refused to ratify the Articles of Confederation until she was assured that the Northwestern Territory should become the common property of the *United States* . . . to be parcelled into free, convenient, and independent *States*.[11]

In the fall of 1780 Washington urged Congress to promise the Revolutionary soldiers half pay for life. Many officers doubted whether the promise would be kept. . . . There was danger that the army would fall to pieces.[12]

On September 3rd, 1780, Alexander Hamilton, in a letter to James Duane, a member of Congress, advised that a convention of all the *States* should meet in the following November, with authority to organize a "vigorous" general confederation.[13]

On November 11th, 1780, representatives from the New England States and New York assembled at Hartford. A circular letter [14] to all the *States* said: "Our embarrassments arise from a defect in the present Government of the *United States*. All government sup-

[11] Fiske's *The Critical Period of American History*, p. 192.
[12] Fiske's *The Critical Period of American History*, p. 106.
"During the Revolution a common fear kept the *States* working together. But they were so intoxicated by their individual sovereignty, that no strong sentiment in favor of 'a more perfect union' developed." (Lee's *Story of the American Constitution*, p. 11.)
[13] Bancroft's *History of the Constitution of the United States*, Vol. I, p. 13. Hamilton to Duane, September 3, 1780. Hamilton, i, 157.
[14] That was their only way to communicate with the people.

poses the power of coercion."[15] The proceedings of the Convention were sent to all the *States*, the Congress, and to General Washington.[16]

Philip Schuyler of New York, in a letter to Washington dated January 21st, 1781, stated that he perceived the necessity for the *States* to surrender some part of *their sovereignty* "and adopt another system of government."[17]

"In the Senate of New York (in January, 1781) Schuyler moved to request the Eastern *States* to join in an early convention, which should form a perpetual league of incorporation, subservient, however, to the common interest of *all the States* . . . and invest the Confederacy with powers of coercion."[18]

On January 29th, 1781, John Sullivan suggested Hamilton for the Treasury,[19] but Robert Morris was chosen.

In a letter (January, 1781) Hamilton expressed his wish for a "convention of all the *States*, with full power to amend, finally and irrevocably, the present futile and senseless *Confederation.*"[20]

---

[15] Bancroft's *History of the Constitution of the United States*, Vol. I, p. 14.

[16] *Ibid.*, p. 15. Papers of the Old Congress xxxiii, containing copies of the credentials of the Commissioners, the resolutions of the Convention, and its letters to the several *States*, to Congress, and to Washington. MS.

[17] Bancroft's *History of the Constitution of the United States*, Vol. I, p. 29. Philip Schuyler to Washington, January 21, 1781. Letters to Washington, iii, 213.

[18] Bancroft's *History of the Constitution of the United States*, Vol. I, p. 29.

[19] *Ibid.*, p. 30. Sullivan to Washington, January 29, 1781. MS.

[20] Bancroft's *History of the Constitution of the United States*, Vol. I, p. 32.

CHAPTER VI

ARTICLES OF CONFEDERATION ADOPTED BY THE STATES —THEIR AMENDMENT DISCUSSED

IN FIFTEEN months (from November, 1777) all the *States* had adopted the Articles of Confederation except Maryland, which *State,* as already stated, had refused to sign until the *States* laying claim to the Northwestern lands, and especially Virginia, should surrender their claims to the *Confederation.* After carrying her point, Maryland ratified the Articles of Confederation on March 1st, 1781, and thus, in the last and most brilliant period of the Revolutionary War, while Greene was leading Cornwallis on his fatal chase across North Carolina, the *Confederation* proposed at the time of the Declaration of Independence was finally consummated. Then the man from Georgia could deal with the man from New Hampshire on an equal footing before the law. This was almost the only effect of the cohesion provision in the whole instrument. Throughout the remainder of the Articles of Confederation, its language was largely devoted to reconciling the theory that the *States* were sovereign with the possible fact that they were already merged to some extent in a larger political body. The *sovereignty* of this larger body was vested in the Congress of Delegates appointed yearly by the *States.*"[1]

---

[1] Fiske's *The Critical Period of American History,* pp. 93, 94, 95.

On the 2nd of March, 1781, Congress assembled under the new powers.

Three distinct branches were created, the legislative, the executive, and the judicial, the powers of each clearly defined. This conception of limitation of powers, however, was not original with the Constitution.

After the Revolution, all the *States* had adopted constitutions, many of which embodied the same principle. Massachusetts, in adopting its Constitution in 1780, had declared that "In the government of this Commonwealth the legislative department shall never exercise the executive and judicial powers, or either of them; the executive shall never exercise the legislative and judicial powers, or either of them; the judicial shall never exercise the legislative and executive powers, or either of them —to the end that it may be a government of laws and not of men." [2]

But the Articles of Confederation soon proved entirely inadequate to the situation, and as early as May, 1781, Pelatiah Webster,[3] of Pennsylvania, proposed a Federal convention for overhauling the whole scheme of government from beginning to end.

Madison's proposal in 1781 that "the Legislature of every *State* give authority to employ the force of the *United States* as well by sea as by land to compel the *States* to fulfil their Federal engagements"[4] was referred to a Grand Committee; that is, to a Committee of one from each *State*. This Committee made its report July 20, 1781, "and then only expressed a wish to give Congress power in time of war to lay an embargo at least for sixty days, and to appoint receivers of the

---

[2] Lee's *The Story of the American Constitution*, pp. 30, 35.
[3] Fiske's *The Critical Period of American History*, p. 101.
[4] Madison Papers, Gilpin's Edition, 88–90. Reports of Committees, pp. 20, 22.

money of the *United States* as soon as collected by *State* officers. By their advice the business was then referred to a Committee of Three."[5]

On July 20th, 1781, in Congress, Edmund Randolph, Oliver Ellsworth, and James M. Varnum were selected to "prepare an exposition of the *Confederation* (of *States*), to devise a plan for its complete execution, and to present supplemental articles."[6]

In July and August, 1781, Hamilton published a series of papers called *The Continentalist*. He said that the *Confederation* was too weak, asked for more strength, and said that "we ought without delay to enlarge the powers of Congress."[7]

On March 20th, 1782, Lord North's ministry in England fell. Within two years thereafter the treaty which established the independence of the *United States* was successfully negotiated at Paris.[8]

In May, 1782, the enthusiasm of Europe for the new Republic of the *United States* first manifested itself in a message the King of Sweden sent through Benjamin Franklin, offering to enter into a treaty. And five months before the definitive American peace treaty was signed with England, the treaty was made and ratified with Sweden. Other European countries quickly followed the same course.[9]

In July, 1782, the New York Legislature invited

[5] Bancroft's *History of the Constitution of the United States*, Vol. I, p. 25. Report of the Grand Committee. MS.

[6] Bancroft's *History of the Constitution of the United States*, Vol. I, p. 25. Report of the Committee of Three. MS.

[7] Bancroft's *History of the Constitution of the United States*, Vol. I, p. 25. *Continentalist*. Reprinted in J. C. Hamilton's edition of the *Federalist*, cxl, cxli.

[8] Fiske's *The Critical Period of American History*, p. 1.

[9] Bancroft's *History of the Constitution of the United States*, Vol. I, p. 70.

Congress, for the common welfare, "to recommend, and each *State* to adopt, the measure of assembling a *general convention* of the *States,* especially authorized to revise and amend the *Confederation* of the *States,* reserving a right to the respective Legislatures (of the *States*) to modify their determinations." [10]

July 1st, 1782, the Rockingham ministry in England fell.[11]

In 1782 John Jay said that he was ready to begin negotiations (on the treaty with England) without waiting for the recognition of independence, provided that the (Scotchman) Oswald's Commission should speak of the thirteen *United States of America* instead of calling them *Colonies* and naming them separately.

Early in October, 1782, negotiations were begun. But the treaty was not concluded until the consent of France had been obtained, as it had already been agreed what the treaty should provide. The Mississippi River became the boundary line between the *United States* and the Spanish possessions.[12]

"The treaty of alliance between the *United States* and France expressly stipulated that neither power should ever make peace without the consent of the other. . . . Now we proceeded amiably to divide territory and commercial privileges with the enemy," (Great Britain).

On November 30th, 1782, our Treaty of Paris (with England) was signed. It was stated to be provisional,

---

[10] *Ibid.,* p. 39. MS. of the Journals of the Senate and Assembly of New York for the session of July, 1782. The grounds for believing Hamilton to have been the draftsman of the resolutions are solely the circumstances above related, and that the language bears his impress.
[11] Fiske's *The Critical Period of American History,* p. 6.
[12] *Ibid.,* p. 25.

OUR UNKNOWN CONSTITUTION 39

and not effective until England and France had agreed on terms of peace.

Great Britain in the treaty of peace had recognized the independence of individual *States,* naming them in order, and her Government followed the same system in all its intercourse with its late Colonies.[13]

The Revolutionary soldiers, whose valor had made the new republic possible, had not received their full pay for a considerable time, and one of the principal subjects of discussion was how to satisfy them.

As it seemed at this juncture almost impossible to keep together the representation of the requisite number of *States* in Congress, there were many who believed that there should be short annual sessions, and in the *interim* between these, Congress should appoint commissioners to conduct the executive business. Jefferson favored this.[14]

On June 4th, 1784, the Committee of *States* assembled, but the representatives of four of them did not attend. The vote of nine was necessary to pass any resolution, and therefore the absence of one blocked consideration of any measure.[14]

On August 19th, 1784, the representatives of three New England *States* returned home, and those who were left only sat intermittently. At last they, too, withdrew.[15]

In this situation Robert Morris retired as Superintendent of Finance, after announcing to the French representatives in America that he was unable to pay

[13] Encyclopædia Britannica, Vol. 27, p. 685a.
France's aid to America had cost her 1400 million francs. (Fiske's *The Critical Period of American History,* p. 37.)
[14] Bancroft's *History of the Constitution of the United States,* Vol. I, p. 164.
[15] *Ibid.,* p. 165.

the interest on the Dutch loan, which France had guaranteed, and that he could not pay the interest on the loan due France direct.

In September, 1784, after Washington had been on a tour of inspection to secure "the allegiance of the transmontane woodsmen by improving the channels of communication with the *States* on the Atlantic," he reported to Governor Harrison of Virginia.[16] He met Lafayette in Richmond, where the Virginia Assembly sent Patrick Henry and Madison to Washington and Lafayette to assure them of their lasting gratitude.[17]

In November, 1784, the members-elect of Congress arrived in such a dilatory manner that Richard Henry Lee of Virginia, on the 26th, 1784, wrote Madison that he believed the *States* should be called "to form a convention to revise the *Confederation*, so as to enable Congress to execute with more energy, effect, and vigor the powers assigned to it, than appears by experience that they can do under the present state of things." Madison said: "The union of the *States* is essential to their safety against foreign danger and internal contention; the perpetuity and efficacy of the present system cannot be confided in; the question therefore is, in what mode and at what moment the experiment for supplying the defects ought to be made." [18]

[16] *Ibid.*, pp. 160–69.
[17] *Ibid.*, pp. 170–71.
[18] *Ibid.*, pp. 166–67.

"There were three fatal defects (in the *Confederation*): first, a two-thirds vote was required for any important legislation, so that any five of the *States* could defeat the most sorely needed measure; second, the impossibility of presenting a united front to foreign countries in respect to commerce; third, the greatest defect was the lack of any means of enforcing obedience." (Fiske's *The Critical Period of American History*, p. 99.)

"No *State* could engage in war except by way of defense against

On November 30th, 1784, the Congress met at Trenton. As there were not enough accommodations for its members there, it adjourned to New York on January 11th, 1785. Richard Henry Lee was elected President. The New York representatives were Jay, Robert R. Livingston, Lansing, and Benton. A majority of them believed in creating a nation,[19] but the strong attitude of Richard Henry Lee brought on a rebellion in New York politics. Its Legislature in March appointed three extra delegates to Congress, two of whom "opposed Federal measures."

In the winter of 1784–85 Noah Webster, of Hartford, Connecticut, sought the proper form for a Continental Government. He declared: "So long as any

sudden Indian attack (under the Articles of Confederation).... The Articles of Confederation show that political action was at no time based on the views of the *States* as absolutely sovereign, but they also show that the share of *sovereignty* accorded to Congress was very inadequate even to the purposes of an effective confederation.... Under the Articles of Confederation, the most fundamental attribute of *sovereignty*, the power of tax, was not given to Congress. It could only make requisitions upon the thirteen members in proportion to the assessed value of their real estate, and it was not provided with any means of enforcing these requirements. The Articles contained nothing except a vague promise on the part of the *States* to obey.... The Articles of Confederation could only be amended by unanimous consent." (*Ibid.*, pp. 96, 97, 98.)

"The delegates in Congress were paid by their own *States* under the Articles of Confederation.... Each *State* had one vote under the Articles of Confederation ... but a bare majority was not enough to carry any important measure.

"Under the Articles of Confederation not a single step could be taken without the consent of at least two-thirds of the *States*, and this provision well nigh sufficed of itself to block the wheels of Federal legislation. There was a President of Congress, but he had no more power than any delegate. During a Congressional recess the country was run by an Executive Committee of one from each *State*, known as the Committee of the States." (*Ibid.*, p. 95.)

[19] Bancroft's *History of the Constitution of the United States*, Vol. I, p. 175.

individual *State* has power to defeat the measures of the other twelve (*States*) our pretended *Union* is but a name, and our *Confederation* a cobweb. The *sovereignty* of each *State* ought not to be abridged in any article relating to its own government; in a matter that equally respects all the *States*, a majority of the *States* must decide." [20]

In 1785 ten *States* approved an amendment to the Articles conceding to Congress the exclusive authority to regulate commerce for a period of thirteen years. But three *States* (Georgia, South Carolina, and Delaware) feared that the New England *States* would secure a monopoly of the carrying trade, and rejected the amendment.[21]

When in 1785 a convention was proposed which should give the *United States* greater power over commerce, Gerry, Holten, and Rufus King, contrary to their instructions, suppressed the acts of Massachusetts, saying that such a reform through a convention "is a violation of the rights of Congress, and, as a manifestation of a want of confidence in them, must meet their disapprobation. A further question arises whether the Convention should revise the Constitution generally or only for express purposes. . . . The requirement of the unanimous consent of the *Legislatures* of the *States* for altering the *Confederation* effectually prevents innovations by intrigue or surprise." [22]

On April 6th, 1785, Mr. King's Committee in Congress reported a resolution permitting slavery in the Northwest until 1801, but it was never called up.

---

[20] Lee's *The Story of the American Constitution*, p. 17.

[21] Bancroft's *History of the Constitution of the United States*, Vol. I, pp. 184, 185.

[22] *Ibid.*, p. 198.

CHAPTER VII

A PATRIOTIC SUBTERFUGE TO REORGANIZE THE UNITED STATES

THE two branches of the Massachusetts Legislature on July 1st, 1785, pledged their best endeavors to organize "the Federal Government on a firm basis, and to perfect the *Union*," and the same day the General Court of Massachusetts resolved "that the present powers of the Congress of the *United States* . . . in the Articles of Confederation are not fully adequate to the great purposes they were originally designed to effect."[1]

July 14th, 1785, Monroe's report to Congress was taken up by the Committee of the Whole. Its advocates claimed that it would encourage domestic industry by putting a tax on foreign goods, and that it was necessary to secure reciprocity with foreign nations, but especially because it would permit a navy, and they said these things could never be done unless the *States* acted in concert, "for their regulations would impede and defeat each other."[2]

In August, 1785, Dickinson, President of the Council of Pennsylvania, sent a message to the Pennsylvania Assembly stating that: "We again declare that

---

[1] Bancroft's *History of the Constitution of the United States,* Vol. I, p. 190.
[2] *Ibid.,* p. 195.

further negotiations ought to be vested in the Federal Council." [3]

The entire nation expected from the Congress itself the necessary amendments to strengthen the Government, because the people in Virginia and everywhere else "resented the restrictive policy of England." It is interesting to note that in the Fifth Congress, Monroe, who afterwards became President, was willing to invest the *Confederation* with a perpetual grant of power to regulate commerce, but on the condition that it should not be exercised without the consent of nine *States*. The Congress referred to his Committee the motion on commerce, but he was in no hurry to test it by a vote. He wrote Jefferson: [4] "It will be best to postpone this for the present; its adoption must depend on *the several Legislatures*." Jefferson himself was happy to find "the conviction growing stronger that nothing could preserve the *Confederacy* unless the bond of union, their common council, should be strengthened." [5]

In the summer of 1784 Señor Gardoqui, the Spanish envoy to the *United States*, told Mr. Jay, our Foreign Affairs Secretary, that his King was well disposed towards America, but could only grant us one favor, and that was to sign a treaty of commerce with us.[6] He insisted, though, that not even that could be done until we gave up all our claims to navigation of the Mississippi south of the Yazoo River. After a year of polite

[3] *Ibid.*, p. 191.

In the Appendix at page 261 there appears a parallel comparison of the Articles of Confederation and the Constitution as finally adopted.

[4] Bancroft's *History of the Constitution of the United States*, Vol. I, p. 94. Monroe to Jefferson, New York, April 12, 1785. MS.

[5] Bancroft's *History of the Constitution of the United States*, Vol. I, p. 94. Jefferson to Madison, Boston, July 1, 1784. MS.

[6] Fiske's *The Critical Period of American History*, p. 210.

but fruitless discussion Mr. Jay said he would only consent for the Mississippi to be closed against us for twenty-five years, if the treaty could be secured.

At this there burst forth a flame of indignation. This grew in violence when a North Carolina trader named Armis was stopped at Natchez, and his wares were confiscated.

Then Americans destroyed stores of Spanish traders at Vincennes and the Spanish tried to incite the Indians to attack them. The people threatened not only to capture Natchez and New Orleans, but if that should not prove effectual, and the Northeastern *States* decided to accept Jay's proposal, they openly threatened secession. The East in the summer of 1786 said that if Mr. Jay was not sustained, they would secede. This agitation only blew over when New Jersey, Pennsylvania, and Rhode Island joined the Southern element. The signing of the treaty was postponed.

Washington, ever alert in furthering Pitt's scheme to overthrow the French in America, understood the political implications of the situation. The knowledge he had gained in early days of the possibilities of transportation by water from the east to the west made him see the trend with prismatic clearness. Before resigning in 1783, he had studied the Mohawk Valley, afterwards served by the Erie Canal and later by the New York Central Railroad. So, on arriving at Mount Vernon again, he had time to study the problem of communicating with the West through the Potomac Valley. No man who has failed to traverse this great way can realize its possibilities. For several years he studied this work, and in 1785 became president of a company to extend transportation by the Potomac and the James Rivers. To testify to its "sense of his unexampled merits," the Legislature of Virginia voted him 150 shares of stock, but Washington characteristically declined it, although his own financial condition at that time would have fully justified its acceptance.

To work out the plans, Virginia and Maryland had to act together, and in 1785 a two-state commission consulted Washington at Mount Vernon. Then, as the plan contemplated connecting the headwaters of both the Ohio and the Potomac, Pennsylvania was invited to join the enterprise. Then with great inspiration Washington suggested that the *States* should consider duties and regulations, as well as a standard currency. These suggestions were transmitted to the Legislatures, and this gave Madison the opportunity to accomplish what had long been in his mind. But he dared not present it himself, because his nationalist leanings were too well known. He procured the introduction of the necessary motion by John Tyler a "zealot for *States' Rights*." The scheme was not immediately successful, but shortly after the motion had been laid upon the table, Maryland adopted the Mount Vernon agreement regarding the Potomac. Maryland had suggested that, as the plan should include a canal to connect the Chesapeake Bay and the Delaware River, Pennsylvania and Delaware should be conferred with.[7] Indeed, the Maryland acceptance said that "commissioners" should be invited to join the plan from all the *States*. Then the dormant Virginia resolution of Tyler was carried and the commissioners directed to attend at Annapolis on the first Monday in September in the year 1786.

That resolution read:

[7] *Ibid.*, pp. 214, 215, 216.

PROPOSITION OF THE GENERAL ASSEMBLY OF VIRGINIA

Virginia, ss. In the House of Delegates, January 21, 1786.
Resolved, that Edmond Randolph, James Madison, Jun., Walter Jones, St. George Tucker, Meriwether Smith, David Ross, William Ronald, and George Mason, Esquires, be appointed commissioners, who, or any five of whom, shall meet such commissioners as may be appointed by the other *States* in the *Union,* at a time and place to be agreed on, to take into consideration the trade of the *United States;* to examine the relative situation and trade of the said *States;* to consider how far a uniform system in their commercial regulations may be necessary to their common interest and their permanent harmony; and to report to the several *States* such an act relative to this great object as, when unanimously ratified by them, will enable the *United States* in Congress assembled effectually to provide for the same; that the said commissioners shall immediately transmit to the several *States* copies of the preceding resolution, with a circular letter requesting their concurrence therein, and proposing a time and place for the meeting aforesaid.

Test,   JOHN BECKLEY, C.H.D.
H. BROOKE, C.S.

1786, January 21,
    Agreed to by the Senate.

This was the beginning of the Constitution of the United States.

When they gathered at Annapolis on the 11th of September, 1786, Virginia, Delaware, Pennsylvania, New York, and New Jersey were represented, but New Hampshire, Rhode Island, Massachusetts, and North Carolina, although they had appointed commissioners, were not represented. Neither Connecticut, Georgia, nor South Carolina had acted. So the five *States* represented, after adopting an address by Hamilton to all the *States,* adjourned. In the instructions to her delegates New Jersey had authorized them to "consider how far a uniform system in their commercial regulations and other important matters might be necessary to the common interest and permanent harmony of the several *States*." Hamilton then advised that all the *States* meet in convention in Philadelphia in the following May, "to devise such further provisions as shall appear to them necessary to render the Constitution of the Federal Government adequate to the exigencies of the *Union*, and to report to Congress such an act as when agreed to by them and confirmed by the Legislatures of every *State*, would effectually provide for the same." Congress had up to this time failed to approve the plan of the commissioners at Annapolis.

It had been proposed in 1783 to relieve the country of debt by applying the money from the sales of homesteads in the West to the payment of the principal, but as the interest on the debt also had to be paid, Congress had recommended for a period of twenty-five years the imposition of duties upon teas, sugars, pepper, cocoa, molasses, and coffees. Each *State* was to appoint its own collectors. But the *States* were never able to agree upon the duties to be collected, so all that was left available was the proceeds of the lands in the West. In this situation an amendment was proposed to the Articles of Confederation to collect the duties and appoint the collectors. But only twelve *States* consented, and under the Articles of Confederation it required all of the thirteen. New York was the only recalcitrant, and her system was very oppressive to New Jersey and her other neighboring *States*. New Jersey refused to pay her part as long as New York oppressed her. New Jersey was persuaded to acquiesce, after which there was the final fight over the amendment in New York. The amendment, notwithstanding Hamilton's valiant efforts, was defeated there.

In February, 1786, Charles Pinckney, of South Carolina, in a motion of very great length, said: "They have therefore wisely determined to make the welfare of the *Union* their first object, reflecting that in all Federal regulations something must be yielded to aid the whole, and that those who expect support must be ready to afford it." [8]

Congress (in 1786) had failed to find ways to carry on the Federal Government. Its weakness lay in the fact that the *States* had not yet ceded the necessary power to the Federal Government. Virginia had invited the other *States* to attend a convention at Annapolis for the purpose of recommending "the strengthening of the Federal Government where its points were weakest." [9]

In September, 1786, Daniel Shays, a former Captain in the Continental Army, with 600 insurgents confronted the Supreme Court of Massachusetts at Springfield, and it was prevented from sitting. Shays had drilled and organized 1200 men, and he afterwards attacked General Shepard with 2000 men. But Shays' men became panicky and they retired, and set fire to houses and robbed the inhabitants at Amherst, Massachusetts.

At this time all of New York's representatives were

[8] Bancroft's *History of the Constitution of the United States*, Vol. I, p. 254. Journals of Congress, Vol. IV, p. 617.

Added to this, in 1785 in the *United States* there was no national coinage, and none was issued until 1793. (Fiske's *The Critical Period of American History*, p. 142.)

[9] Bancroft's *History of the Constitution of the United States*, Vol. I, p. 266.

exceedingly busy at home. One of them (Hobart) procured the services of a friend to look after some pressing affairs and attended the convention at Annapolis. Madison was already there (September 11th, 1786), "aiming at a plenipotentiary general convention." Only the Middle *States* were represented. "No *State* north of New York was represented, and no one south of Delaware, with the single exception of Virginia."[10]

Madison said:

> The commissioners . . . have represented the necessity of extending the revision of the Federal system to all its defects, and have recommended that deputies be appointed by the several Legislatures, to meet in convention in Philadelphia on the second of May next (1787)—provision preferable to a discussion of the subject in Congress, where it might be too much interrupted by ordinary business, and where it would, besides, be deprived of the counsels of individuals who are restrained from a seat in that assembly. The General Assembly of this Commonwealth . . . can no longer doubt that the crisis has arrived at which the *people* of America are to decide the solemn question whether they will, by wise and magnanimous efforts, reap the fruits of independence and of union; or whether, by giving way to unmanly jealousies and prejudices, or to partial and transitory interests, they will renounce the blessings prepared for them by the Revolution. The same noble and extended policy, and the same fraternal and affectionate sentiments which originally determined the citizens of this Commonwealth to unite with their brethren of the other *States* in establishing a *Federal* Government, cannot but be felt with equal force now as motives to lay aside every inferior consideration, and to concur in such further concessions and provisions as may be necessary to secure the objects for which that government was instituted, and render the *United States* as happy in peace as they have been glorious in war.[11]

[10] *Ibid.*, p. 268.
[11] *Ibid.*, pp. 270–71.

The Ordinance of 1787 passed by Congress provided that the Northwestern Territory be "carved into *States*, not exceeding five in number, and any one of these might be admitted into the *Union* as soon as its population reached 60,000. In the meantime the whole Territory was to be governed by officers appointed by Congress, and required to take an oath of allegiance to the *United States*. Their laws should conform these fundamental principles then governing the *United States*, and under no circumstances could any of them ever be separated from the *Union*." [12] Slavery was to be forbidden in this Territory.

In February, 1787, "a Grand Committee of the Seventh Congress by a narrow margin of one vote reported that 'they did strongly recommend to the different *Legislatures* to send forward delegates to the proposed convention at Philadelphia.'" But no vote was taken on this report. New York paid no attention to the proposed meeting at Annapolis, but instructed their delegates in Congress to recommend a general convention "to be initiated by Congress itself." But the proposition of the New York delegates was lost by a big majority. Then King, of Massachusetts, offered a substitute that did not refer to the meeting at Annapolis, but recommended a convention "as an original measure." This was accepted because it was adroitly drawn, so as not to invalidate the elections already made. The great Bancroft says: "In this way the self-love of Congress was appeased, and its authority arrayed in favor of a general convention." [13]

When Congress realized that it could not pass an

---

[12] Fiske's *The Critical Period of American History*, pp. 204–5.
[13] Bancroft's *History of the Constitution of the United States*, Vol. I, pp. 273–74.

effective revenue bill, it decided on February 21, 1787, after it had learned that the Virginia Legislature had appointed delegates to the Constitutional Convention, one of whom was George Washington, to accept the Annapolis recommendations and approve the proposed convention. Soon Massachusetts,[14] New Jersey, Pennsylvania, North Carolina, and Delaware chose delegates, and in the following April, May, and June Georgia, South Carolina, Connecticut, Maryland, and New Hampshire trailed along. Only Rhode Island stood out. This resolution (February 21st, 1787) read:

"It is expedient that on the second Monday in May next (1787) a convention of delegates who shall have been appointed (by the Legislatures) by the several *States* be held in Philadelphia, *for the sole and express purpose of revising the Articles of Confederation,* and reporting to Congress and the several Legislatures such alterations and provisions therein as shall, *when agreed to in Congress* and conformed to by the *States,* render the Federal Constitution adequate to the exigencies of the Government and the preservation of the *Union.*"[15]

The ruse of Washington, Madison, and their coadjutors had worked, and their prescience and courage had started the United States on the road to a close-knit, effective, and powerful government under a constitution elastic enough to conciliate the *States'* rights men, and strong enough to satisfy the advocates of a national Federal system.

Rufus King, of Massachusetts, wrote to Gerry, who had also been fighting the proposed Constitutional Con-

---

[14] Beck's *The Constitution of the United States*, p. 50.
[15] Bancroft's *History of the Constitution of the United States,* Vol. I, p. 273. Austin's *Gerry,* ii, 3, 4, 7, and 8.

vention: "Although my sentiments are the same as to the legality of the measure, I think we ought not to oppose, but to coincide with this project. Events are hurrying us to a crisis. Prudent and sagacious men should be ready to seize the most favorable circumstances to establish a more perfect and vigorous government."

CHAPTER VIII

THE PEOPLE AND THE STATES

THE roots of our Constitution go back over a thousand years. Some of its provisions were derived from the Magna Charta, others from the so-called Constitution of England. At the time it was adopted, it was the last word in man's aspiration for human liberty. It looked "to an indestructible *Union* of indestructible *States*."[1]

England constantly boasts of her "Constitution" and her Constitutional monarchy. Of course, England never had a written constitution. Her "Constitution" is derived from the body of the decisions of her courts.

The Preamble to the new Constitution read:

"We, the *people* of the *United States,* in order to form a more perfect union, establish justice, insure domestic tranquillity, provide for the common defense, promote the general welfare, and secure the blessings of liberty to ourselves and our posterity, do ordain and establish this Constitution for the *United States* of America."

"The Preamble, as finally drafted by the Committee of Detail, began, 'We, the *people* of the *States* of New Hampshire, Massachusetts, Rhode Island,' etc., and ended, 'do ordain, declare, and establish the following Constitution for the Government of Ourselves and our

[1] Texas *vs.* White, 7 Wallace 700.

Posterity.' This wording should be contrasted with the Articles of Confederation, which had begun with the words: 'Articles of Confederation and Perpetual Union between the *States* of New Hampshire, Massachusetts Bay, Rhode Island,' etc.

"When, at the close of the Convention, the Committee of Style appointed to prepare a final draft of the Constitution made its report on September 12, it entirely changed the phraseology of the Preamble. The words, 'We, the *people* of the *States* of New Hampshire,' etc., became, 'We, the *people* of the *United States.*' The final clause, 'declare and establish the following Constitution for the Government of Ourselves and our Posterity,' became 'do ordain and establish this Constitution for the *United States* of America.' "[2]

"In later years, an attempt was made to attribute great significance to the change made by the Committee of Style in substituting the phrase 'We, the *people* of the *United States*,' for the phrase, 'We, the *people* of New Hampshire, Massachusetts, Rhode Island,' etc. But this change was not intended by the Convention to be anything more than a matter of form. As the phrase was originally drafted, reciting the *people* of each of the thirteen *States* separately by name, it was then intended by the Convention that this new Constitution, before it should become effective, must be ratified by all the thirteen *States,* and that the requirement of the Articles of Confederation for unanimity of *States* on any Amendment should be complied with, this new Constitution being regarded in the light of such an amendment. But when, on August 31, 1787, the Con-

[2] Warren's *The Making of the Constitution,* pp. 393, 394. (The Confederation was the government which preceded the Constitution.)

vention decided that the new Government should go into operation upon ratification of the Constitution by nine out of thirteen *States,* such action made it necessary to eliminate from the Preamble the names of the specific *States;* for it could not be known, at the date of the signing of the Preamble and the rest of the Constitution by the delegates, just which of the thirteen *States* would ratify. Hence, the language, 'We, the *people of the United States,*' was used, the meaning being, 'We, the *people* of the *States* united,' *i.e.*, the people of those *States* which should agree to unite, by ratifying the new Constitution. 'No other intent was suggested or contemplated' by this change in language. The idea that 'We, the *people of the United States,*' was intended to mean the *people,* as a whole, of the country known as the *United States of America,* irrespective of the *States* of which the *people* were citizens, was an idea which did not enter the heads of the delegates at that time." [3]

"Justice Story said (in Martin *vs.* Hunter's Lessee, I Wheaton 304): 'The Constitution of the *United States* was ordained and established not by the *States* in their sovereign capacities, but emphatically, as the Preamble of the Constitution declares, by the *people of the United States.* So far from saying that it is established by the governments of the several *States,* it does not even say that it is established by the *people* of the several *States,* but it pronounces that it is established by the *people* of the *United States* in the aggregate. . . . Words cannot be plainer than the words used.'

"This last statement is certainly extreme. It is indeed made plain that the Constitution is not ratified

[3] *Ibid.*, pp. 394, 395, 396.

by the governments of the individual *States,* but it is not clearly indicated whether the ratifying parties are to be considered singly or as a composite whole. And in contradiction to the fact that a single political whole was meant is the fact that in ratifying the Constitution the *people* did vote by *States.*

"The only way by which the force of this fact is avoided is by the proposition that the ratifying *State* Conventions acted *ad hoc*[4] as agents of a single united *people.* But this argument is greatly weakened, if not absolutely destroyed, by the fact that only those *States* were to be considered members of the new *Union* whose respective *peoples,* acting in convention, should ratify the Constitution.

"The use of the phrase, 'We, the *People* of the United States,' as indicating the ordainers and establishers of the *Union,* is, however, of significance in determining the nature of the *Union* that was intended to be created, when taken in connection with the provision of Article VII that the Constitution was to be ratified, not by the *State* Legislatures, but in conventions, for it indicates that the *Union* was one which the *State Legislatures* were not competent to create; that, in other words, it was to be not a mere league or confederacy, such as the existing *State* governments might enter into, but a fundamental *Union* resulting in the creation of a new *National State* which, according to the political philosophy of that date, only the *people* acting in their original sovereign capacity were able to create."[5]

"But whether by 'We, the *People,*' was meant all

---

[4] *Ad hoc* means "to this, hereunto."
[5] Willoughby's *The Constitutional Law of the United States,* Vol. I, pp. 63, 64.

the *people* of the ratifying *States* considered as one body politic, or whether it referred to the *people* as organized in several Commonwealth communities, it is, so far as the language is concerned, impossible to say.

"The framers of the Constitution of the Southern Confederacy avoided this ambiguity by declaring in the Preamble: 'We, the *People* of the Confederate *States*, each *State* acting in its sovereign and independent character, in order to form a permanent federal government, . . . do ordain and establish this Constitution for the Confederate *States* of America." [6]

[6] *Ibid.,* p. 62.

CHAPTER IX

ARE WE A NATION OF PEOPLE, OR A UNION OF STATES, OR BOTH?

FULLY half of the ablest discussions about American political history have centered upon whether we are a *nation* of *people*, or a *confederacy* of *States*.[1]

The Civil War was fought largely over that question, and the great debates of Lincoln and Douglas covered every phase of it. The South, in a numerical minority of citizens, insisted that the *Union* was a *union* of *States*, that each of the *States* was sovereign, and that the *Union* could not force upon a *State* laws repugnant to the beliefs of a majority of the citizens of that *State*.

The Southern *States* claimed that slavery was a *State* question, and that the *United States* could not enforce the abolition of slavery in the Southern *States* against their wishes, and that if a slave escaped from a *State* where slavery was permitted by law to a *State* where slavery was not permitted, he could be brought back to his owner in the slave *State* from which he had escaped. That this was the law was settled by the

[1] "Madison authoritatively declared the real meaning of the words: 'Who are the parties to it? The *people*—but not the *people* as composing one great body; but the *people* as composing thirteen *sovereignties*. . . . Should all the *States* accept it, it will be then a government established by the thirteen *States* of America, not through the intervention of the Legislatures, but by the *people at large*.'" (Warren's *The Making of the Constitution*, p. 396.)

Supreme Court of the United States in the famous Dred Scott case.[2] That case was never overruled by the Supreme Court, but after four years' War between the *States* the Emancipation Proclamation emancipated the slaves[3] and thus changed the law. But even the change in the law has never stopped the discussion about *"State sovereignty"* and *"States' Rights."* It is as rife today in connection with the prohibition question as it ever was about slavery.

In this book I have in every instance italicized the words "States," "people," "Confederacy," "United States," "States' Rights," "sovereignty," and "Union," because it is quite apparent that the distinctions in using those words were considered as important at the time of the founding of the Government as they are now.

While it may be an open question as to whether our Government is one of *States* or of *people*, there can be no doubt of the present enormous veto power of one-fourth of the *States*. This negative control through the provisions of Article V of the Constitution that requires three-fourths of the *States* to amend any article or amendment of the Constitution, or to repeal any article or amendment, is so firmly embedded in the Constitution that it is impossible to dislodge it except by the votes of three-fourths of the *States* as

---

[2] Scott *vs.* Sandford, 19 How. 393.

[3] Strangely enough, they were emancipated by this Proclamation only in the *States* in insurrection against the *United States*. Later on, the constitutional amendment (the Thirteenth Amendment, ratified December 18, 1865) abolishing slavery, was passed by three-fourths of the *States*. It read: "Neither slavery nor involuntary servitude, except as a punishment for crime whereof the party shall have been duly convicted, shall exist within the *United States,* or any place subject to their jurisdiction." (Black's "Lincoln, the Democrat.")

States. And this regardless of whether those three-fourths of the *States* have more or less citizens entitled to vote under the Constitution than the other one-fourth of the *States*.

But many claim that the application of the amending Article V to constitutional questions may frequently be impracticable.

No man can, as as original proposition, argue that the majority should not rule, but nevertheless we must bear in mind that under the Constitution itself it takes three-fourths of the *States* to repeal any amendment to the Constitution of the *United States*, or to amend any section, or to adopt any new section, just as in the beginning it took three-fourths of the *States* acting through *State* Conventions, to enact every provision in the Constitution.

As an illustration apply this proposition to the prohibition question. It required the votes of three-fourths of the *States* to adopt the Eighteenth Amendment. It will likewise require the votes of three-fourths of the *States*, acting separately *as States*, to repeal it. To state the proposition negatively, neither the prohibition amendment nor any other amendment, nor any article, nor any part of any article or amendment of the Constitution, can be repealed or amended if one more than one-fourth of the *States acting as States* votes against it, and this regardless of the fact that the total population of the *States* which want the repeal or the amendment may be ten, twenty, or even a hundred times as large as the total population of the thirteen *States* which may not want the repeal or amendment.

Mr. James M. Beck, in his *The Constitution of the United States*, says:

"Thus it is that today some *States*, which have less population than some wards of the City of New York, have as many votes in the Senate as the great *State* of New York. It is unquestionably a palpable [4] negation of majority rule, for a combination of the little *States*, whose aggregate population is not a fifth of the American people, can defeat the will of the remaining four-fifths. Pennsylvania and New York, with nearly one-sixth of the entire population of the *United States*, have only four in ninety-six votes in the Senate."

The situation regarding the prospect of the repeal or amendment of any article or amendment must remain just as it is until the method of amending the Constitution or repealing any section of it is changed by constitutional amendment. And such constitutional amendment, changing the present method of amending the Constitution, must be adopted in exactly the method pointed out in Article V of the Constitution itself, which says:

Article V: "The Congress, whenever two-thirds of both Houses shall deem it necessary, shall propose amendments to this Constitution, or, on the application of the Legislatures of two-thirds of the several *States*, shall call a convention for proposing amendments, which, in either case, shall be valid to all intents and purposes, as part of this Constitution, when ratified by the Legislatures of three-fourths of the several *States*, or by conventions in three-fourths thereof, as the one or the other mode of ratification may be proposed by the Congress; provided that no amendment which may be made prior to the year one thousand eight hundred and eight shall in any manner affect the first and fourth

---

[4] Mr. Beck (p. 140) might have added after the word "palpable" the words "and intentional."

clauses in the ninth section of the first article; and that no *State,* without its consent, shall be deprived of equal suffrage in the Senate."

When any amendment is proposed that will take away from one-fourth of the *States* the veto power that they now have over any proposed amendment or repeal, the *States* with small populations will be slow to vote for it, because it would curtail their power to block any amendment to the Constitution that was not to their liking. The power these small *States* have is a veto power, but it is a great power.

States with small populations, compared with the population of *States* like Illinois, Pennsylvania, and New York, will be slow to change the instrument that has weathered so many stormy discussions. Nevertheless, it is entirely possible to change the method of amending our Constitution by repealing or amending Article V by the vote of three-fourths of the *States.*[5]

I do not know any great writer who has told just how Article V of the Constitution, providing for the passage of a constitutional amendment, shall be amended.

[5] It will be observed that no *State,* however small, *without its own consent* (even though every other *State* should decree it), shall be deprived of two members of the Senate, just as every *State* with large population has.

CHAPTER X

TROUBLES WITH THE ARMY—HELPLESSNESS OF THE GOVERNMENT

THE officers of the main Army of the Revolution sent to the Congress at Philadelphia as their Committee Major General MacDougall and Colonels Ogden and Brooks, who, on January 6th, 1783, presented the following address:[1]

"To the *United States* in Congress assembled: We, the officers of the army of the *United States,* in behalf of ourselves and our brethren the soldiers, beg leave freely to state to the supreme power, our head and sovereign, the distress under which we labor. Our embarrassments thicken so fast that many of us are unable to go further. Shadows have been offered to us, while the substance has been gleaned by others. The citizens murmur at the greatness of their taxes, and no part reaches the Army. We have borne all that men can bear. Our property is expended; our private resources are at an end. We therefore beg that a supply of money may be forwarded to the Army as soon as possible.

"The uneasiness of the soldiers for want of pay is great and dangerous; further experiments on their patience may have fatal effects. There is a balance

---

[1] Bancroft's *History of the Constitution of the United States,* Vol. I, pp. 76, 77, 78. Journals of Congress, iv, 206.

due upon the account for retained rations, forage, and arrearages on the score of clothing. Whenever there has been a want of means, defect in system, or neglect in execution, we have invariably been the sufferers by hunger and nakedness and languishing in a hospital. We beg leave to urge an immediate adjustment of all dues.

"We see with chagrin the odious point of view in which too many of the *States* endeavor to place men entitled to half pay. For the honor of human nature we hope that there are none so hardened in the sin of ingratitude as to deny the justice of the reward. To prevent altercations, we are willing to commute the half pay pledged. And in this we pray that the disabled officers and soldiers, with the widows and orphans of those who have expended, or may expend, their lives in the service of their country, may be fully comprehended.

"General dissatisfaction is gaining ground in the Army, from evils and injuries which, in the course of seven long years, have made their condition in many instances wretched. They therefore entreat that the Congress, to convince the Army and the world that the independence of America shall not be placed on the ruin of any particular class of her citizens, will point out a mode for immediate redress."

The memorial was referred to the Grand Committee, who conferred with the Superintendent of Finance. He said that any present payment to the Army was impossible, and that it would be imprudent to give assurances with regard to future pay; that he had no money, and had overdrawn his European accounts three and a half million livres. He therefore asked whether it was expedient to make further drafts on the proceeds of the Dutch loan and the French loan. On January 10th, 1783, he was authorized to "draw bills on the credit of applications for loans in Europe." The representatives of the Army told the Committee that if there was not an immediate payment of some of the amount due, a mutiny might ensue, and that the Army "is verging to that state which, we are told, will make a wise man mad." They taunted the Committee with the fact that the legislators always paid themselves before adjourning, and that they as regularly left unpaid those on the military lists. Their spokesman, General MacDougall, said that the most intelligent part of the Army "were deeply touched by the debility of the Federal Government and the unwillingness of the state to invigorate it." While Hamilton in a report of the Grand Committee, which he had drafted, renounced his claims for the half pay, he advised some present payment, and as for the balance, he said, the soldiers would have to wait, like other creditors.[2]

The helplessness of the national Government, together with the general feeling that more power should be given to the *United States,* led to great activity among the statesmen of the day in suggesting tentative plans for a stronger government.

There was a long discussion in regard to the proposed general tax by the national Government. There was almost endless debate on this subject. Bancroft says that "the public mind was ripening for a transition from a *confederation* (of *States*) to a real government." [3]

[2] Bancroft's *History of the Constitution of the United States,* Vol. I, pp. 78–79.
[3] *Ibid.,* p. 86.

On February 21st, 1783, when Madison was arguing for the necessity of a permanent revenue, Mercer, of Maryland, said: "If the Federal compact is such as has been represented, I will immediately withdraw from Congress and do everything in my power to destroy its existence." To which Gorham, of Massachusetts, replied: "The sooner this is known the better, that some of the *States* may form other confederacies adequate to their safety." [4]

In February, 1783, in England, Pitt won against Shelburne by seventeen votes. Shelburne resigned. The King offered Pitt the Treasury. Pitt refused, without a majority which he could not get except by the aid, or at least the neutrality, of Lord North.[5]

In March, 1783, Washington said in a letter to Governor Harrison of Virginia: "I am decided in my opinion that if these powers of Congress are not enlarged and made competent to all the general purposes, the blood which has been spilled, the expense that has been incurred, and the distresses which have been felt will avail nothing, and that the bond which holds us together, already too weak, will soon be broken; when anarchy and confusion will prevail." [6]

On March 15th, 1783, as Washington concluded his address at Newburgh, N. Y., upon the subject of the petition which the soldiers had presented through his "brother officers" in the army, he started in to read a letter, but after the first paragraph he asked leave to put on his spectacles, which he had never yet worn in public, saying: "I have grown gray in your service, and now find myself growing blind." The letter, which

[4] *Ibid.*, p. 91.
[5] *Ibid.*, pp. 54–55.
[6] *Ibid.*, p. 93.

was from Joseph Jones, of Virginia, detailed the vexations of Congress regarding how the Army should be dealt with. The officers who had listened to anonymous addresses now abandoned them and rallied to the advice of Washington, whom they had assured "they loved with the greatest sincerity of which the human heart is capable," and they resolved that "no circumstances of distress or danger shall induce a conduct that may tend to sully the reputation and glory which they (we) have acquired at the price of blood and eight years' faithful services." They made no demands, but declared their unwavering confidence in the justice of the country and of Congress. They merely asked Washington to urge Congress to quickly decide upon their memorial. Before the day ended (March 15th, 1783), Congress resolved to commute the half pay which the officers had been promised into five years' full pay, covered by certificates bearing 6 per cent interest.[7]

Peace was concluded March 19th, 1783, just "eight years from the day when the embattled farmers of Concord 'fired the shot heard round the world.'"[8]

In March, 1783, "William Pitt, the younger, of England, introduced into Parliament the bill which would have secured mutual unconditional free trade between the two countries, which was what Franklin, Jefferson, and Madison desired. Could this bill have been passed, the commercial progress of both countries would have been promoted, and the War of 1812 would have been prevented. But Pitt was defeated on this

[7] *Ibid.*, p. 98.
[8] *Ibid.*, p. 101.

proposal, and the regulation of commerce was left to the King in Council." [9]

Great Britain's national debt when her war with us began was £136,000,000. When the war ended, it was twice that. Our debt was about $46,000,000, the interest on which was about $2,500,000 annually.[10]

The total cost of the war to the Colonies up to the general orders of Washington proclaiming peace in April, 1783, was reckoned by Jefferson at $140,-000,000.

France forwent the payment of interest on its obligations up to 1784.

In 1784 the cost of the Colonial Government was $450,000.[11]

On June 8th, 1783, Washington's famous letter, before "the approaching disbandment of the Army," insisted that there must be "an indissoluble union of all the *States* under a single Federal Government" possessing "the power of enforcing its decrees," that "the debts incurred by Congress for . . . carrying on the war, and securing independence" must be fully paid; thirdly, the "militia must be organized throughout the thirteen *States* on uniform principles"; fourthly, "the people must . . . sacrifice, if need be, some of their local interests, . . . discord, . . . prejudices, and regard one another as fellow citizens." [12]

"In the summer of 1783, Congress ordered the Army disbanded because the Government was afraid of it.

---

[9] Fiske's *The Critical Period of American History*, p. 136.
[10] Bancroft's *History of the Constitution of the United States*, Vol. I, p. 103.
[11] *Ibid.*, pp. 159, 160.
[12] Fiske's *The Critical Period of American History*, p. 54.

... The British had not then evacuated New York City." [13]

On June 9th, 1783, a few hundred mutinous infantrymen stacked their arms in front of the State House in Philadelphia, where Congress was sitting, threw rocks at the building, and refused to disperse, which so alarmed Alexander Hamilton that he told Congress to "think of eternity," as he did not believe they had "more than an hour to live." The government of Pennsylvania refused Congress the protection it asked, because its own militia was insubordinate. So Congress at night fled to Princeton, where it held sessions, and to New York, where it sat during the Constitutional Convention." [14]

"The men of 1783 dwelt in a long, straggling series of republics, fringing the Atlantic coast, bordered on the north and south and west by two European powers (England and Spain), whose hostility they had some reason to dread." [15]

About this time the *States* were requested to pledge their internal revenues for twenty-five years to pay the *nation's* indebtedness, but this required unanimous consent of the *States,* and Rhode Island refused.[16]

"On September 3rd, 1783, the definitive treaty was signed which formally ended the Revolution and established the independence of the *United States.* . . . During the war the united efforts of the *States* were directed by a Continental Congress which sat from 1774 until 1781 without its powers having been defined by any written instrument, and without any authority

---

[13] Lee's *The Story of the American Constitution,* p. 14.
[14] Fiske's *The Critical Period of American History,* p. 43.
[15] *Ibid.,* p. 56.
[16] Beck's *The Constitution of the United States,* p. 43.

to enforce its decrees."[17] It was signed, for the United States by Adams, Franklin, and Jay, and for England by a coalition ministry, which afterwards fell.[18] When the coalition ministry fell, Pitt, who had been Lord of the Treasury and Chancellor of the Exchequer in 1783 when he was just twenty-five, got the biggest majority ever given to an English minister, 160 members of the coalition losing their seats in Parliament. Pitt really ruled seventeen years, with the greatest power since Elizabeth.[19]

In 1783 the last British soldier left New York, which was the last stronghold of King George in America.

On December 4th, 1783, Washington, who had spent $64,315 out of his own pocket, refused any pay for his revolutionary services. He left New York City from South Ferry for Paulus Hook, to go to Annapolis to resign to Congress.[20]

[17] Lee's *The Story of the Constitution*, p. 11.
[18] Fiske's *The Critical Period of American History*, p. 37.
[19] *Ibid.*, p. 45.
[20] *Ibid.*, p. 52.

CHAPTER XI

THE DELEGATES TO THE CONSTITUTIONAL CONVENTION

THE twelve *States* (Rhode Island sending no delegates) through Governors or Legislatures selected seventy-four delegates. Nineteen did not attend, or declined the appointment. Thirty-nine had been in the Confederation Congress, eight had been signers of the Declaration of Independence, five had been in the Annapolis Convention in September, 1786; there were seven Governors and twenty-one soldiers of the Revolution; thirty-three were lawyers, ten had been judges, six, farmers; three, doctors; nine were Princeton men, and there were students from Harvard, Columbia, Pennsylvania, William and Mary University; Oxford and the Scotch universities were also represented.[1]

The delegates attending the Constitutional Convention were fifty-five in number, thirty-nine of whom (those in the list that follows with a star after their names) signed the Constitution. The delegates by *States*, who attended the Convention, were as follows:

CONNECTICUT:
    William Samuel Johnson,* age over 54.
    Roger Sherman,* age 66.
    Oliver Ellsworth, age 42.

---

[1] Warren's *The Making of the Constitution*, p. 55.

"Sixty-five delegates were chosen by twelve participating *States*, but ten failed to take their seats. Among these were Patrick Henry,

DELAWARE:
  Jacob Broom.*
  George Read,* age over 54.
  John Dickinson,* age over 54.
  Gunning Bedford, Jun.*
  Richard Basset.*
GEORGIA:
  William Few.*
  Abraham Baldwin.*
  William Pierce.
  William Houstoun.
MARYLAND:
  James McHenry.*
  Daniel of St. Thomas Jenifer,* age 64.
  Daniel Carroll,* age over 54.
  John Francis Mercer, age under 31.
  Luther Martin.

of Virginia, and Willie Jones, of North Carolina, both of whom declined, and Richard Caswell, of North Carolina, who resigned. Neither Madison's *Journal* nor the records of the secretary gave any reason for the absence of John Pickering and Benjamin West, of New Hampshire; Francis Dana, of Massachusetts; John Neilson and Abraham Clark, of New Jersey, and George Walton and Nathaniel Pendleton, of Georgia. Of the fifty-five who actually participated in the deliberations of the Convention, on the last day thirteen had either gone home or were absent because of illness or other reasons. Of those present, three, Edmund Randolph and George Mason, of Virginia, and Elbridge Gerry, of Massachusetts, refused to sign the completed document, leaving only thirty-nine who immortalized themselves by signing the final draft of the Constitution. Each of the twelve participating *States,* however, was represented among the signers, Hamilton signing alone for New York." (Lee's *The Story of the Constitution,* p. 22.)

"Washington and Madison each became President; Ellsworth and Rutledge, Chief Justices; Wilson, Blair and Paterson, Associate Justices; Hamilton, Secretary of the Treasury; Bedford, Attorney General; Randolph, Attorney General and Secretary of State; Gerry, Vice President; while others became United States Senators, members of Congress, Judges of Federal Courts and of *State* Supreme Courts,

MASSACHUSETTS:
  Elbridge Gerry.
  Nathaniel Gorham.*
  Rufus King,* age 32.
  Caleb Strong.
NEW HAMPSHIRE:
  John Langdon.*
  Nicholas Gilman.*
NEW JERSEY:
  William Livingston,* age over 54.
  David Brearly.*
  William C. Houston.
  William Paterson.*
  Jonathan Dayton,* age 26.
NEW YORK:
  Robert Yates.
  Alexander Hamilton,* age under 31.
  John Lansing.

Governors, etc. History is silent as to any later political activity of eleven. Seven delegates died shortly after the Convention. Madison was the last survivor. He lived to see 'the great American experiment,' as John Ruskin called our country, so largely his brain child, pass into lusty youth and become firmly established among the nations of the earth. Full of years and honors, he passed away at the ripe old age of eighty-five—nearly fifty years after the adjournment of the great Convention." (*Ibid.*, p. 47.)

"The Constitutional Convention was composed of comparatively young men. Jonathan Dayton, the youngest member, was twenty-six years of age; John Francis Mercer, twenty-eight; Charles Pinckney, twenty-nine; Hamilton, whose genius had been touched into a flame by the grim chemistry of war, thirty; Davie, thirty-one; Randolph, thirty-four; Gouverneur Morris, thirty-three; Madison, who contributed so largely to the plan that he was afterwards known as 'The Father of the Constitution,' thirty-six; McClurg, the substitute for Patrick Henry and the most skillful surgeon in the Revolution, forty; Ellsworth, forty-two; Paterson, forty-two; Mifflin, forty-three; Wilson, forty-five; Washington, the Ulysses of the Revolution, fifty-five; Franklin, the Nestor of the Convention, eighty-one; while the average was only forty-two. But, regardless of age

NORTH CAROLINA:
  Alexander Martin.
  William R. Davie.
  William Blount.*
  Richard D. Spaight.*
  Hugh Williamson.*
PENNSYLVANIA:
  Benjamin Franklin,* age 81.
  Thomas Mifflin.*
  Robert Morris.*
  George Clymer.*
  Thomas Fitzsimons.*
  Jared Ingersoll.*
  James Wilson,* age 45.
  Gouverneur Morris,* age 33.
SOUTH CAROLINA:
  John Rutledge,* age 48.
  Charles C. Pinckney,* age under 31.
  Charles Pinckney,* age 29.
  Pierce Butler.*

or occupation, they were patriots and statesmen of the highest order and, in their deliberations, displayed none of the cowardice of time-servers or the low cunning of demagogues." (*Ibid.*, p. 45.)

"The lawyers (in the Convention), however, predominated, numbering thirty-one. Twenty-five (delegates) were from north of the Mason and Dixon line, and thirty from the Southern *States*. Of the thirty-nine who signed the Constitution, nineteen were from the North and twenty from the South. Eight were of foreign birth; these were Alexander Hamilton, William Paterson, James Wilson, Robert Morris, James McHenry, Thomas Fitzsimons, William R. Davie, and Pierce Butler. Eight had the honor of signing the Declaration of Independence; these were Benjamin Franklin, James Wilson, Robert Morris, Roger Sherman, George Read, George Clymer, George Wythe, and Elbridge Gerry. In addition, Franklin had also signed the Treaties of Alliance and Commerce with France in 1778, and the Treaty of Peace with Great Britain in 1783." (*Ibid.*, p. 43.)

"In prestige and influence, Washington ranked first among the delegates. Franklin was the wisest; Hamilton, the most brilliant;

VIRGINIA:
George Washington,* age over 54.
Edmund Randolph, age 34.
John Blair,* age over 54.
James Madison, Jun.,* age 36.
George Mason, age over 54.
George Wythe, age over 54.
J. McClurg.

The Convention sat four months, and Gouverneur Morris spoke 173 times, James Wilson, 169; Madison, 161; Roger Sherman, 138; Mason, 136; Gerry, 119, and George Washington, *once*.

In May, 1787, in Virginia, Patrick Henry, Richard Henry Lee, and Thomas Nelson, having refused to serve as delegates to the Convention, Governor Edmund Randoph (who himself was a delegate) named to one vacancy Professor McClurg, of William and Mary College.[2]

Madison, the most sagacious; while the others, for the most part, were national figures. Seven had been Governors of *States,* while all but twelve had been members of Congress. . . . Thirty were college men, and twenty-six had degrees from the leading colleges of Europe and America." (*Ibid.,* p. 44.)

[2] Bancroft's *History of the Constitution of the United States,* Vol. II, p. 3.

"*Mr. Randolph* is Governor of Virginia—a young gentleman in whom unite all the accomplishments of the scholar and the statesman. He came forward with the postulata, or first principles, on which the Convention acted, and he supported them with a force of eloquence and reasoning that did him great honor. He has a most harmonious voice, a fine person, and striking manners. Mr. Randolph is about thirty-two years of age." (*Character Sketches of the Delegates to the Federal Convention,* by William Pierce, a delegate from Georgia to the Federal Convention.)

"*Mr. McClurg* is a learned physician, but having never appeared before in public life, his character as a politician is not sufficiently known. He attempted once or twice to speak, but with no great

In May, 1787, Washington was met at Chester, thirteen miles from Philadelphia, and the city light horse escorted him to Philadelphia amid the chiming of bells. He immediately called on Benjamin Franklin, the President of Pennsylvania.[3]

The Journal of the Federal Convention shows that on May 14th, 1787, eleven years after the Declaration of Independence, in the plain brick building where the Declaration of Independence was adopted eleven years before,[4] there gathered in Philadelphia "sundry deputies." But a majority of the *States* was not present, so the Convention adjourned to May 25th, 1787.[5]

On May 14th, 1787, the only *States* fully represented were Pennsylvania and Virginia. The others arrived slowly, and pending their coming, the Virginians conferred together many hours a day, in order to be able to present a definite plan. Washington and others favored a new constitution, rather than an effort

---

success. It is certain that he has a foundation of learning, on which, if he pleases, he may erect a character of high renown. The Doctor is about thirty-eight years of age, a gentleman of great respectability, and of a fair and unblemished character." (*Ibid.*)

"*Dr. Franklin* is well known to be the greatest philosopher of the present age; all the operations of nature he seems to understand—the very heavens obey him, and the clouds yield up their lightning to be imprisoned in his rod. But what claim he has to the politician, posterity must determine. It is certain that he does not shine much in public council; he is no speaker, nor does he seem to let politics engage his attention. He is, however, a most extraordinary man, and tells a story in a style more engaging than anything I ever heard. Let his biographer finish his character. He is eighty-two years old, and possesses an activity of mind equal to a youth of twenty-five years of age." (*Ibid.*)

[3] Bancroft's *History of the Constitution of the United States*, Vol. II, p. 4.

[4] Fiske's *The Critical Period of American History*, p. 222.

[5] Bancroft's *History of the Constitution of the United States*, Vol. II, p. 4.

to try to amend the *Confederation*. His position was quickly strengthened by the accession of Randolph and Madison. Randolph was selected to bring forward the Virginia plan.[6]

[6] *Ibid.*, p. 5.

CHAPTER XII

PROCEEDINGS IN THE CONSTITUTIONAL CONVENTION, AND IN CONGRESS

THE question that laid at the very root of all government was the right of the citizens to vote, and how that voting should be registered in the national Legislature. This, of course, should be based on "some equitable ratio." Gouverneur Morris and his followers from Pennsylvania, one of the largest *States,* urged that the large *States* should unite to refuse to the smaller *States* in the Convention the same equal vote [1] they had in the *Confederacy* Congress, but Virginia, the largest in territory and population, sided with the small *States,* and insisted that the small *States* would be "more willing to renounce this unequal privilege in return for an efficient government." [2]

At last, on the 25th of May, 1787, the New Jersey delegates arrived. Four *States* from the South were

[1] The large *States* said it was absurd to give Georgia's 100,000 people the same representation as Virginia's 750,000. . . . Under the Constitution, when Congress was apportioning taxes, the North contended that slaves should be counted. The South said they should not. Now the contention was reversed. The matter was finally compromised, and slavery was permitted for another twenty-five years, and the Southern *States* agreed that Congress should have absolute control over foreign and interstate commerce. (Lee's *The Story of the American Constitution,* pp. 28, 29.)

[2] Bancroft's *History of the Constitution of the United States,* Vol. II, p. 7.

represented with nineteen members, and three from the North with ten members.[3]

Upon motion of Charles Pinckney, of South Carolina, a Committee composed of Mr. Wythe, Charles Pinckney, and Mr. Hamilton was appointed to draw up rules to be observed as the standing orders of the Convention . . . and report to the Convention. The Convention usually sat, irregularly, from 10 to 4.[4]

James Madison's notes show that the Convention

---

[3] *Ibid.*, p. 8.
[4] Farrand's *The Records of the Federal Convention of 1787*, Vol. I, p. 2.

"*Mr. Wythe* is the famous Professor of Law at the University of William and Mary. He is confessedly one of the most learned legal characters of the present age. From his close attention to the study of general learning he has acquired a complete knowledge of the dead languages and all the sciences. He is remarked for his exemplary life, and is universally esteemed for his good principles. No man, it is said, understands the principles of government better than Mr. Wythe, nor anyone who understands the fluctuating condition to which all societies are liable better than he does, yet from his too favorable opinion of men, he is no great politician. He is a neat and pleasing speaker, and a most correct and able writer. Mr. Wythe is about fifty-five years of age." (*Character Sketches of Delegates to the Federal Convention,* by William Pierce, a delegate from Georgia to the Constitutional Convention.)

"*Mr. Charles Pinckney* is a young gentleman of most promising talents. He is, although only twenty-four years of age, in possession of a very great variety of knowledge. Government, law, history, and philosophy are his favorite studies, but he is intimately acquainted with every species of polite learning, and has a spirit of application and industry beyond most men. He speaks with great neatness and perspicuity, and treats every subject as fully, without running into prolixity, as it requires. He has been a member of Congress, and served in that body with ability and *éclat.*" (*Ibid.*)

"In reference to this part of his life, Mr. Pinckney frequently spoke of the deep diffidence and solemnity which he felt, being the youngest member of the body, whenever he addressed the Federal Convention." (J. B. O'Neall, *Biographical Sketches of the Bench and Bar of South Carolina,* Charleston, 1859, II, 140.)

"*Mr. Madison* is a character who has long been in public life; and what is very remarkable, every person seems to acknowledge was called "to revise the Federal system of Government," and that the delegates from Delaware were "prohibited from changing the article in the Confederation establishing an equality of votes among the States."[5]

May 25th, 1787, twenty-eight delegates gathered as the representatives of New York, New Jersey, Pennsylvania, Delaware, Virginia, North Carolina, South Carolina, and Georgia. Rhode Island alone was absent.[6]

---

his greatness. He blends together the profound politician with the scholar. In the management of every great question he evidently took the lead in the Convention, and although he cannot be called an orator, he is a most agreeable, eloquent, and convincing speaker. From a spirit of industry and application which he possesses in a most eminent degree, he always comes forward the best informed man of any point in debate. The affairs of the *United States* he, perhaps, has the most correct knowledge of, of any man in the *Union*. He has been twice a member of Congress, and was always thought one of the ablest members that ever sat in that council. Mr. Madison is about thirty-seven years of age, a gentleman of great modesty—with a remarkably sweet temper. He is easy and unreserved among his acquaintances, and has a most agreeable style of conversation." (*Character Sketches of Delegates to the Federal Convention*," by William Pierce, a delegate from Georgia to the Constitutional Convention.)

[5] Farrand's *The Records of the Federal Convention of 1787*, Vol. I, pp. 3, 4.

[6] *Ibid.*, p. 5, shows that the delegates were tabulated by *States*, as follows:

NEW YORK,	Alexander Hamilton,
	Robert Yates.
NEW JERSEY,	David Brearly,
	William Churchill Houston,
	William Paterson.
PENNSYLVANIA,	Robert Morris,
	Thomas FitzSimons,
	James Wilson,
	Gouverneur Morris.
DELAWARE,	George Read,
	Richard Bassett,
	Jacob Broom.

On that day (May 25th, 1787), upon nomination of Robert Morris, of Pennsylvania, George Washington was unanimously elected President of the Convention. Upon Washington's suggestion, William Jackson was elected Secretary.[7]

VIRGINIA,	George Washington,
	Edmund Randolph,
	George Wythe,
	George Mason,
	James Madison,
	John Blair,
	James McClurg.
NORTH CAROLINA,	Alexander Martin,
	William Richardson Davie,
	Richard Dobbs Spaight,
	Hugh Williamson.
SOUTH CAROLINA,	John Rutledge,
	Charles Cotesworth Pinckney,
	Charles Pinckney,
	Pierce Butler.
GEORGIA,	William Few.

[7] *Ibid.*, p. 2.

"*Robert Morris* is a merchant of great eminence and wealth; an able financier, and a worthy patriot. He has an understanding equal to any public object, and possesses an energy of mind that few men can boast of. Although he is not learned, yet he is as great as those who are. I am told that when he speaks in the Assembly of Pennsylvania, he bears down all before him. What could have been his reason for not speaking in the Convention I know not—but he never once spoke on any point. This gentleman is about fifty years old." (*Character Sketches of Delegates to the Federal Convention,* by William Pierce, a delegate from Georgia to the Constitutional Convention.)

"*General Washington* is well-known as the Commander-in-chief of the late American Army. Having conducted these *States* to independence and peace, he now appears to assist in framing a government to make the people happy. Like Gustavus Vasa, he may be said to be the deliverer of his country; like Peter the Great, he appears as the politician and the statesman; and like Cincinnatus, he returned to his farm, perfectly contented with being only a plain citizen, after enjoying the highest honor of the *Confederacy,* and now only seeks for the approbation of his countrymen by being virtuous and useful. The General was conducted to the chair as

On the 28th of May, 1787, the delegates from two more *States* (Maryland and Massachusetts) arrived. Rhode Island was not represented, and did not sign the Constitution which was afterwards adopted, until 1790. In all there were fifty-five delegates.[8]

On May 28th, 1787, the delegates resolved that there should not be recorded the votes of individuals, and that they would sit behind closed doors, "lest the publication of their debates should rouse the country to obstinate conflicts before they themselves had reached their conclusions."

May 28th, 1787, Mr. Wythe reported that his Committee had directed him to report the rules. Two of them were not adopted; others were amended. They provided that a quorum should consist of the deputies of at least seven *States;* that no deputy should speak more than twice without permission; that the Committee should be appointed by ballot, and that a vote may be postponed until the next day "if the deputies of any *State* desire it."

Mr. Randolph, the Governor of Virginia, who called the Convention to order, drew attention to the fact that the then *Confederacy* "cannot be claimed to be paramount to the *State* Constitutions."[9]

Mr. Butler, of South Carolina, made a motion that

President of the Convention by the unanimous voice of its members. He is in the fifty-second year of his age." (*Ibid.*)

[8] Bancroft's *History of the Constitution of the United States,* Vol. II, p. 8.

[9] Farrand's *The Records of the Federal Convention of 1787,* Vol. I, p. 19.

"*Mr. Butler* is a character much respected for the many excellent virtues which he possesses. But as a politician or an orator, he has no pretentions to either. He is a gentleman of fortune, and takes rank among the first in South Carolina. He has been appointed to Congress, and is now a member of the Legislature of the House "provide against . . . licentious publication of their proceedings," [10] and on May 29th, 1787, among the other rules adopted, it was resolved that nothing said in the Convention be printed, or otherwise published, or communicated without permission.[11]

Mr. Madison's notes show that on this day (May 28th, 1787) Mr. King, of Massachusetts, said that as the acts of the Convention were to have no binding force on the constituents, it was unnecessary for any member to call for the yeas and nays.[12]

Robert Morris, of Pennsylvania, and Gouverneur Morris, of the same *State*, argued that the large *States* should refuse an equal vote to the small *States*, because to do so would permit them "to negative every good system of government," but the delegates from Virginia fought this.[13]

South Carolina. Mr. Butler is about forty years of age; an Irishman by birth." (*Character Sketches of Delegates to the Federal Convention*, by William Pierce, a delegate from Georgia to the Constitutional Convention.)

"*Mr. King* is a man much distinguished for his eloquence and great parliamentary talents. He was educated in Massachusetts, and is said to have good classical as well as legal knowledge. He has served for three years in the Congress of the *United States* with great and deserved applause, and is at this time high in the confidence and approbation of his countrymen. The gentleman is about thirty-three years of age, about five feet, ten inches high, well formed, an handsome face, with a strong, expressive eye, and a sweet, high-toned voice. In his public speaking there is something peculiarly strong and rich in his expression, clear and convincing in his arguments, rapid and irresistible at times in his eloquence, but he is not always equal. His action is natural, swimming, and graceful, but there is a rudeness of manner sometimes accompanying it. But take him *tout ensemble*, he may with propriety be ranked among the luminaries of the present age." (*Ibid.*)

[10] Farrand's *The Records of the Federal Convention of 1787*, Vol. I, p. 9.
[11] *Ibid.*, p. 15.
[12] *Ibid.*, p. 10.
[13] *Ibid.*, p. 11.

On May 29th, 1787, the first additional rule agreed to was "that no member be absent from the House and thereby interrupt the representation of the *State*, without leave." [14]

On May 29th, 1787, Governor Randolph of Virginia opened the business of the Convention with the observation that "it is our duty to inquire into the defects of the *Confederation* and the requisite properties of the government now to be framed; the danger of the situation and its remedy." He said further: "The *Confederation* was made in the infancy of Constitutions . . . when no commercial discord had arisen among *States;* when no rebellion like that in Massachusetts had broken out; when foreign debts were not urgent. . . . But it offered no security against foreign invasion, for Congress could neither prevent nor conduct a war, nor punish infractions of treaties . . . nor control particular *States* from provoking war. The Federal Government has no constitutional power

---

[14] *Ibid.*, p. 15.

"*Mr. Gouverneur Morris* is one of those geniuses in whom every species of talents combine to render him conspicuous and flourishing in public debate. He winds through all the mazes of rhetoric, and throws around him such a glare that he charms, captivates, and leads away the senses of all who hear him. With an infinite stretch of fancy he brings to view things when he is engaged in deep argumentation, that render all the labor of reasoning easy and pleasing. But with all these powers he is fickle and inconstant, never pursuing one train of thinking, nor ever regular. He has gone through a very extensive course of reading, and is acquainted with all the sciences. No man has more wit, nor can anyone engage the attention more than Mr. Morris. He was bred to the law, but I am told he disliked the profession, and turned merchant. He is engaged in some great mercantile matters with his namesake, Mr. Robert Morris. This gentleman is about thirty-three years old; he has been unfortunate in losing one of his legs, and getting all the flesh taken off his right arm by a scald, when a youth." (*Character Sketches of Delegates to the Federal Convention,* by William Pierce, a delegate from Georgia to the Constitutional Convention.)

to check a quarrel between *separate States;* nor to suppress a rebellion in any one of them, nor to defend itself against the encroachments of the *States.* From the manner in which it has been ratified, it cannot be claimed to be paramount to the *State* Constitutions, so that there is a prospect of anarchy, from the inherent laxity of the Government. As a remedy, the government to be established must have for its basis the republican principle." [15]

Governor Randolph then proposed the following resolutions, each of which he explained:

> The Articles of Confederation ought to be so corrected and enlarged as to accomplish the objects proposed by their institution; namely, "common defense, security of liberty, and general welfare."
>
> The rights of suffrage in the national Legislature ought to be

[15] Bancroft's *History of the Constitution of the United States,* Vol. II, pp. 10, 11. Fiske's *The Critical Period of American History,* pp. 235, 236.

> The Virginia delegates' plan was very improperly called a "national plan." It was a "large *State*" plan proposed by those *States* which had or hoped for a large population. It meant to base representation in both Houses on population, so that the large *States* could control both of them, and it left the appointment of a president or other executive, and the Federal judges, to Congress, so that the whole administration of the Government would fall under the large *State* control.
>
> The New Jersey plan continued the old federation with its single House and equal *State* vote, but added the power to regulate commerce and raise revenue, and to compel the *States* to obey requisitions.
>
> The Connecticut delegates from their first appearance had favored a compromise. They had been trained under the New England system, in which the Assemblies were made up of two Houses, one representing the *people* of the whole *State* in proportion to population, the other giving an equal representation to the towns.
>
> The deadlock (between the three plans) was referred to a Committee which reported in favor of the Connecticut compromise. The Senate obtained its power to act as executive council as a restraint on the President in appointments and treaties. (*Encyclopædia Britannica,* Vol. 27, p. 685b.)

proportioned to the quotas of contribution, or to the number of free inhabitants.

The national Legislature ought to consist of two branches, of which the members of the first or democratic House ought to be elected by the *people* of the several *States;* of the second, by those of the first, out of persons nominated by the individual Legislatures.

The national Legislature, of which each branch ought to possess the right of originating acts, ought to enjoy the legislative rights vested in Congress by the *Confederation,* and moreover to legislate in all cases to which the separate *States* are incompetent,[16] or in which the harmony of the *United States* might be interrupted by the exercise of individual legislation; to negative all laws passed by the several *States* contravening the Articles of Union; and to call forth the force of the *Union* against any member of the *Union* failing to fulfil its duty under the articles thereof.

A national executive, chosen by the national Legislature and ineligible a second time, ought to enjoy the executive rights vested in Congress by the *Confederation,* and a general authority to execute the national laws.

The executive and a convenient number of the national judiciary ought to compose a council of revision, with authority to examine every act of the national Legislature before it shall operate.

A national judiciary ought to be established; to consist of supreme and inferior tribunals, to be chosen by the national Legislature; to hold their offices during good behavior, with jurisdiction to hear and determine all piracies and felonies on the high seas; captures from an enemy; cases in which foreigners and citizens, a citizen of one *State* and a citizen of another *State,* may be interested; cases which respect the collection of national revenue; impeachments of national officers; and questions which may involve the national peace and harmony.

Provision ought to be made for the admission of *States* lawfully arising within the limits of the *United States.*

A republican government and the territory of each *State* ought to be guaranteed by the *United States* to each *State.*

Provision ought to be made for the completion of all the en-

[16] Bancroft's *History of the Constitution of the United States,* Vol. II, p. 11.

gagements of Congress, and for its continuance until after the Articles of Union shall have been adopted.

Provision ought to be made for the amendment of the Articles of Union; to which the assent of the national Legislature ought not to be required.

The legislative, executive, and judiciary powers within the several States ought to be bound by oath to support the Articles of Union.

The amendments which shall be offered to the *Confederation* by the Convention ought, after the approbation of Congress, to be submitted to the assemblies of representatives, recommended by the several Legislatures to be expressly chosen by the *people* to consider and decide thereon.[17]

These resolutions were referred to a Committee of the Whole Convention.[18]

[17] *Ibid.*, pp. 12, 13.
[18] Elliott's *Debates on the Federal Constitution*, Vol. I, pp. 123, 124.

The first ten amendments were acted on by Congress in 1790, and became part of the Constitution in 1791. (Fiske's *The Critical Period of American History*, p. 330.)

"In order to follow with clear understanding the course of the proceedings of the Convention, particular attention is required to the following papers, which, except the third, successively formed the general text of their debates:

"1. May 29, 1787. *The Fifteen Resolutions* offered by Mr. Edmund Randolph to the Convention, and by them referred to a Committee of the Whole.

"2. June 13. *Nineteen Resolutions* reported by this Committee of the Whole, on the 13th, and again on the 19th of June, to the Convention.

"3. July 26. *Twenty-three Resolutions,* adopted and elaborated by the Convention, in debate upon the above nineteen, reported from the Committee of the Whole; and on the 23rd and 26th of July, referred, together with the plan of Mr. C. Pinckney, and the propositions of Mr. Paterson, to a Committee of Five, to report a draft of a Constitution.

"4. August 6. *The Draft of a Plan of a Constitution,* reported by the Committee to the Convention; and debated from that time until the 12th of September.

"5. September 13. *Plan of a Constitution,* brought in by a Committee of Revision, appointed on the 8th of September, consisting of

These were the provisions for a truly representative *republic,* where in the choice of the second branch of the Legislature "the *States* were only to nominate candidates."

One provision was absolutely necessary, to have a national Legislature in which the American *people* instead of the American *States* should be represented —and there must be an Assembly, as our present House of Representatives, standing in the same immediate relation to the *people* of the whole country as was sustained by the Assembly of each separate *State* to the *people* of that *State.*

Madison conceived the idea of two governments operating at one and the same time upon the same individuals, harmonious with each other, but each separate in its own sphere.

"Under the Articles of the Confederation each *State* had an equal vote, and two-thirds were required for every important measure. Under the Virginia plan, each *State* was to have a number of representatives proportionate either to its wealth or to the number of its free inhabitants, and a bare majority of votes was to suffice to pass all measures in the ordinary course of business, and these rules were to apply both to the lower House and to the Senate." [19]

This would overthrow the equality of the *States* altogether, and give Virginia sixteen representatives, where Georgia, the smallest *State* in population, had but one, and would permit combinations by individual members of every *State,* irrespective of *State* lines.[20]

five members, to revise the style and arrange the articles agreed to by the Convention." (Elliott's *Debates on the Federal Constitution,* Vol. I, pp. 123, 124.)

[19] Fiske's *The Critical Period of American History,* pp. 236–40.
[20] *Ibid.,* pp. 236–40.

90   OUR UNKNOWN CONSTITUTION

On May 29th, 1787, William Paterson, of New Jersey, noted that *"sovereignty* is an integral thing." This was one of the earliest suggestions of *State sovereignty*.[21]

On May 30th, 1787, after Charles Pinckney, a South Carolinian of only twenty-nine, had presented on the same day his constitutional plan for the form of a "Federal" government to be adopted by the "free and independent *States*," "grounded on the principles of Virginia," both plans were referred to a Committee of the Whole, appointed to consider the state of the *Union*. But none of Pinckney's plan was used, and no copy of it is now extant.[21]

On May 30th, 1787, Governor Randolph introduced the Gouverneur Morris plan for a national government of a "supreme legislative, executive, and judiciary."[22] Here was a suggestion that in case of conflict the *"sovereignty"* of the *States* must yield to the supreme powers of [23] the *national* Government, and Morris declared that "there must be one supreme power, and

---

[21] Bancroft's *History of the Constitution of the United States*, Vol. II, p. 14. Paterson MSS. Gilpin, 735. Elliot, 128. Yates in Elliot, i, 391.

[22] Bancroft's *History of the Constitution of the United States*, Vol. II, p. 14. Gilpin, 747. Elliot, 132.

[23] Bancroft's *History of the Constitution of the United States*, Vol. II, p. 14. Yates in Elliot, i, 392.

"Mr. Paterson is one of those kind of men whose powers break in upon you, and create wonder and astonishment. He is a man of great modesty, with looks that bespeak talents of no great extent —but he is a classic, a lawyer, and an orator—and of a disposition so favorable to his advancement that every one seemed ready to exalt him with their praises. He is very happy in the choice of time and manner of engaging in a debate, and never speaks but when he understands his subject well. This gentleman is about thirty-four years of age, of a very low stature." (*Character Sketches of Delegates to the Federal Convention*, by William Pierce, a delegate from Georgia to the Constitutional Convention.)

one only. A confederacy is a mere compact, resting on the good faith of the parties; a *national,* supreme government must have a complete and compulsive operation." [24]

On the same day Gouverneur Morris said: (1) "We are not now under a Federal government. (2) There is no such thing. A Federal government is that which has a right to compel every part to do its duty. A Federal government which each party may violate at pleasure cannot answer the purpose." [25]

On May 30th, 1787, Hamilton moved that "suffrage in the national Legislature ought to be proportioned to the number of free inhabitants," [26] but Madison moved

---

[24] Bancroft's *History of the Constitution of the United States,* Vol. II, p. 15.

[25] Farrand's *The Records of the Federal Convention of 1787,* Vol. I, p. 43.

[26] Bancroft's *History of the Constitution of the United States,* Vol. II, p. 15. Journal, Elliot, i, 151.

"*Colonel Hamilton* is deservedly celebrated for his talents. He is a practitioner of the law, and reputed to be a finished scholar. To a clear and strong judgment he unites the ornaments of fancy, and whilst he is able, convincing, and engaging in his eloquence, the heart and head sympathize in approving him. Yet there is something too feeble in his voice to be equal to the strains of oratory; it is my opinion that he is rather a convincing speaker than a blazing orator. Colonel Hamilton requires time to think; he inquires into every part of his subject with the searchings of philosophy, and when he comes forward, he comes highly charged with interesting matter; there is no skimming over the surface of a subject with him—he must sink to the bottom to see what foundation it rests on. His language is not always equal, sometimes didactic like Bolingbroke's, at others light and tripping like Stern's. His eloquence is not so defusive as to trifle with the senses, but he rambles just enough to strike and keep the attention. He is about thirty-three years old, of small stature, and lean. His manners are tinctured with stiffness, and sometimes with a degree of vanity that is highly disagreeable." (*Character Sketches of the Delegates to the Federal Convention,* by William Pierce, a delegate from Georgia to the Constitutional Convention.)

that "the equality of suffrage established by the Articles of Confederation ought not to prevail in the national Legislature, but that an equitable ratio of representation ought to be substituted." [27]

On May 31st, 1787, the Virginia resolution for two legislative branches was passed by the Committee of the Whole, "partly to prevent the fatal conflict which might one day take place between a single legislative body and a single executive," [28] and partly to "check haste in legislation by reciprocal watchfulness." The popular legislative branch was to represent the democratic principle of government.[29]

"The clauses of the Virginia plan, giving to the national Legislature the powers necessary to preserve harmony among the *States,* to negative all *State* laws contravening, in the opinion of the national Legislature, the Articles of Union, or, as Benjamin Franklin said, 'contravening treaties subsisting under the authority of the *Union,*' were agreed to without debate." [30]

Madison attempted to confer on the (proposed) *national* Legislature the right to veto any law passed by a *State,* but this the Convention refused to do.[31]

On June 1st, 1787, the Convention in Committee of the Whole discussed whether there should be one or more executives, and whether he (or they) should be chosen directly by the *people,* by *State legislatures,* by electors, by one branch or by both branches of the

---

[27] Bancroft's *History of the Constitution of the United States,* Vol. II, p. 15. Gilpin, 751. Elliot, 134.
[28] Bancroft's *History of the Constitution of the United States,* Vol. II, p. 16.
[29] *Ibid.,* p. 17. Gilpin, 754. Elliot, Vol. v, p. 136.
[30] Bancroft's *History of the Constitution of the United States,* Vol. II, p. 18.
[31] *Ibid.,* pp. 18, 19.

OUR UNKNOWN CONSTITUTION

national Legislature. Further, there was discussed the executive's absolute, unqualified right to veto legislation.[32] Replying to a suggestion for one executive, Governor Randolph declared that "unity in the executive is the *foetus* of monarchy." [33] During the discussion as to how long the executive should hold office, Sherman said that the executive should be dependent on "that body whose will it (the executive) is to execute. Independence of the executive over the supreme legislature is the very essence of tyranny." [34]

The Convention in Committee of the Whole decided on a seven-year term for the executive, and they voted against the proposition that the executive should not be re-elected.

On June 4th, 1787, in the Convention seven *States* out of ten voting, voted for a single executive.[35]

On the same day, when Wilson [36] advocated the Virginia plan of veto by the "executive and a convenient number of the judiciary," Elbridge Gerry referred to

---

[32] *Ibid.*, p. 20.
[33] *Ibid.*, p. 21. Gilpin, 764. Elliot, 141. Farrand's *The Records of the Federal Convention of 1787*, Vol. I, p. 66.
[34] Bancroft's *History of the Constitution of the United States*, Vol. II, p. 22.
[35] *Ibid.*, p. 25.
[36] *Ibid.*, p. 25. Farrand's *The Records of the Federal Convention of 1787*, Vol. I, p. 94.

"*Mr. Gerry's* character is marked for integrity and perseverance. He is a hesitating and laborious speaker, possesses a great degree of confidence, and goes extensively into all subjects that he speaks on, without respect to elegance or flower of diction. He is connected and sometimes clear in his arguments, conceives well, and cherishes as his first virtue, a love for his country. Mr. Gerry is very much of a gentleman in his principles and manners; he has been engaged in the mercantile line and is a man of property. He is about thirty-seven years of age." (*Character Sketches of Delegates to the Federal Convention*, by William Pierce, a delegate from Georgia to the Constitutional Convention.)

the fact that "judges in some *States* . . . with general approbation had set aside laws as being against the Constitution (of the *Confederacy*); and he proposed to confide the veto power to the executive alone, and subject it to be overruled by two-thirds of each national legislative branch.[37] This was carried.

The Committee of the Whole then agreed that "a *national* judiciary be established . . . of one supreme tribunal, and one or more inferior bodies." [38]

On June 6th, 1787, in the Committee of the Whole, the proposition to elect the first branch (now the House of Representatives) by the *State Legislatures* was negatived, there being three votes for it and eight against it.

On June 6th, 1787, in the Committee of the Whole, Charles Pinckney urged electing the popular branch of the *national* Legislature by the *Legislatures of the States,* and not by the *people.* Wilson said that "representation ought to be the exact transcript of the

[37] Bancroft's *History of the Constitution of the United States,* Vol. II, p. 25. Farrand's *The Records of the Federal Convention of 1787,* Vol. I, p. 95.

[38] *Ibid.,* pp. 137–38.

"*Mr. Wilson* ranks among the foremost in legal and political knowledge. He has joined to a fine genius all that can set him off and show him to advantage. He is well acquainted with man, and understands all the passions that influence him. Government seems to have been his peculiar study; all the political institutions of this world he knows in detail, and can trace the causes and effects of every revolution from the earliest stages of the Grecian commonwealth down to the present time. No man is more clear, copious, and comprehensive than Mr. Wilson, yet he is no great orator. He draws the attention not by the charm of his eloquence, but by the force of his reasoning. He is about forty-five years old." (*Character Sketches of Delegates to the Federal Convention,* by William Pierce, a delegate from Georgia to the Constitutional Convention.)

whole society." [39] Roger Sherman, of Connecticut, said: "If it is in view to abolish the *State* governments, the elections ought to be by the *people*. If they are to be continued, the elections to the *national* Government should be made by them." [40] Mason said: "Under the existing *Confederacy* Congress represents the *States,* and not the *people* of the *States;* their acts operate on the *States,* not on individuals. In the new plan of government the *people* will be represented. They ought, therefore, to choose the representatives." [41]

[39] Bancroft's *History of the Constitution of the United States,* Vol. II, p. 27. Gilpin, 801, 802. Elliot, Vol. V, p. 160.
[40] Bancroft's *History of the Constitution of the United States,* Vol. II, p. 27. Gilpin, 802, 803. Elliot, Vol. V, p. 161.
[41] Bancroft's *History of the Constitution of the United States,* Vol. II, p. 27. Gilpin, 803. Elliot, Vol. V, p. 161.

"*Mr. Sherman* exhibits the oddest shaped character I ever remember to have met with. He is awkward, unmeaning, and unaccountably strange in his manner. But in his train of thinking there is something regular, deep, and comprehensive; yet the oddity of his address, the vulgarisms that accompany his public speaking, and that strange New England cant which runs through his public as well as his private speaking make everything that is connected with him grotesque and laughable; and yet he deserves infinite praise; no man has a better heart or a clearer head. If he cannot embellish, he can furnish thoughts that are wise and useful. He is an able politician, and extremely artful in accomplishing any particular object; it is remarked that he seldom fails. I am told he sits on the Bench in Connecticut, and is very correct in his discharge of his judicial functions. In the early part of his life he was a shoemaker, but despising the lowness of his condition, he turned almanac maker, and so progressed upwards to a judge. He has been several years a member of Congress, and discharged the duties of his office with honor and credit to himself, and advantage to the *State* he represented. He is about sixty." (*Character Sketches of Delegates to the Federal Convention,* by William Pierce, a delegate from Georgia to the Constitutional Convention.)

"*Mr. Mason* (of Virginia) is a gentleman of remarkably strong powers, and possesses a clear and copious understanding. He is able and convincing in debate, steady and firm in his principles, and undoubtedly one of the best politicians in America. Mr. Mason is about sixty years old, with a fine, strong constitution." (*Ibid.*)

"It is essential," said Dickinson, "that one branch of the Legislature should be drawn immediately from the *people;* and it is expedient that the other should be chosen by the *Legislatures of the States.* This combination of the *State* Governments with the national Government is as politic as it is unavoidable."[42] William Pierce, of Georgia, declared in favor of the citizens being represented individually in the popular branch, and collectively, through the *States.*[43]

---

[42] Bancroft's *History of the Constitution of the United States,* Vol. II, p. 28.

[43] *Ibid.,* p. 28. Gilpin, 807. Elliot, Vol. V, p. 163.

"Mr. Dickinson has been famed through all America for his Farm Letters; he is a scholar, and said to be a man of very extensive information. When I saw him in the Convention, I was induced to pay the greatest attention to him whenever he spoke. I had often heard that he was a great orator, but I found him an indifferent speaker. With an affected air of wisdom he labors to produce a trifle; his language is irregular and incorrect; his flourishes (for he sometimes attempts them) are like expiring flames—they just show themselves and go out. No traces of them are left on the mind to cheer or animate it. He is, however, a good writer, and will ever be considered one of the most important characters in the *United States.* He is about fifty-five years old, and was bred a Quaker." (*Character Sketches of Delegates to the Federal Convention,* by William Pierce, a delegate from Georgia to the Constitutional Convention.)

"William Pierce. My own character I shall not attempt to draw, but leave those who may choose to speculate on it, to consider it in any light that their fancy or imagination may depict. I am conscious of having discharged my duty as a soldier through the course of the late Revolution with honor and propriety; and my services in Congress and the Convention were bestowed with the best intention towards the interest of Georgia, and towards the general welfare of the *Confederacy.* I possess ambition, and it was that, and the flattering opinion which some of my friends had of me, that gave me a seat in the wisest council in the world, and furnished me with an opportunity of giving these short sketches of the characters who composed it." (*Ibid.*)

The Virginia plan was later adopted.[44]

On June 6th, 1787, in the Committee of the Whole, Mr. Pinckney, according to previous notice and rule obtained, moved "that the first branch of the national Legislature be elected by the *State* Legislatures, and not by the *people*," contending that the *people* were less fit judges (in such a case), and that the Legislatures would be less likely to promote the adoption of the new Government if they were to be excluded from all share in it.

Mr. Rutledge seconded the motion. Mr. Gerry said: "Much depends on the mode of election. In England the *people* will probably lose their liberty from the smallness of the proportion having a right of suffrage. Our danger arises from the opposite extreme; hence in Massachusetts the worst men get into the Legislature. Several members of that body had lately been convicted of infamous crimes. Men of indigence, ignorance, and baseness spare no pains, however dirty, to carry their point against men who are superior to the artifices practiced. He was not disposed to run into extremes. He was as much principled as ever against aristocracy and monarchy. It was necessary on the one hand that the *people* should appoint one branch of the Government in order to inspire them with the necessary confidence. But he wished the election on the other hand to be so modified as to secure more effectually a just preference of merit. His idea was that the *people* should nominate certain persons in certain districts, out of whom *State* Legislatures should make the appointment."

Mr. Wilson: "He wished for vigor in the Govern-

[44] Farrand's *The Records of the Federal Convention of 1787*, Vol. I, pp. 132, 133.

ment, but he wished that vigorous authority to flow immediately from the legitimate source of all authority. The Government ought to possess not only first the *force,* but secondly, the *mind or sense* of the *people* at large. . . . Representation is made necessary only because it is impossible for the *people* to act collectively. The opposition was to be expected, he said, from the Governments, not from the citizens, of the *States.* The latter had parted, as was observed (by Mr. King) with all necessary powers; and it was immaterial to them by whom they were exercised, if well exercised. The *people* he supposed would be rather more attached to the national Government than to the *State* Governments, as being more important in itself, and more flattering to their pride. There is no danger of improper elections if made by *large* districts. Bad elections proceed from the smallness of the districts which give an opportunity to bad men to intrigue themselves into office."

Mr. Sherman: . . . "If the *State* Governments are to be continued, it is necessary, in order to preserve harmony between the national and *State* Governments, that the elections to the former should be made by the latter. The right of participating in the national Government would be sufficiently secured to the *people* by their election to the *State* Legislatures. The objects of the *Union,* he thought, were few: 1, defense against foreign danger; 2, against internal disputes and a resort to force; 3, treaties with foreign nations; 4, regulating foreign commerce, and drawing revenue from it. These and perhaps a few lesser objects rendered a *Confederation* of the *States* necessary. All other matters, civil and criminal, would be much better in the hands of the *States.* The *people* are more happy in small than in large *States*. *States* may indeed be too small, as Rhode Island, and thereby be, too, subject to faction. Some others were perhaps too large, the powers of the Government not being able to pervade them. He was for giving the general Government power to legislate and execute within a defined province."

Col. Mason: "Under the existing *Confederacy*, Congress represent the *States*, not the *people* of the *States;* their acts operate on the *States*, not on the individuals. The case will be changed in the new plan of government. The *people* will be represented; they ought therefore to choose the representatives. The requisites in actual representation are that the representatives should sympathize with their constituents; should think as they think, and feel as they feel; and that for these purposes should even be residents among them. Much, he said, had been alleged against democratic elections. He admitted that much might be said; but it was to be considered that no government was free from imperfections and evils; and that improper elections in many instances were inseparable from republican governments. But compare these with the advantages of this form in favor of the rights of the *people*, in favor of human nature. He was persuaded that there was a better chance for proper elections by the *people*, if divided into large districts, than by the *State* Legislatures. Paper money had been issued by the latter when the former were against it. Was it to be supposed that the *State* Legislatures then would not send to the national Legislature patrons of such projects, if the choice depended on them?" [45]

[45] *Ibid.*, pp. 132, 133, 134.

On June 7th, 1787, Dickinson, of Delaware, in the Committee of the Whole, moved that members of the second branch (now the Senate) ought to be chosen by the individual (State) Legislatures.[46] It was carried by unanimous vote. Bancroft says: "In this way the *States* as *States* found their lodgement in the new Constitution." [47]

In this debate Wilson said: "I wish to keep the *States* from devouring the national Government." [48]

To the remark of Randolph, that the *States* ought to be one *nation,* Paterson replied: "The idea of a *national* Government as contradistinguished from a *Federal* one never entered into the mind of any of the *States.* If the *States* are as *States* still to continue in union, they must be considered as equals. Thirteen sovereign and independent *States* can never constitute one nation, and at the same time be *States.* If we are to be formed into a nation, the *States* as *States* must be abolished,[49] and the whole must be thrown into hotchpot, and when an equal division is made, there may be fairly an equality of representation. New Jersey will never confederate on the plan before the Committee. I would rather submit to a despot than to such a fate. I will not only oppose the plan here, but on my return home will do everything in my power to defeat it there." [50]

---

[46] Bancroft's *History of the Constitution of the United States,* Vol. II, p. 29. Gilpin, 812. Elliot, Vol. V, p. 166.

[47] Bancroft's *History of the Constitution of the United States,* Vol. II, p. 31.

[48] *Ibid.,* p. 30. Gilpin, 817, 818. Elliot, Vol. V, p. 168, 169.

[49] Bancroft's *History of the Constitution of the United States,* Vol. II, pp. 31, 32. Paterson MSS.

[50] Bancroft's *History of the Constitution of the United States,* Vol. II, p. 32. Gilpin, 831, 832; and compare 870, 902, 903. Elliot, Vol. V, p. 176, 177, 194, 211.

In *The Making of the Constitution,* Warren says: "Nor was the Senate established to be a body particularly representing property, as was the case with the *State* Senates, under the various *State* Constitutions which required high property qualifications for Senators and for those who voted for them; for though Madison, Gerry, Mason, and a few others thought that the Senate should represent wealth, the Convention expressly refused to adopt this idea, and voted against any property qualification." [51]

"The actual theory on which the Senate was established was that there might be a body which should act as a check or curb on the House. It was expressed in homely fashion in the anecdote of the conversation between Jefferson and Washington when breakfasting together on the former's return from France. In answer to Jefferson's inquiry why a Senate was agreed to, Washington asked: "Why did you pour that coffee into your saucer?" "To cool it," replied Jefferson. "Even so," said Washington, "we pour legislation into the senatorial saucer to cool it." [52] (Later, it was evidently thought the coffee was getting too cool, because the Constitution was amended May 31, 1913, so as to permit election of *United States* Senators by direct vote of the *people* of each *State*.)

[51] Warren's *The Making of the Constitution,* p. 193.
[52] *Ibid.,* p. 194. Farrand's *The Records of the Federal Convention of 1787,* Vol. III, p. 359.

"Originally Senators were chosen by the Legislatures of their respective *States,* but since the adoption of the Seventeenth Amendment in 1913 they have been elected by popular vote. One-third of the members of the Senate are elected every two years, and hold their office for a term of six years." (Lee's *The Story of the American Constitution,* p. 30.)

On June 9th, 1787,[53] Mr. Paterson, of New Jersey, said that he considered the proposition for a proportional representation (in both Houses) as striking at the existence of the lesser *States;* . . . that the Convention was formed in pursuance of an Act of Congress; that this Act was stated in several of the Commissions, particularly that of Massachusetts, which he required to be read.[54]

In *The Making of the Constitution,* Warren says on page 223:

"The precise powers which the delegates possessed, in attending the Convention, were as follows: The Articles of Confederation had provided that they should 'be inviolably observed by every *State,* and the *Union* shall be perpetual; nor shall any alteration at any time hereafter be made in them, unless such alteration be agreed to in a Congress of the *United States,* and be afterwards confirmed by the Legislature of every *State.*' In accordance with this Article, the credentials of the delegates from every *State* (except New Jersey) had expressly provided that any Act determined upon by the Convention should be reported to Congress and when agreed to therein, be

[53] Edward Carrington this day wrote from New York to Thomas Jefferson: "All the *States* have elected representatives except Rhode Island, whose apostasy from every moral, as well as political, obligation has placed her perfectly without the views of the *Confederation;* nor will her absence or concurrence occasion the least impediment in any stage of the intended business." (Warren's *The Making of the Constitution,* p. 202.)

[54] This Act reads: ". . . for the sole and express purpose of revising the Articles of Confederation, and reporting to Congress and the several Legislatures such alterations and provisions therein as shall when agreed to in Congress and confirmed by the *States* render the Federal Constitution adequate to the exigencies of government and the preservation of the *Union.*" (Farrand's *The Records of the Federal Convention of 1787,* Vol. I, p. 177.)

duly confirmed by the several *States*. The purposes for which the delegates were to meet were expressed in their credentials in every *State,* as, in substance, 'to render the Federal Constitution adequate to the exigencies of Government and the preservation of the *Union.*' Under this broad power, it is clear that (except in New Jersey and Delaware) there was no limitation whatever upon the kind of amendment or change in the Articles of Confederation which the delegates might adopt, provided they reported it to Congress for acceptance and to the *States* for unanimous confirmation. The delegates did not, in fact, exceed their powers, until the crucial day (August 31), when they decided, without requiring the acceptance by Congress, to submit their work directly to conventions of the *people* in the respective *States*. This was a revolutionary step. When the delegates took that action, they threw off entirely the restrictions of their credentials, and acted solely on their own authority."

Mr. Paterson said: "Our powers do not extend to the abolition of the *State* Governments, and the erection of a national Government." [55]

Mr. Wilson, of Pennsylvania, said at this sitting of the Committee of the Whole, "if no *State* will part with any of its *sovereignty,* it is in vain to talk of a national Government." [56]

On June 11th, 1787, in the Committee of the Whole, there was a resolution that provision for the amendment of the "Articles of *Union*" ought to be made "whensoever it should seem necessary." It passed in the affirmative.

On the same day, although Gerry said, in the Com-

[55] *Ibid.,* p. 178.
[56] *Ibid.,* p. 183.

mittee of the Whole, that "the *people* of New England will never give up annual elections,"[57] Madison's proposition to elect members of the popular branch for three years was changed to two years, and the restriction to one election was removed, and the minimum age of the members was fixed at twenty-five. The minimum age of Senators was fixed at thirty. No restriction was put upon their right to re-election.[58]

On June 13th, 1787, in the Committee of the Whole, Mr. Gorham, of Massachusetts, who was in the chair, said the Committee of the Whole had directed him to report to the House,[59] that the Virginia plan was recommended. One of the main objections to it came from the smaller *States,* which had been deprived of their equality of suffrage *they had since the foundation of the Union* (under the *Confederacy*). The Connecticut plan ranked next in importance to the Virginia plan.

By June 14th, 1787, the *"States' Rights"* group had decided that they would submit a definite alternative plan, and Mr. Paterson on June 14th, 1787, moved that

[57] Gilpin, 847. Elliot, Vol. V, p. 184.
[58] Bancroft's *History of the Constitution of the United States,* Vol. II, pp. 34, 35.
[59] Farrand's *The Records of the Federal Convention of 1787,* Vol. I, p. 223.

"*Mr. Gorham* is a merchant in Boston, high in reputation, and much in the esteem of his countrymen. He is a man of very good sense, but not much improved in his education. He is eloquent and easy in public debate, but has nothing fashionable or elegant in his style; all he aims at is to convince, and where he fails, it never is from his auditory not understanding him, for no man is more perspicuous. He has been President of Congress, and three years a member of that body. Mr. Gorham is about forty-six years of age, rather lusty, and has an agreeable and pleasing manner." (*Character Sketches of Delegates to the Federal Convention,* by William Pierce, a delegate from Georgia to the Constitutional Convention.)

the Convention adjourn to give them time to do so.[60]

All the *States* had come to the Convention as sovereigns, and the smaller ones demanded in the new Constitution the same equality that prevailed in the deliberations of the Convention, i.e., that any *State*, large or small, or however many delegates it had in the Convention, vote as a unit. The big *States* did not favor this, so when the Committee of the Whole rose it reported the Virginia plan, with the proviso that representation in the bi-chambered Congress should be "according to some equitable ratio of representation." [61]

On June 15th, 1787, in the Committee of the Whole,[62] Paterson, of New Jersey, presented the New Jersey plan, which was a "revision of the Articles of Confederation." [63] Lansing, of New York, said in the Committee of the Whole, on June 15th, 1787: "The New Jersey system is *Federal;* the Virginia system, *national*. In the first, the powers flow from the *State* Governments; in the second, they derive authority from the *people* of the *States,* and must *ultimately annihilate the State Governments*. We are invested with power only to alter and amend defective parts of the present *Confederation*." [64]

[60] Beck's *The Constitution of the United States,* p. 101.
[61] *Loc. cit.*
[62] Warren's *The Making of the Constitution,* p. 221.
[63] Bancroft's *History of the Constitution of the United States,* Vol. II, p. 39.
[64] Paterson MSS. Bancroft's *History of the Constitution of the United States,* Vol. II, pp. 40, 41.

A parallel comparison of the Virginia and New Jersey plans appears in the Appendix at page 251.

"With Yates and Lansing, of New York; Martin, of Maryland; Gerry, of Massachusetts, and Mason, of Virginia, the *States* were supreme, and they resisted every effort to create a strong central

One of the earliest prophecies of the battle that afterwards raged in the United States occurred when Paterson, of New Jersey, said in the Committee of the Whole, June 16th, 1787: "If no *confederation* at present exists, all the *States* stand on the footing of equal *sovereignty;* and *all* must concur before any *one* can be bound. If a *Federal* Constitution exists on equal *sovereignty* as its basis, and the dissent of *one State* renders every amendment null . . . can any *State,* unless by the consent of the whole . . . withdraw its powers? . . . Give Congress the same powers that are intended for the two branches, and I apprehend that they will act with more energy and wisdom than the latter. Congress is the sun of our political system." [65]

On June 16th, 1787, one of the Pinckneys said in the Committee of the Whole: "The whole case comes to this: Give *New Jersey* an equal vote, and she will dismiss her scruples and concur in the national system." [66]

On the same day Randolph declared in the Committee of the Whole: "We must resort to a *national* legislation over individuals. To vest such power in the Congress of the *Confederation* would be blending the legislative with the executive. Elected by the Legislatures who retain even a power of recall, they are a mere diplomatic body, with no will of their own, and always obsequious to the *States* who are ever en-

---

government. . . . They also defeated Hamilton's scheme to elect the President and Senators for life." (Lee's *The Story of the American Constitution,* p. 42.)

[65] *Ibid.,* pp. 40, 41. Paterson MSS.

[66] Bancroft's *History of the Constitution of the United States,* Vol. II, p. 41. Gilpin, 875. Yates in Elliot, Vol. I, 415. Elliot, Vol. V, p. 197. Paterson MSS.

croaching on the authority of the *United States*.[67] A *national* government, properly constituted, will alone answer the purpose; and this is the only moment when it can be established." [68]

The following paper was read in the Committee of the Whole by Colonel Hamilton, as containing his ideas of a suitable plan of government for the *United States*, in a speech June 18th, 1787, upon the motion of Mr. Dickinson that the Committee of the Whole "consider the state of the American *Union*."

"1. The supreme legislative power of the *United States* of America to be vested in two distinct bodies of men, the one to be called the Assembly, the other the Senate, who, together, shall form the Legislature of the *United States*, with power to pass all laws whatsoever, subject to the negative hereafter mentioned.

"2. The Assembly to consist of persons elected by the *people* to serve for three years.

"3. The Senate to consist of persons elected to serve during good behavior; their election to be made by electors chosen for that purpose by the *people*. In order to this, the *States* to be divided into election districts. On the death, removal, or resignation of any Senator, his place to be filled out of the district from which he came.

"4. The supreme executive authority of the *United States* to be vested in a governor, to be elected to serve during good behavior. His election to be made by electors, chosen by the *people* in the election districts

---

[67] Bancroft's *History of the Constitution of the United States*, Vol. II, p. 41. Gilpin, 876, 877. Elliot, Vol. V, p. 198.

[68] Bancroft's *History of the Constitution of the United States*, Vol. II, pp. 41, 42. Yates in Elliot, Vol. I, p. 417. Gilpin, 877–879. Elliot, Vol. V, p. 198. Paterson MSS.

aforesaid. His authorities and functions to be as follows:

"To have a negative upon all laws about to be passed, and the execution of all laws passed; to have the entire direction of war, when authorized or begun; to have, with the advice and approbation of the Senate, the power of making all treaties; to have the sole appointment of the heads or chief officers of the departments of finance, war, and foreign affairs; to have the nomination of all other officers (ambassadors of foreign nations included), subject to the approbation or rejection of the Senate; to have the power of pardoning all offenses except treason, which he shall not pardon without the approbation of the Senate.

"5. On the death, resignation, or removal of the Governor, his authorities to be exercised by the President of the Senate, until a successor be appointed.

"6. The Senate to have the sole power of declaring war; the power of advising and approving all treaties; the power of approving or rejecting all appointments of officers, except the heads or chiefs of the departments of finance, war, and foreign affairs.

"7. The supreme judicial authority of the *United States* to be vested in —— judges, to hold their offices during good behavior, with adequate and permanent salaries. This court to have original jurisdiction in all causes of capture; and an appellate jurisdiction in all causes in which the revenues of the general Government, or the citizens of foreign nations, are concerned.

"8. The Legislature of the *United States* to have power to institute courts in each *State,* for the determination of all matters of general concern.

"9. The Governors, Senators, and all officers of

the *United States* to be liable to impeachment for mal and corrupt conduct; and, upon conviction, to be removed from office, and disqualified from holding any place of trust or profit. All impeachments to be tried by a court, to consist of the chief or senior judge of the superior court of law, in each *State;* provided, that such judge hold his place during good behavior, and have a permanent salary.

"10. All laws of the particular *States* contrary to the Constitution or laws of the *United States* to be utterly void. And the better to prevent such laws being passed, the Governor or President of each *State* shall be appointed by the general Government, and shall have a negative upon the laws about to be passed in the *State* of which he is Governor or President.

"11. No *State* to have any forces, land or naval; and the militia of all the *States* to be under the sole and exclusive direction of the *United States;* the officers of which to be appointed and commissioned by them." [69]

June 18th, 1787, Mr. Hamilton said: "I confess that this (New Jersey) plan and that from Virginia are very remote from the idea of the *people*. Perhaps the Jersey plan is nearest their expectation. But, the *people* are gradually ripening in their opinions of government—they begin to be tired of an excess of democracy." [70]

Hamilton stated his belief to be that the British Government was the best in the world, and that he doubted much whether anything short of it would do in America. He concluded by submitting a sketch of

---

[69] Elliot, Vol. I, pp. 179, 180.
[70] Farrand's *The Records of the Federal Convention of 1787*, Vol. I, p. 301.

a plan, which, he admitted, "went beyond the ideas of most members," but which embodied principles necessary to check and control the existing evils. This sketch provided, amongst other things, for a Senate and an executive, both elected to serve during good behavior, and for the appointment of *State* Governors by the general Government. Such provisions alone would have made it impossible of acceptance. Hence, it is not singular that this Hamilton sketch was neither referred to any Committee, nor taken up by the Convention for action in any way. "The gentleman from New York is praised by all, but supported by no gentleman," observed Dr. William Samuel Johnson." [71]

Hamilton, in referring to the "vital defects of the *Confederation*," said it could not be amended except by investing it with most important powers. "To do so would establish a general government in one hand without checks; a *sovereignty* of the worst kind, the *sovereignty* of a single body. This is a conclusive objection to the New Jersey plan." [72] "I have great doubts," he continued, "whether a *national* government on the Virginia plan can be effectual.[73] Gentlemen say we need to be rescued from the democracy. But what are the means proposed? A democratic Assembly is to be checked by a democratic Senate, and both these by a democratic chief magistrate.[74] The Virginia plan is but pork still with a little change of

[71] Warren's *The Making of the Constitution*, p. 228.
[72] Bancroft's *History of the Constitution of the United States*, Vol. II, p. 42. Hamilton's Works, Vol. II, p. 412. Yates in Elliot, Vol. I, pp. 420, 421.
[73] Bancroft's *History of the Constitution of the United States*, Vol. II, p. 43. Yates in Elliot, Vol. I, p. 417.
[74] Bancroft's *History of the Constitution of the United States*, Vol. II, p. 43. Hamilton, Vol. II, p. 415.

the sauce.[75] It will prove inefficient, because the means will not be equal to the object."[76]

How correct or how incorrect Hamilton's prophecy was, the subsequent history of the *United States* has demonstrated.

On the same day, commenting on his outline for a Constitution, Hamilton proceeded: "This constitutes an elective monarchy; but by making the executive subject to impeachment the term 'monarchy' cannot apply."[77] His outline provided for an Assembly elected directly by the *people* for three years. It was to be counterbalanced by a Senate elected by the *people* through electors.

Hamilton's speech lasted about five hours, after which the Convention adjourned. He began with a modest explanation of his previous silence by saying that it was "from respect to others whose superior abilities, age, and experience render me unwilling to bring forward ideas dissimilar to theirs, and partly from my delicate situation with respect to my own *State*, to whose sentiments, as expressed by my own colleagues, I can by no means accede. The crisis, however, which now marks our affairs is too serious to permit any scruples whatever to prevail over the duty imposed on every man to contribute his efforts for the public safety and happiness."[78]

---

[75] Bancroft's *History of the Constitution of the United States*, Vol. II, p. 43. Yates in Elliot, Vol. I, p. 423. Gilpin, 893, note. Elliot, Vol. V, p. 205.

[76] Bancroft's *History of the Constitution of the United States*, Vol. II, p. 43. Hamilton, Vol. II, p. 415.

[77] Bancroft's *History of the Constitution of the United States*, Vol. II, p. 44. Yates in Elliot, Vol. I, p. 422.

[78] Beck's *The Constitution of the United States*, pp. 105, 106, 107, 108.

"He thereupon announced his opposition either to the Virginia or the New Jersey plans, and in so doing he confessed that he was 'much discouraged by the amazing extent of country in expecting the desired blessing from any general *sovereignty* that could be substituted.'

"He announced that an effective government must depend upon the following requisites: 1, an active and constant interest in support of it; 2, the love of power; 3, an habitual attachment of the *people;* 4, force, whether by the coercion of laws or the coercion of arms; 5, influence, by which he explained that he 'did not mean corruption, but a dispensation of those regular honors and emoluments which produce an attachment to the government.' . . . 'What, then, is to be done? I am much embarrassed. The extent of the country to be governed discourages me. The expense of a general government is also formidable, unless there were such a diminution of expense on the side of the *State* Governments as the case would admit. *If they were extinguished,* I am persuaded that great economy might be obtained by substituting a general government. I do not mean to shock the public opinion by proposing such a measure. On the other hand, I see no necessity for declining it.' . . . 'I have no scruple in declaring, supported as I am by the opinion of so many of the wise and good, that the British Government is the best in the world; and I doubt much whether anything short of it would do in America. . . . We ought to go as far, in order to attain stability and permanency, as republican principles will admit. Let one branch of the Legislature hold their places for life, or at least during good behavior. Let the executive, also, be for life.'

"With this preliminary explanation he then proceeded to submit the outline of a plan which, in effect, carried out his view of assimilating the new government to the English Constitution.

"According to this plan, the Legislature was to consist of two branches, of which the first, called the Assembly, was to consist of persons elected to serve for three years. The Senate was to consist of persons elected for an indefinite tenure of office, themselves to be selected by electors chosen for that purpose by the *people*. The supreme executive authority was to be a 'governor,' who likewise was to serve for life, and he was also to be elected by electors. The executive was to have a negative on all laws about to be passed *and upon the execution of all laws already passed*. The Senate was to have the sole power to declare war and of approving or rejecting all appointments of officers except the heads of the departments of finance, war, and foreign affairs. The judicial authority of the nation was to be vested in judges who would sit for life, and the Congress could institute other courts in each *State* 'for the determination of all matters of general concern.' Under Clause X, all laws of the particular *States* which were contrary to the Constitution or laws of the *United States* were to be void, 'and the better to prevent such laws being passed the Governor or President of each *State* shall be appointed by the general Government and shall have a negative upon the laws about to be passed in the *State* of which he is the Governor or President.'

"Apparently some of the delegates understood his speech, not unnaturally, to advocate the virtual abolition of the *States,* for on the next day Mr. Hamilton corrected this misunderstanding by saying: 'By an abolition of the *States* I meant that no boundary could be drawn between the national and *State* Legislatures, and that the former must therefore have *indefinite* authority. If it were limited at all, the rivalship of the *States* would gradually subvert it. As *States* I think they ought to be abolished, but I admit the necessity of leaving in them subordinate jurisdictions.' " [79]

"Hamilton clearly wished to impose an imitation monarchy upon the American *people,* not necessarily for the love of that form of government, but on account of his intense distrust of the *people,* whom he once called 'a great beast.' " [80]

June 19th, 1787, Hamilton said: "I agree to the proposition (not to annihilate the *State* Governments). I did not intend yesterday a total extinguishment of *State* Governments; but my meaning was, that a national government ought to be able to support itself without the aid or interference of the *State* Governments, and that therefore it was necessary to have full *sovereignty.* Even with corporate rights the *States* will be dangerous to the national Government, and ought to be extinguished, new modified, or reduced to a smaller scale." [81]

June 19th, 1787, Mr. King, of Massachusetts, said: "The only criterion of determining what is Federal and what is national is this, those acts which are for the government of the *States* only are purely Federal;

---

[79] *Ibid.,* pp. 108, 109, 111, 112.

[80] *Ibid.,* p. 115.

"When Congress asked power to regulate the commerce for fifteen years, the *States* refused it." (*Encyclopædia Britannica,* Vol. 27, p. 685a.)

[81] Farrand's *The Records of the Federal Convention of 1787,* Vol. I, p. 328.

those which are for the government of the citizens of the individual *States* are national and not Federal." [82]

June 19th, 1787, in the Committee of the Whole, "Mr. King, of Massachusetts, conceived that the import of the terms *'States,' 'sovereignty,' 'national,' 'Federal,'* had been often used and applied in the discussion inaccurately and delusively. These *States* were not 'sovereigns' in the sense contended for by some. They did not possess the peculiar features of *sovereignty*. They could not make war, nor peace, nor alliances, nor treaties. Considering them as political beings, they were dumb, for they could not speak to any foreign sovereign whatever. They were deaf, for they could not hear any propositions from such sovereign. They had not even the organs or faculties of defense or offense, for they could not of themselves raise troops, or equip vessels, for war. On the other side, if the *Union* of the *States* comprises the idea of a *confederation*, it comprises that also of consolidation. A union of the *States* is a union of the men composing them, from whence a *national* character results to the whole." [83]

[82] *Ibid.*, pp. 331, 332.
[83] *Ibid.*, p. 323.
Here follows a letter from James Varnum to General Washington.
Newport, June 18th, 1787.
Sir:—
... The upper house, or Governor, and Council, embraced the measure, but it was negatived in the house of Assembly by a large majority, notwithstanding the greatest exertions were made to support it. ...
Permit me, Sir, to observe that the measures of our present Legislature do not exhibit the real character of the *State*. They are equally reprobated and abhorred by gentlemen of the learned professions, by the whole mercantile body, and by most of the respectable farmers and mechanicks. The majority of the administration is composed of a licentious number of men, destitute of

In reply to Hamilton, Wilson said on June 19th, 1787: "I am for a *national* government, but not one that will swallow up the *State* Governments; these are absolutely necessary for purposes which the *national* Government cannot reach." [84] "I did not intend yesterday," answered Hamilton, "a total extinguishment of *State* Governments; but that a national government must have indefinite *sovereignty;* for if it were limited at all, the rivalship of the *States* would gradually subvert it.[85] The *States* must retain subordinate jurisdictions." [86]

On June 19th, 1787, the Committee of the Whole reported the amended Virginia plan. It then dissolved. Connecticut joined the six nationally-minded *States* to make up the necessary vote. New York, New Jersey, and Delaware voted no, and Maryland was divided.

education, and many of them, void of principle. From anarchy and confusion they derive their temporary consequence, and this they endeavor to prolong by debauching the minds of the common people, whose attention is wholly directed to the abolition of debts both public and private. With these are associated the disaffected of every description, particularly those who were unfriendly during the war. . . . It is fortunate however that the wealth and resources of this *State* are chiefly in possession of the well affected, and that they are entirely devoted to the public good.

I have the honor of being, Sir,
    with the greatest veneration and esteem,
        Your excellency's very obedient and
            most humble servant
His excellency,
    Genl. Washington.
(*Ibid.*, Vol. III, pp. 47, 48.)

[84] Bancroft's *History of the Constitution of the United States,* Vol. II, p. 47. Gilpin, 904. Elliot, Vol. V, p. 212.

[85] Bancroft's *History of the Constitution of the United States,* Vol. II, p. 47. Gilpin, 905. Elliot, Vol. V, p. 212.

[86] Bancroft's *History of the Constitution of the United States,* Vol. II, p. 47. Yates in Elliot, Vol. I, p. 426.

Georgia, with less than 60,000 people, voted with the large *States*.[87]

On June 19th, 1787, "a vote was taken on the plain proposition whether the Randolph Resolutions 'should be adhered to as preferable to those of Mr. Paterson.' Seven *States* favored such adherence, while New York, New Jersey, and Delaware voted 'no,' and Maryland was divided.

"It is to be remarked that in all the votes thus far, the *State* of Georgia, with less than 60,000 inhabitants, voted with the large *States*. This was due to the fact that, as her area exceeded that of Virginia and North Carolina, and was only 14,000 square miles less than all the other ten *States* together, Georgia expected in the near future to develop into one of the most important and populous *States* of the *Union*."[88]

On June 19th, 1787, in the Committee of the Whole, Mr. Luther Martin, of Maryland, said the Revolution "placed the thirteen *States* in a state of nature toward

---

[87] Bancroft's *History of the Constitution of the United States*, Vol II, p. 46. Gilpin, 904. Elliot, Vol. V, p. 212. Yates in Elliot, Vol. I, p. 425.

"Finally (1787) in the Convention it was decided that the Federal Constitution, as now adopted, should be presented to the Continental Congress, and then referred to special conventions in all the *States* for ratification, and then when nine *States*, or two-thirds of the whole number, should have ratified, it should at once go into operation as between such ratifying *States*" (and all *States*). (Fiske's *The Critical Period of American History*, p. 302.)

[88] Warren's *The Making of the Constitution*, p. 232.

"*Mr. Martin* was educated for the bar, and is Attorney General for the *State* of Maryland. This gentleman possesses a good deal of information, but he has a very bad delivery, and so extremely prolix, that he never speaks without tiring the patience of all who hear him. He is about thirty-four years of age." (*Character Sketches of Delegates to the Federal Convention*, by William Pierce, a delegate from Georgia to the Constitutional Convention.)

each other." [89] But Wilson replied: "In the Declaration of Independence the United Colonies were declared to be free and independent *States*, independent, not *individually*, but *unitedly*." [90]

Bancroft says: "Connecticut, which was in all sincerity partly Federal and partly national, was now compelled to take the lead." [91] That *State* was represented by Roger Sherman, William Samuel Johnson, and Oliver Ellsworth, a delegation superior in age and experience. The latter delegate threw his best efforts into obtaining "the equal representation of the *States* in the Senate." [92]

The Virginia plan, which Paterson, of New Jersey, called "the *Federal* Government of the United States," was described nineteen times as "national." [93]

But on June 20th, 1787, Judge Ellsworth said in the Convention: "I propose, and therefore move, to expunge the word 'national' in the first resolve, and to place, in the room of it, 'the Government of the *United*

---

[89] Bancroft's *History of the Constitution of the United States*, Vol. II, pp. 47, 48. Gilpin, 906, 907. Elliot, Vol. V, p. 213.

[90] Bancroft's *History of the Constitution of the United States*, Vol. II, pp. 47, 48. Gilpin, 906, 907. Elliot, Vol. V, p. 213.

[91] Bancroft's *History of the Constitution of the United States*, Vol. II, p. 48.

[92] *Ibid.*, p. 51. Gilpin, 908. Elliot, Vol. V, p. 214.

[93] Bancroft's *History of the Constitution of the United States*, Vol. II, p. 51. Paterson, MSS.

"*Mr. Ellsworth* is a Judge of the Supreme Court in Connecticut; he is a gentleman of clear, deep, and copious understanding; eloquent and connected in public debate, and always attentive to his duty. He is very happy in a reply, and choice in selecting such parts of his adversary's arguments as he finds make the strongest impressions, in order to take off the force of them, so as to admit the power of his own. Mr. Ellsworth is about thirty-seven years of age, a man much respected for his integrity, and venerated for his abilities." (*Ibid.*)

States'"; which was agreed to, *nem. con.* (No one against.) [94]

On June 20th, 1787, Mason, of Virginia, said in the Convention: "On two points the American mind is well settled: an attachment to republican government, and an attachment to more than one branch in the Legislature. The general accord of their Constitutions in both these circumstances must either have been a miracle, or must have resulted from the genius of the *people*. Congress is the only single Legislature not chosen by the *people* themselves, and in consequence they have been constantly averse to giving it further powers. (Mr. Mason, of course, referred to the Congress as selected under the Articles of Confederation by the *State* Legislatures.)[95] They never will, they never can, intrust their dearest rights and liberties to one body of men not chosen by them, and yet invested with the sword and the purse; a conclave, transacting their business in secret and guided in many of their acts by factions and party spirit." [96]

On June 21st, 1787, it was resolved (nine *States* voting "yes," New Jersey, "no"; Maryland, divided) that the members of the first branch of the Legislature ought to be elected by the *people* of the several *States*.[97]

On June 25th, 1787, in the Convention, in the course of the debate, Wilson, of Pennsylvania, said: "A citi-

[94] Yates Records in Elliot, Vol. I, p. 427.
[95] Fiske's *The Critical Period of American History*, p. 95.
[96] Bancroft's *History of the Constitution of the United States*, Vol. II, p. 52. Gilpin, 912–915. Elliott, Vol. V, pp. 216, 217. Yates in Elliot, Vol. I, pp. 428, 429.

On June 20th, 1787, Jefferson, writing to Madison from Paris, first suggested the (afterwards) Supreme Court of the *United States* as an appeal court from *State* courts. (Warren's *The Making of the Constitution*, p. 235.)

[97] Elliot, Vol. IV, p. 224.

zen of America is a citizen of the *general Government*, and is a citizen of the particular *State* in which he may reside.[98] The *general Government* is meant for them in the first capacity; the *State* Governments in the second. Both Governments are derived *from the people,* both meant *for the people;* both, therefore, ought to be regulated on the same principles. In forming the *general Government* we must forget our local habits and attachments, lay aside our *State* connections, and act for the general good of the whole. The *general Government* is not an assemblage of *States*, but of *individuals,* for certain political purposes; it is not meant for the *States*, but for the *individuals* composing them; the *individuals*, therefore, not the *States*, ought to be represented in it."[99] "He persisted to the last in demanding that the Senate should be elected by electors chosen by the *people.*"[100]

On June 25th, 1787, in the Convention, Charles Pinckney, of South Carolina, said: "It (the *United States*) should have an adequate system of government —a country in which every member of the society almost will enjoy an equal power of arriving at the supreme office, and consequently of directing the strength and sentiments of the whole community—a country in which the whole community will enjoy in the fullest sense that kind of political liberty which consists in the power the members of the *States* reserve to themselves of arriving at the public offices, or at least of having votes in the nomination of those who

---

[98] Bancroft's *History of the Constitution of the United States,* Vol. II, pp. 54, 55. Yates in Elliot, Vol. I, pp. 445, 446.

[99] Bancroft's *History of the Constitution of the United States,* Vol. II, p. 55. Gilpin, 957. Elliot, Vol. V, p. 239.

[100] Bancroft's *History of the Constitution of the United States,* Vol. II, p. 55.

fill them—a new extensive country containing within itself the materials of forming a government capable of extending to its citizens all the blessings of civil and religious liberty, capable of making them happy at home. This is the great end of a republican form of government. In such a country, though there might be three classes of men—the professional, the commercial, and the landed (or owners and cultivators of the soil), there is, after all, but one great and equal body of citizens among whom there are no distinctions of rank, and very few or none of fortune." [101]

On June 27th and 28th, 1787, in the Convention, Martin denounced "any general government that could reach individuals." [102]

On June 28th, 1787, in the Convention, Madison said: "The two extremes before us are, a perfect separation, and a perfect incorporation of thirteen *States*. In the first case, they will be independent *nations*, subject only to the law of *nations;* in the last, they will be mere counties of one entire republic, subject to one common law. In the first, the smaller *States* will have everything to fear from the larger; in the last, nothing. Their true policy, therefore, lies in promoting that form of government which will most approximate the *States* to the condition of counties." [103]

After opening the debate which followed, Johnson said: "A *State* exists as a political society, and it exists as a district of individual citizens. The aristocratic and other interests, and the interests of the *States*, must be armed with some power of self-defense.

[101] Warren's *The Making of the Constitution*, p. 239.
[102] Bancroft's *History of the Constitution of the United States*, Vol. II, pp. 57, 58.
[103] *Ibid.*, p. 58. Gilpin, 982. Elliot, Vol. V, p. 252.

In one branch of the *general Government,* the *people* ought to be represented; in the other, the *States.*"[104]

Rather than accept the Virginia plan, Martin said he preferred two confederacies, one composed of the large *States,* and one composed of the small *States.*

On June 29th, 1787, in the Convention, after the rule of suffrage had been discussed, "it was then decided, by the six national *States* to four, Maryland being divided, that the first branch ought to bear proportion to the population of the several *States.*"[105]

On the same day, Abraham Baldwin, who had moved to Georgia from Connecticut, said: "The second branch (the Senate) ought to be the representation of property,[106] and ought not to be elected as the first."[107]

Madison, with his rare prescience, said: "Defensive power ought to be given, not between the large and small *States,* but between the Northern and Southern." He further suggested "that the *States* should be represented in one branch according to the number of free inhabitants only; and in the other according to the

[104] Bancroft's *History of the Constitution of the United States,* Vol. II, p. 59. Gilpin, 987. Elliot, Vol. V, p. 255.
[105] Bancroft's *History of the Constitution of the United States,* Vol. II, p. 61.
[106] *Ibid.,* p. 62. Gilpin, 998. Elliot, Vol. V, p. 260.
[107] Bancroft's *History of the Constitution of the United States,* Vol. II, p. 62. Yates in Elliot, Vol. I, p. 465.

"*Mr. Baldwin* is a gentleman of superior abilities, and joins in a public debate with great art and eloquence. Having laid the foundation of a complete classical education at Harvard College, he pursues every other study with ease. He is well acquainted with books and characters, and has an accommodating turn of mind, which enables him to gain the confidence of men and to understand them. He is a practicing attorney in Georgia and has been twice a member of Congress. Mr. Baldwin is about thirty-eight years of age." (*Character Sketches of Delegates to the Federal Convention,* by William Pierce, a delegate from Georgia to the Constitutional Convention.)

whole number. The Southern scale would have the advantage in one House, and the Northern in another." [108]

Finally, the smaller *States* served notice upon the larger *States* that "unless representation in both branches of the proposed Legislature should be on the basis of equality, each *State*, whether large or small, having one vote, they would forthwith leave the Convention." [109]

On July 2nd, 1787, the Convention, upon the motion of Franklin, adjourned over the ensuing holiday, until July 5th, 1787, to give a Committee (appointed upon the suggestion of Charles Cotesworth Pinckney) time to consider how the *States* should be represented in the second branch.[110]

On "July 3rd, 1787, the Grand Committee accepted as a basis for a compromise [111] the proposal of Franklin [112] that in the first branch of the First Congress there should be one member for every 40,000 in-

[108] Bancroft's *History of the Constitution of the United States*, Vol. II, pp. 63, 64. Gilpin, 1006. Elliot, Vol. V, pp. 264, 265.
[109] Beck's *The Constitution of the United States*, p. 125.
[110] Bancroft's *History of the Constitution of the United States*, Vol. II, p. 67. Gilpin, 1023, 1024. Elliot, Vol. V, p. 273. Beck's *The Constitution of the United States*, p. 264.
[111] Bancroft's *History of the Constitution of the United States*, Vol. II, p. 68. Yates in Elliot, Vol. I, p. 478.
[112] Bancroft's *History of the Constitution of the United States*, Vol. II, p. 68. Martin in Elliot, Vol. I, p. 358.

"*Mr. Charles Cotesworth Pinckney* is a gentleman of family and fortune in his own *State*. He has received the advantage of a liberal education, and possesses a very extensive degree of legal knowledge. When warm in debate, he sometimes speaks well, but he is generally considered an indifferent orator. Mr. Pinckney was an officer of high rank in the American Army, and served with great reputation through the War. He is now about forty years of age." (*Character Sketches of Delegates to the Federal Convention,* by William Pierce, a delegate from Georgia to the Constitutional Convention.)

habitants, counting all the free and three-fifths of the rest; that in the second branch each *State* should have an equal vote; and that in return for this concession to the small *States*, the first branch should be invested with the sole power of originating taxes and appropriations." [113]

On July 5th, 1787, Elbridge Gerry brought into the Convention the report of the Grand Committee.[114]

On the same day Gouverneur Morris in the course of the discussion said: "Not liberty—property is the main object of society. The savage state is more favorable to liberty than the civilized, and was only renounced for the sake of property." [115]

On July 7th, 1787, in the Convention, "the clause allowing each *State* an equal vote in the Senate was retained as part of the report by a majority of six to three, New York being present and voting with the majority, Massachusetts and Georgia being divided." [116]

"July 10th, 1787, in the Convention, Randolph, following the precedent of 1781, insisted on an absolute constitutional requirement of a census of population and an estimate of wealth, to be taken within one year after the first meeting of the Legislature (national Congress), and ever thereafter periodically; and that the representation be arranged accordingly." [117]

On July 11th, 1787, in the Convention, "by a majority of two to one the first Legislature under the new

[113] Bancroft's *History of the Constitution of the United States*, Vol II, p. 68.
[114] *Ibid.*, p. 68.
[115] *Ibid.*, pp. 69, 70. Gilpin, 1034. Elliot, Vol. V, pp. 278, 279.
[116] Bancroft's *History of the Constitution of the United States*, Vol. II, p. 71.
[117] *Ibid.*, pp. 78, 79. Gilpin, 1063. Elliot, Vol. V, p. 293.

Constitution was required to provide for a census;[118] a periodical census ever after was then accepted without a division. Its period, first fixed at fifteen years, after repeated debates, was reduced to ten."[119]

The representation in the first branch might have been fixed[120] at one for every 40,000 of free inhabitants

[118] Bancroft's *History of the Constitution of the United States,* Vol. II, p. 80. Gilpin, 1078. Elliot, Vol. V, p. 301.

[119] Bancroft's *History of the Constitution of the United States,* Vol. II, p. 80. Gilpin, 1086. Elliot, Vol. V, p. 305.

[120] When the Constitution was finally adopted, Article I, Section 2, Subdivision 1, read: "Representation and direct taxes shall be apportioned among the several *States* which may be included within this *Union,* according to their respective numbers, which shall be determined by adding to the total number of free persons, including those bound to service for a term of years, and excluding Indians not taxed, three-fifths of all other persons. The actual enumeration shall be made within three years after the first meeting of the Congress of the *United States,* and within every subsequent term of ten years, in such manner as they shall by law direct. The number of representatives shall not exceed one for every 30,000, but each *State* shall have at least one representative." ...

The Fourteenth Amendment to the Constitution, adopted July 28th, 1868, reads (Section 2): "Representatives shall be apportioned among the several *States* according to their respective numbers, *counting the* whole number of persons in each *State,* excluding Indians not taxed. But when the right to vote at any election for the choice of electors for President and Vice President of the *United States,* Representatives in Congress, the executive and judicial officers of a *State,* is denied to any of the male inhabitants of such *State,* being twenty-one years of age, and citizens of the *United States,* or in any way abridged, except for participation in rebellion, or other crime, the basis of representation therein shall be reduced in the proportion which the number of such male citizens shall bear to the whole number of male citizens twenty-one years of age in such *State.*"

"*Mr. Yates* is said to be an able judge. He is a man of great legal abilities, but not distinguished as an orator. Some of his enemies say he is an anti-Federal man, but I discovered no such disposition in him. He is about forty-five years old, and enjoys a great share of health." (*Character Sketches of Delegates to the Federal Convention,* by William Pierce, a delegate from Georgia to the Constitutional Convention.)

and three-fifths of the slaves, if Morris had not proposed on the morning of July 12th, 1787, that "taxation should be in proportion to representation."[121] To this the Convention unanimously agreed, after the word "direct" had been placed before the word "taxation." This was done after Mason had declared that taxation based on representation "would so embarrass the (national) Legislature in raising a revenue that they would be driven back to requisitions on the States."[122]

"The final motion to make blacks equal with whites in fixing the ratio of representation received no support but from South Carolina and Georgia;[123] and the compromise, proportioning representation to direct taxation, and both to the number of the free and three-fifths of the others, was established by the Southern *States,* even Georgia approving, and South Carolina relenting so far as to divide its vote."[124]

Madison's compromise provided that "in counting population, whether for direct taxation or for representation in the Lower House of Congress, five slaves should be reckoned as three individuals. . . . Henceforth, so long as slavery lasted (unless the Constitution should be changed) the vote of a Southerner

"*Mr. Lansing* is a practicing attorney at Albany, and Mayor of that Corporation. He has a hesitation in his speech that will prevent his being an orator of any eminence; his legal knowledge, I am told, is not extensive, nor his education a good one. He is, however, a man of good sense, plain in his manners and sincere in his friendships. He is about thirty-two years of age." (*Ibid.*)

[121] Bancroft's *History of the Constitution of the United States,* Vol. II, p. 83. Gilpin, 1079. Elliot, Vol. V, p. 302.

[122] Bancroft's *History of the Constitution of the United States,* Vol. II, p. 83.

[123] *Ibid.*, p. 84. Gilpin, 1084–1087. Elliot, Vol. V, p. 305.

[124] Bancroft's *History of the Constitution of the United States,* Vol. II, p. 84. Gilpin, 1086–1087. Elliot, Vol. V, p. 306.

counted for more than the vote of a Northerner. . . .
In South Carolina there soon came to be more blacks
than whites. . . . Every five slaveholders down there
were equal in political weight to not less than eight
farmers or merchants in the North." [125]

On July 12th, 1787, Rufus King, of Massachusetts,
said in the Convention, in a discussion on whether
three-fifths of the slave population were to be counted
in figuring the representation: "The Southern *States*
threaten to separate now in case injury shall be done
them. There will be no point of time at which they
will not be able to say 'Do us justice or we will separate.'" [126]

I merely quote the above because it has some bearing on the question as to whether the members of the
Constitutional Convention considered that they were
forming a confederacy of *States*, or a *nation* of the
people of those *States*.

At this early stage of the discussions (July 13th,
1787) Gouverneur Morris, of Pennsylvania, stated in
the Convention "as the result of his deep meditation":
"The Southern gentlemen will not be satisfied unless
they see the way open to their gaining a majority in
the public councils. The consequence of such a trans-

[125] Fiske's *The Critical Period of American History*, pp. 261, 262.
[126] Bancroft's *History of the Constitution of the United States*,
Vol. II, p. 84.

"The delegates (in the Federal Convention) from the Northern
States argued that slaves were not represented in the Legislatures
of the *States* in which they belonged and, therefore, should not be
considered in fixing a basis for representation in the national Legislature; that in such *States* slaves were regarded as property, and
should not be represented any more than other species of property;
that slaves did not vote, and that such a basis would make the vote
of a Southern white man count for more than that of a white man
in the North." (Lee's *The Story of the American Constitution*,
p. 27.)

fer of power from the maritime to the interior and landed interest will, I foresee, be an oppression to commerce. In this struggle between the two ends of the *Union,* the Middle *States* ought to join their Eastern brethren. If the Southern *States* get the power into their hands and be joined, as they will be, with the interior country, everything is to be apprehended." [127]

On the same day in the Convention Mr. Butler, of South Carolina, replied: "The Southern *States* want security that their negroes may not be taken from them. . . . The *people* and strength of America are evidently bearing to the South and Southwest." [128]

Mr. Wilson said in the Convention on this occasion: "Property is not the sole nor the primary end of government and society; the improvement of the human mind is the most noble object." [129]

Every State voted on the same day, in the Convention, for "the apportionment of representation to numbers" except Delaware, whose vote was divided.[130]

The preservation of the rights of the smaller *States* by allowing them the same representation in the Senate (of two members each) as the larger *States,* continued to occupy the attention of the Convention in July.

Many of the members had against their better judgment voted for the equal representation in the Senate of all the *States,* large and small, because they realized

[127] Bancroft's *History of the Constitution of the United States,* Vol. II, pp. 84, 85.
[128] *Ibid.,* p. 85. Gilpin, 1091–1093. Elliot, Vol. V, pp. 308, 309.
[129] Bancroft's *History of the Constitution of the United States,* Vol. II, p. 85.
[130] *Ibid.,* p. 86. Gilpin, 1094. Elliot, Vol. V, p. 309.

that if they did not so vote, the Constitution could not be put through.[131]

The real conflict of interest, Mr. Madison declared in the Convention, July 13th, 1787, was between the Northern and the Southern *States*, not between the large and small *States*. He said the institution of slavery constituted the line of discrimination, and "should a proportional representation take place, the Northern will still outnumber the other; but every day will tend toward an equilibrium."[132]

The great Bancroft declares that: "Had the South joined with the smaller *States* to establish the suffrage by *States* in both branches of the general Legislature, it would, in less than ten years,[133] have arrived at an equality, alike in the House and in the Senate. But it believed that swarms of emigrants were about to throng every path to the Southwest, bearing with them affluence and power. It did not yet know the dynamic energy of freedom in producing wealth, and attracting and employing and retaining population. The equality of the vote in the Senate, which Virginia and South Carolina vehemently resisted, was to gain and preserve for the slaveholding *States* a balance in one branch of the Legislature; in the other, where representation was apportioned to population, the superiority of the free Commonwealths would increase from decade to decade till slavery in the *United States* should be no more."[134]

On July 13th, 1787, a statute was passed by Con-

[131] Bancroft's *History of the Constitution of the United States*, Vol. II, p. 86.
[132] *Ibid.*, pp. 86, 87. Gilpin, 1104. Elliot, Vol. V, p. 315.
[133] Bancroft's *History of the Constitution of the United States*, Vol. II, p. 87. (On the admission of Tennessee.)
[134] *Ibid.*, p. 87.

gress, "forbidding slavery to cross the Ohio River," by the votes of Georgia, South Carolina, North Carolina, Virginia, Delaware, New Jersey, New York, and Massachusetts—all the *States* that were then present in the Congress. Maryland was the only Southern *State* absent. Pennsylvania and three New England *States* were also absent.[135]

On July 16th, 1787, the Convention voted for equal representation of *every State* in the Senate.[136] Jefferson over ten years before had suggested this very thing.

When the vote was taken on this proposition, July 16th, 1787, six of the Southern *States* and four Northern *States* were present.[137] "Four of the six *States* which demanded a proportional (to population) representation" in the upper branch refused to vote that every *State*, large and small, should have two members. The deciding vote was North Carolina's. She voted with the small *States* for equal representation in the Senate, and the proposition was carried by a majority of one. So the prophecy of Thomas Jefferson, in his letter to John Adams,[138] became true, that "the good Whigs will so far cede their opinions for the sake of the *Union*."

[135] *Ibid.*, pp. 115, 116.
[136] *Ibid.*, p. 87. Gilpin, 1107. Elliot, Vol. V, p. 316. Warren's *The Making of the Constitution*, p. 309.
[137] Bancroft's *History of the Constitution of the United States*, Vol. II, pp. 87, 88.
[138] *Ibid.*, p. 88. Works of John Adams, IX, 465–467.

"A compromise was finally effected by the Northern *States* agreeing to the importation of slaves for an additional period of twenty years, and the Southern *States* conceding to Congress absolute control over both foreign and interstate commerce, with authority to enact navigation laws by a majority vote." (Lee's *The Story of the American Constitution*, p. 28.)

The most important question of representation in the lower and upper branches having been voted, Sherman and other members began to worry over the action of the Convention.

On July 17th, 1787, in the Convention, a motion of Bedford, from Delaware, was seconded by Gouverneur Morris, "to empower the national Legislature to legislate for the general interests of the *Union,* for cases to which the *States* are separately incompetent, and for cases in which the harmony of the *United States* might be interrupted by the exercise of individual legislation,"[139] and was adopted by the vote of every *State* except South Carolina and Georgia.

On July 17th, 1787, "It was moved and seconded . . . to take up the following: 'To make the laws binding on the *people* of the *United States* in all cases which may concern the common interests of the *Union:* but not to interfere with the government of the individual *States* in any matters of internal police which respect the government of such *States* only, and wherein the general welfare of the *United States* is not concerned,' which 'passed' in the negative: Ayes, two; noes, eight. (That is to say, it was lost.)

"It was moved and seconded to alter the second clause of the sixth resolution so as to read as follows, namely, 'and moreover to legislate in all cases for the general interests of the *Union,* and also in those to

[139] Bancroft's *History of the Constitution of the United States,* Vol. II, p. 90. Gilpin, 1116. Elliot, Vol. V, p. 320.

"*Mr. Bedford* was educated for the bar, and in his profession, I am told, has merit. He is a bold and nervous speaker, and has a very commanding and striking manner, but he is warm and impetuous in his temper, and precipitate in his judgment. Mr. Bedford is about thirty-two years old, and very corpulent." (*Character Sketches of Delegates to the Federal Convention,* by William Pierce, a delegate from Georgia to the Constitutional Convention.)

which the *States* are separately incompetent, or in which the harmony of the *United States* may be interrupted by the exercise of individual legislation,' which passed in the affirmative: Ayes, six; noes, four. (To agree to the second clause of the sixth resolution as amended. Ayes, eight; noes, two.)

"On the question to agree to the following clause of the sixth resolution, reported from the Committee of the Whole House, namely, 'to negative all laws passed by the several *States* contravening in the opinion of the national Legislature the Articles of Union, or any treaties subsisting under the authority of the *Union*,' it passed in the negative: Ayes, three *States;* noes, seven *States*."[140]

On July 18th, 1787, the Convention adopted the report of the Committee of the Whole that there be one supreme tribunal (the now Supreme Court at Washington), and that the national Legislatures be empowered to institute inferior tribunals.[141]

The important question still remained as to how the new Constitution should be ratified. The point was

[140] Farrand's *The Records of the Federal Convention of 1787*, Vol. II, pp. 21, 22.
[141] Warren's *The Making of the Constitution*, p. 325.

In the articles concerning the judiciary there was great care to exclude from the jurisdiction of the *Federal* courts every question regarding occurrences within the borders of a *State*. The Virginia, the New Jersey, and the Connecticut "plans" all agreed upon this point.

Originally, the draft of the Constitution only gave the Supreme Court jurisdiction of cases concerning "ambassadors, other ministers, and consuls." Later that court was given jurisdiction where a *State* was a party plaintiff. In admiralty and maritime cases there was a right of appeal to the Supreme Court. The Supreme Court was designed to be "the bulwark of a limited Constitution against encroachment." (The Federalist, LXXVIII.)

whether the *Legislatures* of the *States,* or the *people* direct, should ratify.[142]

Mason of Virginia said: "The *Legislatures* of the *States* have no power to ratify it. And, if they had, it would be wrong to refer the plan to them, because succeeding Legislatures, having equal authority, could undo the acts of their predecessors, and the national Government would stand in each *State* on the tottering foundation of an act of Assembly. Whither, then, must we resort? To the *people,* with whom all power remains that has not been given up in the constitutions derived from them." [143]

Randolph said: "The consideration of this subject (ratification) should be transferred from the *Legislatures,* where local demagogues have their full influence, to a field in which their efforts can be less mischievous. Moreover, some of the *States* are averse to any change in their Constitution, and will not take the requisite steps unless expressly called upon to refer the question to the *people.*" [144]

On July 20th, 1787, the next discussion of importance about the power of the *States* as opposed to the power of the *people* of those *States* occurred over the method of electing the executive. There were seven methods suggested: 1. By the *people* at large. 2. By the *Legislatures of the States.* 3. By the *executives of the States.* 4. By *electors* chosen by the *people.* 5. By electors chosen by lot. 6. By the Legislature (Congress) on the nomination of three (or two) candidates by each *several States.* 7. By the Legislature (Con-

[142] Bancroft's *History of the Constitution of the United States,* Vol. II, p. 93.
[143] *Ibid.,* p. 93.
[144] *Ibid.,* pp. 93, 94. Gilpin, 1177–1179. Elliot, Vol. V, pp. 352, 353.

gress) on the nomination of one candidate for each *State*. Washington, Madison, Wilson, Morris, and Gerry disapproved the choice of one executive by the legislature. Rutledge, Mason, and Strong favored it.[145]

On July 23rd, 1787, in the Convention, Gerry, of Rhode Island, said: "The last Article (of the Confederation) authorizes alterations only by the unanimous concurrence of the *States*." [146]

On the same day, in the Convention, Mr. Gorham, another Rhode Island delegate, replied that "provision ought to be made for giving effect to the system, without waiting for the unanimous concurrence of the *States*." [147]

Ellsworth said during this debate that when the Articles of Confederation were established, there was no thought of "conventions of the *people,* with power derived expressly from the *people*." [148]

King insisted that "the authority of the *people* expressly delegated to conventions is most likely to draw forth the best men in the *States* to decide on the new Constitution." [149]

On July 23rd, 1787, nine *States* in the Convention voted for, and only Delaware voted against, submitting the ratification of the new Constitution to assemblies in each *State,* chosen specially for that purpose by the *people*.[150]

---
[145] Bancroft's *History of the Constitution of the United States,* Vol. II, pp. 172, 173.
[146] *Ibid.,* p. 94.
[147] *Ibid.,* p. 94. Gilpin, 1180. Elliot, Vol. V, pp. 353, 354.
[148] Bancroft's *History of the Constitution of the United States,* Vol. II, p. 94. Gilpin, 1181. Elliot, Vol. V, p. 354.
[149] Bancroft's *History of the Constitution of the United States,* Vol. II, p. 94. Gilpin, 1182, 1183. Elliot, Vol. V, p. 355.
[150] Bancroft's *History of the Constitution of the United States,* Vol. II, p. 95. Gilpin, 1185. Elliot, Vol. V, p. 356.

On July 24th, 1787, the Convention appointed a Committee of "two Southern, two Northern, and one Middle Western" representatives "to report a constitution conformable to the resolutions passed by the Convention."[151]

On July 26th, 1787, in the Convention, the twenty-three resolutions which had been passed, were referred to a Committee of Detail of five to prepare and report them in the form of a constitution. Gorham, Ellsworth, and Wilson, of the Committee, represented the North; Randolph and Rutledge represented the South.[152]

Many of the Articles were framed by the Committee of Detail out of the twenty-three resolutions of the Constitutional Convention.[153]

The people of the *Colonies* each had a "separate home government. . . . It was their first care to see of whom they were composed. The question they agreed to investigate and decide by a joint act of them all. For this end Congress selected from its numbers five of its ablest jurists and most trusted statesmen:

---

[151] Warren's *The Making of the Constitution*, p. 353.
[152] Bancroft's *History of the Constitution of the United States*, Vol. II, p. 95.
[153] *Ibid.*, p. 119.

"Mr. Rutledge is one of those characters who was highly mounted at the commencement of the late Revolution; his reputation in the First Congress gave him a distinguished rank among the American worthies. He was bred to the law, and now acts as one of the Chancellors of South Carolina. The gentleman is much famed in his own *State* as an orator, but in my opinion he is too rapid in his public speaking to be denominated an agreeable orator. He is undoubtedly a man of abilities, and a gentleman of distinction and fortune. Mr. Rutledge was once Governor of South Carolina. He is about forty-eight years of age." (*Character Sketches of Delegates to the Federal Convention*, by William Pierce, a delegate from Georgia to the Constitutional Convention.)

John Adams, Thomas Jefferson, Edward Rutledge, James Wilson, and Robert R. Livingston. . . . Their unanimous report, unanimously accepted by Congress, was: 'All persons abiding within any of the *United Colonies,* and deriving protection from the laws of the same, owe allegiance to the said laws, and are members of such *Colony.*' " [154]

"Madison pointed out that the true difference between a league or treaty and a constitution was, that the one system was founded on the *Legislatures* only, and the other on the *people;* that in point of political operation there were important distinctions in favor of the latter: 'A law violating a treaty ratified by a pre-existing law might be respected by the Judges, as a law, though an unwise and perfidious one. A law violative of a constitution established by the *people* themselves would be considered by the Judges as null and void.' " [155]

On August 6th, 1787, the Committee of Detail reported to the Convention its draft of the Constitution consisting of a "preamble and twenty-three articles divided into forty-one sections." [156]

One of the features of the new Constitution reported to the Convention by the Committee was that representatives were not required to reside in the district they might be elected to represent; but, of course, they had to be inhabitants of the *State* they represented.

On "August 20th, 1787, the power 'to make all laws necessary and proper for carrying to execution the powers vested by this Constitution in the Government

---

[154] Bancroft's *History of the Constitution of the United States,* Vol. II, p. 120. Journals of Congress for June 5th, 17th, and 24th, 1776.
[155] Warren's *The Making of the Constitution,* p. 350.
[156] *Ibid.,* p. 388.

of the *United States,* or in any department or office thereof,' was so clearly necessary that, without cavil or remark, . . . was unanimously agreed to." [157]

"When the Convention voted to refer the Constitution to Conventions of the *people* for adoption, rather than to the *State* Legislatures, it voted directly in opposition to the propertied interests. For, as will be shown in detail *infra,* practically all the *State* Constitutions, at that time, required voters for members of the *State* Legislature to possess a certain amount of property (some *States* requiring possession of more property to vote for *State* Senator than for Representative); and they required the members of the Legislature to have property qualifications (in some *States* larger for Senators than for Representatives). On the other hand, in all the *States,* whoever was qualified to vote for *State* Representative could vote for members of a Convention; and in Massachusetts and some other States, every freeman of a town (irrespective of possession of property) could vote for a member of a Convention. Moreover, members of Conventions themselves were not obliged to possess any property qualifications. Hence, the vote by which the Federal Convention referred ratification to the *people* was a democratic vote, and not in the interests of property." [158]

"Every *State* at that time had property and religious qualifications both for the electors of the *State* Legislatures, and for the Representatives and Senators to be elected to the same; moreover, in some *States* certain classes of men, such as clergymen, were en-

---

[157] Bancroft's *History of the Constitution of the United States,* Vol. II, p. 149. Gilpin, 1370. Elliot, Vol. V, p. 447.
[158] Warren's *The Making of the Constitution,* pp. 351, 352.

tirely excluded from the Legislature. Hence a much more general representation of the *people* might then have been expected in a *State* Convention than in a *State* Legislature. Moreover, though the size of the *State* Legislature was limited by the *State* Constitutions, there was no restriction as to size of Conventions; and Conventions did not present the difficulty of action which the two branches of a Legislature with their varying interests might occasion. Since the rise, in subsequent years, of universal manhood and womanhood suffrage and the abolition of property qualifications, the necessity of Conventions is at the present time less apparent. Consideration of an amendment by a Convention, however, presents one advantage which is as applicable today as in 1787, namely, that the submission is to a body chosen for the special purpose of considering the amendment, whereas submission to a Legislature may be to a body elected beforehand on entirely different issues and with no view towards its capacity to pass on the amendment." [159]

In discussing in the Convention what should constitute treason, and whether there could be treason against a particular *State,* Mason said, on August 20th, 1787: "The *United States* will have a qualified *sovereignty* only; the individual *States* will retain a part of the *sovereignty*." [160]

On the same day Ellsworth said: "The *United States* are sovereign on one side of the line dividing the jurisdictions, the *States* on the other. Each ought

[159] *Ibid.,* pp. 677, 678.
[160] Bancroft's *History of the Constitution of the United States,* Vol. II, p. 150.

to have power to defend their respective *sovereignties*." [161]

August 24th, 1787, the report of the Committee of Detail relating to the executive came before the Convention. The report was unanimous that the power should be vested in one person, but many plans were advocated for selecting him. It was finally decided to elect him for four years by electors appointed by each *State,* as its Legislature might direct.[162]

On September 12th, 1787, it was proposed by Gerry and Mason that a Bill of Rights be prepared by a Committee for insertion in the Constitution, but Sherman said "the *State* Declarations of Rights are not repealed by this Constitution; and being in force, are sufficient." The proposition was then unanimously rejected.[163]

Hamilton had a similar thought when he said afterwards in Number 84 of the *Federalist:* "The Constitution is itself in every rational sense a bill of rights. . . . The proposed government is one of enumerated powers. . . . Why declare that things shall not be done which there is no power to do? Why, for instance, should it be said that liberty of the press shall not be restrained when no power is given by which restrictions may be imposed?"

September 12th, 1787, the Committee on Style made its final revised draft of the Constitution, and reported it to the Convention on "four folio pages printed on one side." [164]

[161] *Ibid.,* p. 150. Gilpin, 1375. Elliot, Vol. V, p. 450.
[162] Bancroft's *History of the Constitution of the United States,* Vol. II, pp. 173-77.
[163] Lee's *The Story of the American Constitution,* p. 59.
[164] Warren's *The Making of the Constitution,* p. 686.

September 13th, 1787, Mr. Johnson had reported from the Committee of Style a draft of a resolution recommending that the Constitution when adopted should be laid before Congress, and expressing "the opinion of this Convention" that it should be submitted to a Convention of delegates chosen in each *State* under the recommendation of its *Legislature* "for their assent and ratification"; that Congress, as soon as the Conventions of nine *States* should have ratified, should fix a date for the election of the new Government; and that after such election "the Congress, together with the President, should, without delay, proceed to execute the Constitution." This resolution was now (September 17th, 1787) voted by the "unanimous order of the Convention.[165]

September 15th, 1787, there was a resolution that "no *State* without its own consent should ever be deprived of its equality in the Senate."

---

[165] Farrand's *The Records of the Federal Convention of 1787*, Vol. II, p. 604.

"*Dr. Johnson* is a character much celebrated for his legal knowledge; he is said to be one of the first classics in America, and certainly possesses a very strong and enlightened understanding. As an orator, in my opinion, there is nothing in him that warrants the high reputation which he has for public speaking. There is something in the tone of his voice not pleasing to the ear, but he is eloquent and clear, always abounding with information and instruction. He was once employed as an agent for the *State* of Connecticut to state her claims to certain landed territory before the British House of commons; this office he discharged with so much dignity, and made such an ingenious display of his powers, that he laid the foundation of a reputation which will probably last much longer than his own life. Dr. Johnson is about sixty years of age, possesses the manners of a gentleman, and engages the hearts of men by the sweetness of his temper, and that affectionate style of address with which he accosts his acquaintances." (*Character Sketches of Delegates to the Federal Convention,* by William Pierce, a delegate from Georgia to the Constitutional Convention.)

September 17th, 1787, "as the document was ready for signature, it became a grave question whether the remnant had sufficient faith in their work to subscribe their names, and if they failed to do so, its adoption by the *people* would have been impossible. Many delegates had left in disgust, and the fifty-five had shrunk to forty-two. Of the latter, three refused to the last to sign. They were Edmund Randolph, George Mason, and Elbridge Gerry." [166]

"It is said that Franklin wept. When he had concluded his address, he moved that the Constitution be signed with the following attestation:

" 'Done in Convention, by the unanimous consent of the *States* present.'

"This was to enable the delegates, who were not convinced as to the wisdom of the proposed Constitution and remained unmoved by Franklin's eloquent appeal, to sign in behalf of their *States* without accepting any personal responsibility." [167]

"A vote was then taken as to the adoption of the Constitution as enrolled, and the *States,* as *States,* unanimously voted in the affirmative." [168]

Alexander Hamilton said: "A few characters of consequence, by opposing, or even refusing to sign the Constitution, might do infinite mischief, by kindling the latent sparks that lurk under an en-

---

[166] Beck's *The Constitution of the United States,* p. 164.
[167] *Ibid.,* p. 165.
[168] *Ibid.,* p. 166.

"When the document (Constitution) had been agreed upon in substance, it was turned over to a Committee headed by Gouverneur Morris, an adept in the use of correct English, to be put in proper form. This Committee freed it of all redundancy and ambiguousness, and reported it to the Convention in its present form on September 17th, 1787." (Lee's *The Story of the American Constitution,* p. 39.)

thusiasm in favor of the Convention which may soon subside. *No man's ideas are more remote from the plan than my own are known to be;* but is it possible to deliberate between anarchy and convulsion on the one side, and the chance of good to be expected from the plan on the other?"

"Mr. Blount thereupon vindicated the wisdom of Gouverneur Morris's adroit expedient by stating that while he would not have signed the Constitution as an individual, he was willing to have it attested as the act of the *States*." [169]

"The vote was then taken, and ten of the eleven *States* then present voted in the affirmative (to sign the Constitution), while the eleventh (South Carolina) did not vote." [170]

Benjamin Franklin looked toward the picture of a rising sun behind the President's chair.

"I have," said he, "often and often in the course of the session, and the vicissitudes of my hopes and fears as to the issue, looked at that behind the President without being able to tell whether it was rising or setting. But now at length I have the happiness to know that it is a rising and not a setting sun."

"Before the Convention adjourned, it resolved:
'That the preceding Constitution be laid before the

[169] Beck's *The Constitution of the United States,* p. 167.
[170] *Ibid.,* p. 169.
"*Mr. Blount* is a character strongly marked for integrity and honor. He has been twice a member of Congress, and in that office discharged his duty with ability and faithfulness. He is no speaker, nor does he possess any of those talents that make men shine; he is plain, honest, and sincere. Mr. Blount is about thirty-six years of age." (*Character Sketches of Delegates to the Federal Convention,* by William Pierce, a delegate from Georgia to the Constitutional Convention.)

United States in Congress assembled, and that it is the opinion of this Convention, that it should afterwards be submitted to a convention of delegates, chosen in each *State* by the people thereof, under the recommendation of its legislature, for their assent and ratification; and that each convention assenting to, and ratifying the same, should give notice thereof to the *United States* in Congress assembled.

GEORGE WASHINGTON,
President.'

"It also suggested to Congress steps which, upon the ratification of the Constitution by nine *States,* should be followed in installing the new Government. Congress was then sitting in New York. By direction of the Convention, Washington sent Congress a copy of the Constitution, and the resolutions just mentioned."[171] His letter follows:

September 17, 1787.

His Excellency, The President of Congress.
Sir:

We have now the honor to submit to the consideration of the *United States,* in Congress assembled, that Constitution which has appeared to us the most advisable.

The friends of our country have long seen and desired that the power of making war, peace, and treaties; that of levying money, and regulating commerce; and the correspondent executive and judicial authorities, should be fully and effectually vested in the general Government of the *Union;* but the impropriety of delegating such extensive trust to one

---

[171] Beck's *The Constitution of the United States,* p. 173.

body of men is evident; hence results the necessity of a different organization.

It is obviously impracticable, in the Federal Government of these *States,* to secure all rights of independent *sovereignty* to each, and yet provide for the interest and safety of all. Individuals entering into society must give up a share of liberty to preserve the rest. The magnitude of the sacrifice must depend as well on situation and circumstance, as on the object to be obtained. It is at all times difficult to draw with precision the line between those rights which must be surrendered, and those which may be reserved; and, on the present occasion, this difficulty was increased by a difference among the several *States* as to their situation, extent, habits, and particular interests.

In all our deliberations on this subject we kept steadily in our view that which appears to us the greatest interest of every true American, the consolidation of our *Union,* in which is involved our prosperity, felicity, safety—perhaps our national existence. This important consideration, seriously and deeply impressed on our minds, led each *State* in the Convention to be less rigid, on points of inferior magnitude, than might have been otherwise expected; and thus the Constitution which we now present is the result of a spirit of amity, and of that mutual deference and concession which the peculiarity of our political situation rendered indispensable.

That it will meet the full and entire approbation of every *State* is not perhaps to be expected; but each will doubtless consider that, had her interest alone been consulted, the consequences might have been particularly disagreeable or injurious to others; that it is liable to as few exceptions as could reasonably have been expected, we hope and believe; that it may promote the lasting welfare of that country so dear to us all, and secure her freedom and happiness, is our most ardent wish.

With great respect, we have the honor to be, sir, your Excellency's most obedient and humble servants. By the unanimous order of the Convention.

GEORGE WASHINGTON, *President*.

The Convention adjourned on September 17th, 1787,[172] after it adopted the Constitution. Its last step was a resolution that the Constitution be sent to the Congress of the *Confederation,* with the recommendation that it be submitted to Conventions elected by the *people* of *each State,* for ratification or rejection. If nine *States* should ratify it, Congress should appoint days for the popular election of electors, and that then the new Congress and President should "without delay proceed to execute the Constitution." [173]

September 20th, 1787, Washington, who was President of the Convention that drafted the Constitution, wrote the President of Congress a letter in which he said: "We kept steadily in view the consolidation of our *Union,* in which is involved our prosperity, felicity, safety, perhaps our national existence. And thus the Constitution which we now present is the result of that mutual deference and concession, which the peculiarity of our political situation rendered indispensable." [174] The following resolution was then passed by Congress:

[172] Elliott's *Debates on the Federal Constitution,* Vol. I, pp. 17, 18.
[173] Fiske's *The Critical Period of American History,* p. 306.
[174] Bancroft's *History of the Constitution of the United States,* Vol. II, pp. 225–27.

THE UNITED STATES IN CONGRESS ASSEMBLED.[175]

Friday, September 28, 1787.

Present—New Hampshire, Massachusetts, Connecticut, New York, New Jersey, Pennsylvania, Delaware, Virginia, North Carolina, South Carolina, and Georgia; and from Maryland, Mr. Ross.

Congress having received the report of the Convention, lately assembled in Philadelphia,—

Resolved, unanimously, That the said report, with the resolutions and letter accompanying the same, be transmitted to the several Legislatures, in order to submit to a Convention of delegates, chosen in each *State* by the *people* thereof, in conformity to the resolves of the Convention made and provided in that case.

CHARLES THOMPSON,
Secretary.

When George Washington finally put the question

---

[175] Elliott's *Debates on the Federal Constitution,* Vol. I, p. 18.

"On September 20, 1787, the proposed Constitution was formally laid before Congress. The first move of the opposition, led by Richard Henry Lee, a member of that body, was to strangle it by preventing Congress from transmitting it to the several *State* Legislatures. In the meantime, James Madison, who had resumed his seat in Congress, successfully met every objection and, after eight days of debate, that body formally transmitted the Constitution to the various *State* Legislatures, to be submitted by them to the people in delegate Conventions. Upon this issue the *people,* for the first time, divided into two national political parties—the Federalist and the Anti-Federalist. . . . The latter opposed its approval with equal zeal, and were directed by three of the greatest pre-Revolutionary patriots—Samuel Adams, 'Father of the Revolution,' the aged but still fiery Patrick Henry, and Richard Henry Lee, who, eleven years before, had moved the adoption of the Declaration of Independence." (Lee's *The Story of the American Constitution,* p. 56.)

of agreeing to the Constitution to the Constitutional Convention, all the *States* present answered "aye." All the *States* had previously voted against another convention.

As it was not known which nine of the thirteen *States* would (first) adopt the Constitution, the names of the *States* were not inserted in the instrument.

Alexander Hamilton "successively inscribed on the great sheet of parchment the name of each *State,* as their delegations came forward in geographical order." [176]

Gouverneur Morris said: "The moment it (the Constitution) goes forth, the great question will be: shall there be a national Government or a monarchy?" [177]

[176] Bancroft's *History of the Constitution of the United States,* Vol. II, p. 221.
[177] *Ibid.*, p. 220.

CHAPTER XIII

RATIFYING THE CONSTITUTION

THE next important question was as to how the Constitution should be ratified. Hamilton thought it would be courteous for Congress to first agree to the Constitution, and then transmit it for ratification by the *State* Legislatures. In this he and Gerry were in accord. Wilson and others opposed. Finally, in the language of the Committee of Detail, it was agreed that it should be laid before the Congress . . . and . . . afterwards submitted to a "Convention chosen in *each State* under the recommendation of its *Legislature,* in order to receive the ratification of such Convention."[1]

After it was voted that "the Constitution should be established on its ratification by the Conventions of nine States" (about three-fourths), a Committee of five was designated to arrange and revise it. They were Johnson, of Connecticut; Hamilton, of New York; Gouverneur Morris, Madison, and King, of Massachusetts.

Richard Henry Lee fought the new proposed Constitution because it did not set out the contract between the *nation* and the *government*. He said: "The Constitution makes no mention but of those who govern,

---

[1] Bancroft's *History of the Constitution of the United States,* Vol. II, p. 205.

and never speaks of the rights of the *people* who are governed."[2]

Lee thought the power of the Government should be qualified by a bill of rights which would relate to the freedom of conscience, freedom of the press, trial by jury in civil as well as criminal cases, "the prohibition of standing armies, freedom of elections, independence of judges, security against excessive bail, fines or punishment, against unreasonable searches and seizures of persons, houses, papers, or property, and the right of petition."[3]

Instead of transmitting the Constitution to *State* Legislatures for action, as the Articles of Confederation provided, it was sent to *State* Conventions of the people to ratify or disapprove it.

Referring to the Constitution, Bancroft says: "Here is no transient contract between parties; it is the institution of government by an act of the highest *sovereignty;* the decree of many who are yet one; their law of laws, inviolably supreme, and not to be changed except in the way which their forecast had provided."

"One charge of the opposition, at least, was true, namely, that the Convention had exceeded its authority. It was called for the purpose of amending the Articles of Confederation. Instead, it discarded the old government entirely, and proceeded to create a new one."[4]

Between September 18th, 1787, and January, 1788, the *people* of the different *States* began to select dele-

[2] *Ibid.*, pp. 225–227.
[3] *Ibid.*, p. 208.
[4] Lee's *The Story of the American Constitution*, p. 57.

gates to *State* Conventions "to pronounce their judgment on the creation of a Federal republic." [5]

On September 28th, 1787, "the old Congress after some debate decided to submit the Constitution to the *States* for action without any recommendation except as follows: 'That the said report, with the resolutions and the letter accompanying the same, be transmitted to the several Legislatures, in order to be submitted to a Convention of delegates chosen in each *State* by the *people* thereof, in conformity to the resolves of the Convention made and provided in that case.'" [6]

This was done in pursuance of the resolution passed by the Convention.[7]

In the Pennsylvania Convention Wilson said that under the proposed Constitution "error in the Legislature may be corrected by the Constitution; error in the Constitution, by the *people*. . . . In this Constitution all authority is derived from the *people*." It would have been more strictly accurate if he had said that the Constitution could be corrected by three-fourths of the *States,* composed of the *people,* or he might have said that one *State* more than one-fourth of the *States,* composed of the *people,* could block any correction of the Constitution. But at that time the makers of the Constitution probably did not have in mind the distinction between the *people* (who composed the *States*) and the *States* composed of the *people,* or the distinction between the *people* who

[5] Bancroft's *The History of the Constitution of the United States,* Vol. II, p. 239.
[6] Beck's *The Constitution of the United States,* p. 176.
[7] Elliott's *Debates on the Federal Constitution,* Vol. I, p. 16.

composed the *Union,* or the *Union* composed of the *people*.

"Not more than 160,000 voted for representatives to the *State* ratifying Conventions—but it will be recalled that at that time suffrage was restricted to freeholders."[8]

In Pennsylvania, as in other *States,* there were many who wanted to amend the Constitution which had been proposed to the *States*. If amended, it would then have gone back to the Convention with such amendments by probably every *State,* and the delegates of no *State* would have been authorized to vote for all the amendments offered by the other *States,* so that it would have then had to be referred back to the *States* again. The *States* would then have sent delegates back to the Convention for other endless votes. This sort of practice has frequently been employed to kill an instrument through endless debates and amendments.

But their opponents realized that this would have been an endless process. They knew that if the instrument was not adopted as it was received by the Conventions of the *States,* there would be no Constitution, so they insisted upon its adoption in the same form that it came to the Conventions. This was eventually done.

The Assembly of Maryland, in November, 1787, summoned its delegates to a Convention. By a majority of one the meeting of the Convention was postponed until April. After Washington in a letter to Thomas Johnson had advised against any further adjournment, a quorum of the Convention met at

[8] Beck's *Constitution of the United States,* p. 178.

Annapolis on April 21st, 1788. The proposed Constitution was ratified by sixty-three to eleven.[9]

On December 7th, 1787, Delaware unanimously ratified the Constitution.[10]

On December 12th, 1787, Pennsylvania ratified, with a vote of forty-six to twenty-three.[10]

On December 18th, 1787, New Jersey, which had opened its convention with prayer, unanimously ratified.[10]

[9] Bancroft's *History of the Constitution of the United States*, Vol. II, pp. 278, 281, 283.

[10] Warren's *The Making of the Constitution*, pp. 819, 820. (Appendix D.)

"It was the plan of the Anti-Federalists in Pennsylvania to wage a vigorous campaign, secure a majority in the new Legislature, and prevent the calling of a convention to consider the new Constitution. But the Federalists were too astute to be caught in a situation that might prove so disastrous. Without waiting even for Congress to submit the Constitution formally to the various Legislatures, George Clymer, Federalist member, who had also sat in the Convention, introduced a resolution calling a convention to consider the proposed form of government.... Nineteen were bitterly Anti-Federalists, and to prevent the passage of the resolution, they absented themselves from the legislative chamber. The forty-five Federalists dispatched the sergeant-at-arms to bring in the absentees, but they defied him. An adjournment was then taken until the next morning, when a number of citizens broke into their room, seized two Anti-Federalist members, forcibly took them to the legislative chamber, and held them in their seats until the resolution was passed.... The chief objections of the Pennsylvania Anti-Federalists to the Constitution were ... that it provided for the payment of the salaries of members of Congress out of the Federal treasury, thus rendering them independent of their respective States; that it required an oath of all Federal officers to support it.

"The Anti-Federalists in Pennsylvania branded Washington as a 'born fool' and Franklin as an 'old dotard.' Finding themselves hopelessly outnumbered in the Convention, they resorted to filibustering, but the eloquence and logic of that great Scotchman, James Wilson, who later became an Associate Justice of the Supreme Court, beat down all opposition, and the Constitution was ratified on December 12, 1787, by a vote of forty-six to twenty-three." (Lee's *The Story of the American Constitution*, pp. 62, 64.)

On January 2nd, 1788, Georgia unanimously ratified the Constitution.[10]

"In the Massachusetts Convention the Federalists were ably assisted by Fisher Ames, whose eloquence was soon to become so famous. The irreconcilable Elbridge Gerry marshalled the forces of the Anti-Federalists, and was covertly assisted by Samuel Adams, 'Father of the Revolution,' and Governor John Hancock, President of the Convention. . . . It was argued that a two-year term for members of Congress was entirely too long; that a Federal district ten miles square was too large an area in which to permit Congress to 'wreak its tyrannical will without let or hindrance—a district one mile square would be large enough'; that the power vested in the proposed government to maintain a standing army foreboded tyranny; that the 'President as Commander-in-chief of such army could make himself a Cromwell'; that the Constitution did not recognize the existence of a God; that it required no religious test for Federal officers; that under it 'a Papist or Infidel was as eligible to hold office as a Christian'; that too much power was delegated to the Federal Government; that the *people* could not support such an elaborate system; that it did not contain a bill of rights; and, finally, that the entire system was conceived by lawyers who expected to get into Congress, manage the Government to suit themselves, and 'swallow up us little folks just like the whale swallowed Jonah.'"[11]

On January 9th, 1788, after considering the proposed Constitution, first, section by section, and afterwards as a whole, Connecticut ratified it by 128 to 40.[10]

[10] *Loc. cit.*
[11] Lee's *The Story of the American Constitution*, p. 65.

On February 16th, 1788, Massachusetts ratified the Constitution by a vote of 187 to 168.[10]

After a strong fight had been made on the Constitution because "an unalienable power resides in the *people* to amend their form of government," and after the instrument had been read and debated, Maryland's ratification on April 26th, 1788 (the seventh *State* to ratify), gave a majority of the thirteen *States* in favor of the Constitution. Maryland's action caused Washington to say: "The fiat of your Convention will most assuredly raise the edifice. . . . Should everything proceed with harmony and consent according to our actual wishes and expectations, it will be so much beyond anything we had a right to imagine or expect eighteen months ago that it will, as visibly as any possible event in the course of human affairs, demonstrate the finger of Providence."[12]

When South Carolina was considering the objection of its James Lincoln, that the proposed Constitution contained no bill of rights, Charles Cotesworth Pinckney replied: "By delegating express powers, we certainly reserve to *ourselves* every power and right not mentioned in the Constitution. Another reason weighed particularly with the members from this *State*. Bills of right generally begin with declaring that all men are by nature born free. Now, we should make that declaration with a very bad grace when a large part of our property consists in men who are actually born slaves."

On May 23rd, 1788, South Carolina, due to the powerful Pinckney and Rutledge support, ratified the Constitution, 149 to 73. Here aged Christopher Gads-

[10] *Loc. cit.*
[12] Bancroft's *History of the Constitution of the United States*, Vol. II, pp. 283, 284, 285.

den said: "I can have but little expectation of seeing the happy effects that will result to my country from the wise decisions of this day, but I shall say with old Simeon: 'Lord, now lettest Thou Thy servant depart in peace, for mine eyes have seen the salvation of my country.'"[13]

New Hampshire, after adjourning from February until June, 1788, to give them time to consider, and see what the other *States* would do, ratified the Constitution June 21st, 1788, while the Anti-Federalists in New York and Virginia were wrangling over the question of ratification.[14]

After New Hampshire (the ninth *State* to ratify) had ratified the Constitution by fifty-seven to forty-seven, it then became a fact, and Congress named the first Wednesday of January, 1789, as the day for the choice by the *States* of electors, the first Wednesday in February for the choice of President and Vice President, and the first Wednesday in March for the inauguration of the new Government, at New York City. The last date fell on March 4th, which has been the limit of each President's term since that time. Washington was unanimously elected President, and John Adams, standing next on the list, was Vice President.

"Among the leaders in the Virginia Convention, which met June 2nd, 1788, were James Madison, master spirit of the Federalists and a future President; John Marshall, later Chief Justice; Edmund Randolph, Governor of the State; Edmund Pendleton, President of the Convention; George Wythe, Chancellor of Virginia; and General Henry (Light Horse Harry) Lee,

[13] *Ibid.*, p. 291.
[14] *Ibid.*, p. 278.

Revolutionary hero and father of Robert E. Lee. At the head of the Anti-Federalists was Patrick Henry, the chief critic and most savage assailant of the Constitution. He was ably supported by James Monroe, later President; George Mason, William Grayson, John Tyler, and Benjamin Harrison, the last two, fathers of future Presidents.

"Besides sincerely opposing a strong national government, there was a strong element of selfishness in Virginia's opposition to the proposed form of government. At that time, her planters owed English merchants over $10,000,000, and her Legislature had passed an act suspending the right of such merchants to sue for their money in the *State* courts. The *State*, therefore, was particularly opposed to Section 10, Article I, of the Constitution, which forbids a *State* to pass any 'law impairing the obligation of contracts,' and which would deprive her citizens of the advantage secured by the *State* statute.

"On their respective sides Henry and Madison bore the brunt of the fight which lasted twenty-three days. The former spoke on eighteen separate days. On each of several days he made three speeches; on one day, five, and on another, eight. One of his speeches lasted seven hours. While Madison spoke less often, his labors were no less onerous. Of the two, Henry was the more eloquent, but Madison surpassed him in reasoning power and logic. Governor Randolph although he did not sign the Constitution in Philadelphia, patriotically and brilliantly advocated it in the Virginia State Convention. His was the last voice to be raised in its defense in the Virginia Convention." [15]

"Henry savagely attacked the Constitution, saying

[15] Lee's *The Story of the American Constitution*, pp. 67, 68.

that it established a 'covenant among the *people* instead of a league between the *States*'; that the first clause should read 'We the *States*,' instead of 'We the *people*'; and that it contained no bill of rights. In the office of the President he foresaw 'the likeness of a kingly crown.' " [15]

He declared on June 4th, 1788, that the language of the Constitution, "We, the *people*," is the institution of one great consolidated *national* Government of the *people* of all the *States*, instead of a government by compact with the *States* for its agents. The *people* gave the Convention no right to use their name." Pendleton said: "The expression, 'we, the *people*,' is a common one. . . . Who but the *people* can delegate powers, or form a government?" He declared that the *Confederation* then existing was no government at all.[16]

On June 25th, 1788, by eighty-nine to seventy-nine, the Constitution was ratified by Virginia. To their

---

[15] *Loc. cit.*

[16] Bancroft's *History of the Constitution of the United States,* Vol. II, p. 302.

"Of Henry's speech on June 24th, 1788, one delegate said later that as he 'listened to Mr. Henry, he sensed the doors of the dungeon closing upon him, heard the clank of the chains, and felt the fetters tightening on his wrists.' As Henry reached his powerful climax, he cried: 'I see the awful immensity of the dangers with which it (the Constitution) is pregnant. I see it. I feel it. I see beings of a higher order anxious concerning our decision.' . . . Had a vote been taken at the conclusion of Henry's speech, undoubtedly the Constitution would have been rejected. But the next day, the phantoms built up by Henry were beaten down under the crushing blows of Madison's irresistible logic. Henry's substitute resolution was lost, and Wythe's resolution to ratify adopted by a vote of eighty-nine to seventy-nine, and thus ended the most spectacular convention ever held in America." (Lee's *The Story of the American Constitution*, p. 69.)

ratification were added "a few declaratory truths not affecting the validity of the Act."

"The Legislature (of New York) finally called a Convention to meet at Poughkeepsie on June 17, 1778, to consider the Constitution. The Anti-Federalists had an overwhelming majority of the delegates. They were led by Governor George Clinton, who had been the *State's* Chief Executive for nine years. . . . The Federalist position was defended by Hamilton, Jay, and Livingston, but the chief burden fell upon Hamilton. He had also been a delegate to the Philadelphia Convention. . . . With supreme tact and patience, and with an eloquence never surpassed in America, he argued for the greater part of five weeks." [17]

On July 26th, 1788, in the New York Convention, thirty voted for and twenty-seven against ratifying the proposed Constitution (the decision of New Hampshire and Virginia largely influencing the result) [18] only after Hamilton had warned the up-State delegates that if they refused, Manhattan Island, Westchester and Kings Counties would secede from the rest of the *State* and leave it without a seaport. New York refused to call an election or to appoint electors, and did not take part in the first election the first Wednesday in January, 1789.

On August 4th, 1788, North Carolina rejected ratification of the Constitution by a vote of 193 to 75.

The Congress of the *Confederation* had expired of mere inanition,[19] and its record ceased on October 21st,

---

[17] Lee's *The Story of the Amercan Constitution*, pp. 73, 74, 75.
[18] *Encyclopædia Britannica*, Vol. 27, p. 687a.
[19] *Ibid.*, Vol. 23, p. 252.

1788. The *United States* got on without any national government for nearly six months.

Charles Pinckney wrote to Rufus King from Charleston on January 26th, 1789:

"You know I always preferred the election by the Legislature, to that of the *people,* and I will now venture to pronounce that the mode which you and Madison and some others so thoroughly contended for and ultimately carried, is the greatest blot in the Constitution—of this, however, more hereafter." [20]

On April 30th, 1789, George Washington was inaugurated President at New York, amid the huzzahs of a happy and united people.

On November 21st, 1789, North Carolina ratified the Constitution, which it had rejected by 195 to 75 on August 4th, 1788.

"On July 4th, 1788, the *people* of Providence, R. I., were preparing to celebrate the fact that the required number of *States* had ratified the Constitution, when one thousand armed men under the leadership of a Supreme Court Judge came in from the rural districts and prevented the celebration and publicly burned a copy of the Constitution. It was only when Rhode Island was told that unless she entered the *Union,* she would be made to pay her share of the war debt by force, that she adopted the Constitution, and this was upon the further threat that the United States Government would put a tariff on all of their exports to the other twelve States." [21]

On May 29th, 1790, Rhode Island ratified the Constitution by a vote of thirty-four to thirty-two. It had

---

[20] Farrand's *The Records of the Federal Convention of 1787*, Vol. III, p. 355.

[21] Lee's *The Story of the American Constitution,* p. 75.

been referred to the *several towns* instead of to a Convention.[22]

Notwithstanding the fact that the ratification by Maryland and South Carolina had killed the idea of a separate Southern Confederacy, Patrick Henry declared that "Virginia and North Carolina could exist separated from the rest of America." "Virginia, the greatest and most mighty *State* in the *Union*," followed by North Carolina, and New York (which *State* he announced as being in high opposition), should hold the Constitution in suspense until they had compelled the other *States* to adopt the amendments on which she should insist.[23]

Madison told the exact truth when he said: "The Constitution is in part a consolidated *union*, and in part rests so completely on the *States* that its very life is bound upon theirs." [24]

Bancroft, in his chapter on the Constitution, observes that the nationality of the American *people* was "the principle of individuality," which was strengthened by their struggles with Nature in her wildness, by the remoteness from the abodes of ancient institutions, by the war against the traditions of absolute power, and old superstitions, till it developed itself into the most perfect liberty in thought and action." [25]

---

[22] Farrand's *The Records of the Federal Convention of 1787*, Vol. III, p. 355. See Appendix D, p. 283.
[23] Bancroft's *History of the Constitution of the United States*, Vol. II, p. 308.
[24] *Ibid.*, p. 303.
[25] *Ibid.*, p. 323.

"The Federalists, however, had a marked advantage in that they offered a concrete plan for the cure of existing evils. In addition, they had the prestige which came from the powerful influence of Washington, who briefly summed up the whole Federalist argument in a message to the *people* of Massachusetts. 'The Constitution,'

A parallel column comparison of the Articles of Confederation, and the Constitution of the *United States,* appears in Appendix B, page 261.

said he, 'is the best form of government that can be obtained at this time. We must choose between it and disunion and anarchy. If it is imperfect, a constitutional door is open for amendments which may be adopted in a peaceable manner, without tumult or disorder.'

"Three of the 'mere boys'—Hamilton, Madison, and Jay—won immortal fame by the publication of a series of essays explaining every vital clause of the Constitution. Of these eighty-five letters, all signed 'Publius,' Hamilton wrote fifty-one, Jay, five, and Madison, twenty-nine." (Lee's *The Story of the American Constitution,* pp. 59, 61.)

CHAPTER XIV

A BRIEF ANALYSIS OF THE CONSTITUTION AND ITS AMENDMENTS

The Constitution starts with the Preamble already quoted. It consists of twenty-eight "articles" and sixty-four numbered subdivisions of these articles called "sections." Some of these sections are again subdivided into paragraphs.

ARTICLE I
Section 1

"All legislative powers herein granted shall be vested in a Congress of the United States, which shall consist of a Senate and House of Representatives."

Section 2

"The House of Representatives shall be composed of members chosen every second year (the even numbered years) by the people of the several States, and the electors in each State shall have the qualifications requisite for electors of the most numerous branch of the State Legislature." (The "House" or "Assembly.")

(It is significant that the qualifications for a Congressman [of the national Government] who represents the whole *United States,* should be the same as those prescribed by the *States* for Assemblymen or members of the *State* House of Representatives, but it will be seen by paragraph 2 of section 2 below, that in addition he must have been seven years a *citizen* of the *United States,* shall be twenty-five years of age, and shall be an inhabitant of that *State* in which he shall be chosen.)

"No person shall be a Representative who shall not have attained to the age of twenty-five years, and been seven years a citizen of the United States, and who shall not when elected, be an inhabitant of that State in which he shall be chosen."

[A Representative need not be an inhabitant of the district from which he is a candidate provided he lives in the *State.*]

"[Representatives and direct taxes shall be apportioned among the several States which may be included within this Union, according to their respective numbers, which shall be determined by adding to the whole number of free persons, including those bound to service for a term of years, and excluding Indians not taxed, three-fifths of all other persons.] [26] The actual enumeration shall be made within three years after the first meeting of the Congress of the United States, and within every subsequent term of ten years, in such manner as they shall by law direct. The number of Representatives shall not exceed one for every thirty thousand, but each State shall have at least one representative"; . . .

"Filling of vacancies in representation. Whenever vacancies happen in the representation from any State, the Executive Authority thereof shall issue writs to fill such vacancies."

---

[26] The clause in brackets in the last paragraph is amended by the Fourteenth Amendment, section 2.

Note that the word *State* always begins with a capital, as do some other words.

"The House of Representatives shall chuse their speaker and other officers; and shall have sole power, of impeachment."

Section 3

"Senate. [1. The Senate of the United States shall be composed of two Senators from each State, chosen by the Legislature thereof, for six years; and each Senator shall have one vote.]"

The part in brackets is just as it was in the original Constitution because the sections as originally adopted are always inserted, but the law has been changed by the Seventeenth Amendment to the Constitution, which provides that Senators shall be elected by the *people*.

"Immediately after they shall be assembled in consequence of the first election, they shall be divided as equally as may be into three classes. The seats of the Senators of the first class shall be vacated at the expiration of the second years, of the of the second class at the expiration of the fourth year, and of the third class at the expiration of the sixth year, so that one-third may be chosen every second year; and if vacancies happen by resignation, or otherwise during the recess of the Legislature of any State, the Executive thereof may make temporary appointments (until the next meeting of the Legislature, which shall then fill such vacancies)."

"No person shall be a Senator who shall not have attained the age of thirty years, and been nine years a citizen of the United States, and who shall not when elected be an inhabitant of that State for which he shall have been chosen."

"The Vice President of the United States shall be

President of the Senate, but shall have no vote, unless they be equally divided."

"The Senate shall chuse their other officers, and also a President pro tempore, in the absence of the Vice President, or when he shall exercise the office of President of the United States."

"The Senate shall have sole power to try all impeachments. When sitting for that purpose, they shall be on oath or affirmation. When the President of the United States is tried, the Chief Justice shall preside; and no person shall be convicted without the concurrence of two-thirds of the members present."

"Judgment in cases of impeachment shall not extend further than to removal from office, and disqualification to hold or enjoy any office of honor, trust, or profit under the United States; but the party convicted shall nevertheless be liable and subject to indictment, trial, judgment, and punishment, according to law."

Section 4

"The times, places, and manner of holding elections for Senators and Representatives shall be prescribed in each State by the Legislature thereof; but the Congress may at any time by Law make or alter such Regulations, except as to the Places of chusing Senators."

This again is curious. The section starts out by giving the whole subject into the care of the *States*, but the latter part of the sentence provides that Congress may change all of their regulations "except as to the place of chusing Senators."

"The Congress shall assemble at least once in every Year, and such Meeting shall be on the first Monday in December, unless they shall by Law appoint a different Day."

Section 5

"Each House shall be the Judge of the Elections, Returns and Qualifications of its own Members, and a Majority of each shall constitute a Quorum to do Business; but a smaller Number may adjourn from day to day, and may be authorized to compel the Attendance of absent Members, in such Manner, and under such Penalties as each House may provide."

"Each House may determine the Rules of its Proceedings, punish its Members for disorderly Behavior, and, with the Concurrence of two thirds, expel a Member."

"Each House shall keep a Journal of its Proceedings, and from time to time publish the same, excepting such Parts as may in their Judgment require Secrecy; and the Yeas and Nays of the Members of either House on any question shall, at the Desire of one fifth of those Present, be entered on the Journal."

"Neither House, during the Session of Congress shall, without the Consent of the other, adjourn for more than three days, nor to any other Place than that in which the two Houses shall be sitting."

Section 6

"The Senators and Representatives shall receive a Compensation for their Services, to be ascertained by Law, and paid out of the Treasury of the United States. They shall in all Cases, except Treason, Felony and Breach of the Peace, be privileged from Arrest during their Attendance at the Session of their respective Houses, and in going to and returning from the same; and for any Speech or Debate in either

House, they shall not be questioned in any other Place."

"No Senator or Representative shall, during the Time for which he was elected, be appointed to any civil Office under the Authority of the United States, which shall have been created, or the Emoluments whereof shall have been encreased [27] during such time; and no Person holding any Office under the United States, shall be a Member of either House during his Continuance in Office."

Section 7

"All Bills for raising Revenue shall originate in the House of Representatives; but the Senate may propose or concur with Amendments as on other Bills."

"Every Bill which shall have passed the House of Representatives and the Senate, shall before it becomes a Law, be presented to the President of the United States; If he approve he shall sign it, but if not he shall return it, with his Objections to that House in which it shall have originated, who shall enter the Objections at large on their Journal, and proceed to reconsider it. If after such Reconsideration two thirds of that House shall agree to pass the Bill, it shall be sent, together with the Objections, to the other House, by which it shall likewise be reconsidered, and if approved by two thirds of that House, it shall become a Law. But in all such Cases the Votes of both Houses shall be determined by Yeas and Nays, and the Names of the Persons voting for and against the Bill shall be entered on the Journal of each House respectively. If any Bill shall not be returned by the President within ten Days (Sundays excepted) after it shall have been presented to him, the Same shall be a Law, in like

[27] So in original.

Manner as if he had signed it, unless the Congress by their Adjournment prevent its Return, in which Case it shall not be a Law.

"Every Order, Resolution, or Vote to which the Concurrence of the Senate and House of Representatives may be necessary (except on a question of adjournment) shall be presented to the President of the United States; and before the Same shall take Effect, shall be approved by him, or being disapproved by him, shall be repassed by two thirds of the Senate and House of Representatives, according to the Rules and Limitations prescribed in the Case of a Bill."

Section 8

"The Congress shall have Power.—1. To lay and collect Taxes, Duties, Imposts and Excises, to pay the Debts and provide for the common Defence and general Welfare of the United States; but all Duties, Imposts and Excises shall be uniform throughout the United States." [28]

This is known as the "General Welfare Clause," upon which is based the doctrine of "implied powers," that is, powers not expressly set out in the Constitution. Hamilton was the first to so interpret it.

"To borrow money on the credit of the United States."

"To regulate Commerce with foreign Nations, and among the several States, and with the Indian tribes."

"To establish an uniform Rule of Naturalization, and uniform Laws on the subject of Bankruptcies throughout the United States."

More strictly speaking, a national law of bankruptcy, to be administered by the Federal Courts.

[28] By the Sixteenth Amendment to the Constitution, Congress is given the power to lay and collect taxes on incomes.

"To coin Money, regulate the Value thereof, and of foreign Coin, and fix the Standard of Weights and Measures."

"To provide for the Punishment of counterfeiting the Securities and current Coin of the United States."

"To establish Post Offices and post Roads."

"To promote the Progress of Science and useful Arts, by securing for limited Times to Authors and Inventors the exclusive Right to their respective Writings and Discoveries."

"To constitute Tribunals inferior to the supreme Court."

More strictly speaking, this should read "To constitute Federal tribunals inferior to the Supreme Court."

"To define and punish Piracies and Felonies committed on the high Seas, and Offenses against the Law of Nations."

"To declare War, grant Letters of Marque and Reprisal, and make Rules concerning Captures on Land and Water."

"To raise and support Armies, but no Appropriation of Money to that Use shall be for a longer Term than two Years."

"To provide and maintain a Navy."

"To make Rules for the Government and Regulation of the land and naval Forces."

"To provide for calling forth the Militia to execute the Laws of the Union, suppress Insurrections and repel Invasions."

"To provide for organizing, arming, and disciplining the Militia, and for governing such Part of them as may be employed in the Service of the United States, reserving to the States, respectively, the Appointment of the Officers, and the Authority of training the Militia according to the discipline prescribed by Congress."

"To exercise exclusive Legislation in all Cases whatsoever, over such District (not exceeding ten Miles square) as may, by Cession of particular States, and the acceptance of Congress, become the Seat of the Government of the United States, and to exercise like Authority over all Places purchased by the Consent of the Legislature of the State in which the Same shall be, for the Erection of Forts, Magazines, Arsenals, dock-Yards, and other needful Buildings;—and"

(It will be observed that the above notes the concession to *State's Rights* by recognizing the consent of the *State* Legislature.)

"To make all Laws which shall be necessary and proper for carrying into Execution the foregoing Powers, and all other Powers vested by this Constitution in the Government of the United States, or in any Department or Officer thereof."

Section 9

"The Migration or Importation of such Persons as any of the States now existing shall think proper to admit, shall not be prohibited by the Congress prior to the Year one thousand eight hundred and eight, but a tax or duty may be imposed on such Importation, not exceeding ten dollars for each Person."

"The privilege of the Writ of Habeas Corpus shall not be suspended, unless when in Cases of Rebellion or Invasion the public Safety may require it."

"No Bill of Attainder or ex post facto Law shall be passed."

(Under bills of attainder under the early English

law the property of the accused was forfeited to the Crown, and his blood was "corrupted" so that he could not afterwards inherit or transfer lands.)

("Section 9 of Article I says Congress shall not pass *ex post facto* laws, and Section 10 says that the *States* shall not pass them. *'Ex post facto'* means 'after the act is done,' and consequently laws cannot be passed which declare that criminal which was not so when the act was committed, or which inflicts a severer punishment for a crime than the law provided at the time the crime was committed. An *ex post facto* law is also one that deprives accused persons of some legal right or protection that they had at the time the act was done." [29]

Ex post facto laws are:

"1. Every law that makes an act done before its passage, and which was innocent when done, criminal, and punishes such action.

"2. Every law that aggravates a crime, or makes it greater than it was when committed.

"3. Every law that changes the nature of the punishment, or inflicts a greater punishment than the law attached to the crime when committed.

"4. Every law that changes the legal rules of evidence so as to make it less difficult to convict the offender.

"5. Every law which deprives persons accused of crime of some lawful protection or right to which they have become entitled." [29])

To continue the text of the Constitution:

"No capitation, or other direct, Tax shall be laid,

[29] Lee's *The Story of the American Constitution,* pp. 124, 125.
[29] *Loc. cit.*

unless in Proportion to the Census or Enumeration herein before directed to be taken." [30]

"No Tax or Duty shall be laid on Articles exported from any State."

"No Preference shall be given by any Regulation of Commerce or Revenue to the Ports of one State over those of another: nor shall Vessels bound to, or from, one State, be obliged to enter, clear, or pay Duties in another."

"No Money shall be drawn from the Treasury, but in Consequence of Appropriations made by Law; and a regular Statement and Account of the Receipts and Expenditures of all public Money shall be published from time to time."

"No Title of Nobility shall be granted by the United States: And no Person holding any Office of Profit or Trust under them, shall, without the Consent of the Congress, accept of any present, Emolument, Office, or Title, of any kind whatever, from any King, Prince, or foreign State."

Section 10

"No State shall enter into any Treaty, Alliance, or Confederation; grant Letters of Marque and Reprisal; coin Money; emit Bills of Credit; make any Thing but gold and silver Coin a Tender in Payment of Debts; pass any Bill of Attainder, ex post facto Law, or Law impairing the Obligation of Contracts [31] or grant any Title of Nobility."

"No State shall, without the Consent of the Con-

[30] See the Sixteenth Amendment.

[31] These contracts include agreements between *States,* between *States* and individuals, between the *United States* and a *State,* between *States* and corporations or individuals, between individuals, and between corporations. (Lee's *The Story of the American Constitution,* p. 157.)

gress, lay any Imposts or Duties on Imports or Exports, except what may be absolutely necessary for executing its inspection Laws: and the net Produce of all Duties and Imposts, laid by any State on Imports or Exports, shall be for the Use of the Treasury of the United States; and all such Laws shall be subject to the Revision and Control of the Congress."

(I do not know of any *State* ever having laid any imposts, etc., with the consent of Congress.)

"No State shall, without the consent of Congress, lay any duty of Tonnage, keep Troops, or Ships of War in time of Peace, enter into any Agreement or Compact with another State, or with a foreign Power, or engage in War, unless actually invaded, or in such imminent Danger as will not admit of delay."

(This section was to prevent the *States* from encroaching upon the prerogatives of the Federal (national) Government. It was also designed to secure *United States* citizens from discriminatory legislation by *State* Legislatures.[32])

---

[32] "To prevent encroachment upon the powers of the Federal Government by the *States*, as well as to protect citizens of the *United States* from unfair discrimination through *State* legislation, section 10, Article I, provides that *States* may not 'enter into any Treaty, Alliance or Confederation; grant Letters of Marque and Reprisal; coin Money; emit Bills of Credit; make any Thing but gold and silver coin a Tender in the Payment of Debts; pass any Bill of Attainder, ex post facto Law, or Law impairing the Obligation of Contracts, or grant any Title of Nobility.' Nor may any *State*, 'without the Consent of Congress, lay any imposts or Duties on Imports or Exports, . . . or lay any Duty of Tonnage' on shipping.

"Article VI, declares that the Constitution and the *'Laws of the United States which shall be made in Pursuance thereof; and all Treaties made, or which shall be made, under the authority of the United States, shall be the supreme law of the Land.'* It may not be inferred from this, however, that the Federal Government is supreme over the *States*. The *States* are not subordinate to the national Government in the sense that they may be commanded by

ARTICLE II

Section 1

"The executive Power shall be vested in a President of the United States of America. He shall hold his Office during the Term of four Years, and, together with the Vice-President, chosen for the same Term, be elected, as follows:"

"Each State shall appoint, in such Manner as the Legislature thereof may direct, a Number of Electors,

it. The *United States* is a government whose powers are strictly enumerated in the Constitution, and it is only in respect to the powers so enumerated that it is supreme.

"The Tenth Amendment provides that *'The powers not delegated to the United States by the Constitution, nor prohibited by it to the States, are reserved to the States respectively, or to the people.'* Hence, all powers not conferred upon the Federal Government by the Constitution, nor denied to the *States* in that instrument, are reserved or residuary powers of the *States,* and in the exercise thereof the *States* are supreme. This principle was clearly stated by Madison in *The Federalist,* when he wrote: 'The powers delegated by the proposed Constitution to the Federal Government are few and defined. Those which are to remain in the *State* governments are numerous and indefinite. The former will be exercised principally on external objects, as war, peace, negotiation, and foreign commerce, with which last the power of taxation will, for the most part, be connected. The powers reserved to the several *States* will extend to all the objects which, in the ordinary course of affairs, concern the lives, liberties, and properties of the *people,* and the internal order, improvement, and prosperity of the *State*.'

"But why, it is sometimes asked, did the framers of the Constitution enumerate the powers conferred upon the Federal Government and leave those so reserved to the *States* open to conjecture and uncertainty? The answer is simple. The powers reserved to the *States* are too comprehensive for enumeration, for they embrace all those social and business relationships which go to the very foundation of law and order. They include the whole domain of civil and religious liberty, contracts, principal and agent, master and servant, utility regulation, education, suffrage, marriage, divorce, domestic relations, business, property, trade, taxation, and the administration of most of the criminal laws." (Lee's *The Story of the American Constitution,* pp. 37–39.)

equal to the whole Number of Senators and Representatives to which the State may be entitled in the Congress: but no Senator or Representative, or Person holding an Office of Trust or Profit under the United States, shall be appointed an Elector."

(Here it may be observed that in a national matter so important as the election of the President the manner of choosing the electors is left to the *State* Legislatures.)

"[The Electors shall meet in their respective States, and vote by Ballot for two persons, of whom one at least shall not be an Inhabitant of the same State with themselves. And they shall make a List of all the Persons voted for, and of the Number of Votes for each; which List they shall sign and certify, and transmit sealed to the Seat of the Government of the United States, directed to the President of the Senate. The President of the Senate shall, in the Presence of the Senate and House of Representatives, open all the Certificates, and the Votes shall then be counted. The Person having the greatest Number of Votes shall be the President, if such Number be a Majority of the whole Number of Electors appointed; and if there be more than one who have such Majority, and have an equal Number of Votes, then the House of Representatives shall immediately chuse by Ballot one of them for President; and if no Person have a Majority, then from the five highest on the list the said House shall in like Manner chuse the President. But in chusing the President, the Votes shall be taken by States, the Representation from each State having one Vote; A quorum for this Purpose shall consist of a Member or Members from two-thirds of the States, and a Majority of all the States shall be necessary to a Choice. In every Case, after the Choice of the President, the Person having the greatest Number of Votes of the Electors shall be the Vice President. But if there should remain two or more who have equal Votes, the Senate shall chuse from them by Ballot the Vice-President.]" [33]

"The Congress may determine the Time of chusing the Electors, and the Day on which they shall give their Votes; which Day shall be the same throughout the United States."

"No person except a natural born Citizen, or a Citizen of the United States, at the time of the Adoption of this Constitution, shall be eligible to the Office of President; neither shall any Person be eligible to that Office who shall not have attained to the Age of thirty-five Years, and been fourteen Years a Resident within the United States." [34]

"In Case of the Removal of the President from Office, or of his Death, Resignation, or Inability to discharge the Powers and Duties of the said Office, the same shall devolve on the Vice President, and the Congress may by Law provide for the Case of Removal, Death, Resignation or Inability, both of the President and Vice President, declaring what Officer shall then act as President, and such Officer shall act accordingly, until the Disability be removed, or a President shall be elected." [35]

"The President shall, at stated Times, receive for his Services, a Compensation, which shall neither be

---

[33] This clause has been superseded by the Twelfth Amendment. (See page 191.)

[34] For qualifications of the Vice President, see the Twelfth Amendment, page 193.

[35] Amended by Article XX, sections 3 and 4, of the amendments to the Constitution.

encreased nor diminished during the Period for which he shall have been elected, and he shall not receive within that Period any other Emolument from the United States, or any of them."

The expression "or any of them," it has been agreed, throws some light on whether the *United States* was a union of *States,* or a union of the *people* of all the *States.*

"Before he enter on the Execution of his Office, he shall take the following Oath or Affirmation:—"I do solemnly swear (or affirm) that I will faithfully execute the Office of President of the United States, and will to the best of my Ability, preserve, protect and defend the Constitution of the United States."

Section 2

"The President shall be Commander-in-Chief of the Army and Navy of the United States, and of the Militia of the several States, when called into the actual Service of the United States; he may require the Opinion, in writing, of the principal Officer in each of the executive Departments, upon any subject relating to the Duties of their respective Offices, and he shall have Power to grant Reprieves and Pardons for Offenses against the United States, except in Cases of Impeachment."

Here is an anomaly. The President has the command of the Militia of the several *States* when called into the actual service of the *United States,* presumably by the order of the *United States.*

"He shall have Power, by and with the Advice and Consent of the Senate, to make Treaties, provided two-thirds of the Senators present concur; and he shall nominate, and by and with the Advice and Consent of the Senate, shall appoint Ambassadors, other public

Ministers and Consuls, Judges of the supreme Court, and all other Officers of the United States, whose Appointments are not herein otherwise provided for, and which shall be established by Law; but the Congress may by Law vest the Appointment of such inferior Officers, as they think proper, in the President alone, in the Courts of Law, or in the Heads of Departments."

Of course, the expression "provided two-thirds of the Senators present concur" contemplates always that there shall be a quorum present.

"The President shall have Power to fill up all Vacancies that may happen during the Recess of the Senate, by granting Commissions which shall expire at the End of their next Session."

Section 3

"He shall from time to time give to the Congress Information of the State of the Union, and recommend to their Consideration such Measures as he shall judge necessary and expedient; he may, on extraordinary Occasions, convene both Houses, or either of them, and in Case of Disagreement between them, with Respect to the Time of Adjournment, he may adjourn them to such Time as he shall think proper; he shall receive Ambassadors and other public Ministers; he shall take Care that the Laws be faithfully executed, and shall Commission all the Officers of the United States."

Section 4

"The President, Vice-President and all civil Officers of the United States, shall be removed from Office on Impeachment for, and Conviction of, Treason, Bribery, or other high Crimes and Misdemeanors."

ARTICLE III

Section 1

"The judicial Power of the United States, shall be vested in one supreme Court, and in such inferior Courts as the Congress may from time to time ordain and establish. The Judges, both of the supreme and inferior Courts, shall hold their Offices during good Behaviour, and shall, at stated Times, receive for their Services a Compensation which shall not be diminished during their Continuance in Office."

Of course, "inferior courts" refers only to Federal Courts.

Section 2

"The judicial Power shall extend to all Cases, in Law and Equity, arising under this Constitution, the Laws of the United States, and Treaties made, or which shall be made, under their Authority;—to all Cases affecting Ambassadors, other public Ministers and Consuls;—to all Cases of Admiralty and maritime Jurisdiction;—to Controversies to which the United States shall be a Party;—to Controversies between two or more States;—between a State and Citizens of another State;—between Citizens of different States;—between Citizens of the same State claiming Lands under Grants of different States, and between a State, or the Citizens thereof, and foreign States, Citizens or Subjects." [36]

But see the Eleventh Amendment, providing that *States* may not be sued by citizens of another *State*, or by "citizens or subjects of any foreign state." (See page 191.)

---

[36] This section is abridged by the Eleventh Amendment.

"In all Cases affecting Ambassadors, other public Ministers and Consuls, and those in which a State shall be Party, the supreme Court shall have original Jurisdiction. In all the other Cases before mentioned, the supreme Court shall have appellate Jurisdiction, both as to Law and Fact, with such Exceptions, and under such Regulations as the Congress shall make."

"The trial of all Crimes, except in Cases of Impeachment, shall be by Jury; and such Trial shall be held in the State where the said Crimes shall have been committed; but when not committed within any State, the trial shall be at such Place or Places as the Congress may by Law have directed."

Section 3

"Treason against the United States, shall consist only in levying War against them, or, in adhering to their Enemies, giving them Aid and Comfort. No Person shall be convicted of Treason unless on the Testimony of two Witnesses to the same overt Act, or on Confession in open Court."

Professor Lee says:

"To make out that portion of the definition denoted 'levying war,' there must be a gathering of *people* with arms, and with violence or potential violence, to overthrow the Government or defy its laws. The word 'enemies' only refers to inhabitants or citizens of a foreign power in conflict with the *United States,* and the Constitution provides that no person shall be convicted of treason except by two witnesses to the same overt act, or on confession in open court, but the Constitution provides that 'no attainder of treason shall work corruption of blood, or forfeiture except during the life of the person attainted.' The punishment for treason is death, or, in the discretion of the Court, imprisonment at hard labor for not less than five years and a fine of not less than $10,000." [37]

"The Congress shall have power to declare the Punishment of Treason, but no Attainder of Treason shall work Corruption of Blood, or Forfeiture except during the Life of the Person attainted.

ARTICLE IV

Section 1

"Full Faith and Credit shall be given in each State to the public Acts, Records, and judicial Proceedings of every other State. And the Congress may by general Laws prescribe the Manner in which such Acts, Records and Proceedings shall be proved, and the Effect thereof.

Section 2

"The Citizens of each State shall be entitled to all Privileges and Immunities of Citizens in the several States."

The same provision in the Articles of Confederation had no effect, because the authority to enforce it was vested in no one.

"A Person charged in any State with Treason, Felony, or other Crime, who shall flee from Justice, and be found in another State, shall on demand of the executive Authority of the State from which he fled, be delivered up, to be removed to the State having Jurisdiction of the Crime."

"No Person held to Service or Labour in one State, under the Laws thereof, escaping into another, shall, in Consequence of any Law or Regulation therein, be discharged from such Service or Labour, but shall be

[37] Lee's *The Story of the American Constitution*, p. 127.

delivered up on Claim of the Party to whom such Service or Labour may be due." [38]

Section 3

"New States may be admitted by the Congress into this Union; but no new State shall be formed or erected within the Jurisdiction of any other State; nor any State be formed by the Junction of two or more States, or parts of States, without the Consent of the Legislatures of the States concerned as well as of the Congress."

"The Congress shall have Power to dispose of and make all needful Rules and Regulations respecting the Territory or other Property belonging to the United States; and nothing in this Constitution shall be so construed as to Prejudice any Claims of the United States, or of any particular State."

Section 4

"The United States shall guarantee to every State in this Union a Republican Form of Government, and shall protect each of them against Invasion; and on Application of the Legislature, or of the Executive (when the Legislature cannot be convened) against domestic Violence."

This section was invoked by President Cleveland in the Chicago railroad strike of 1894. The strike was broken because its continuance tied up the *United States* mail.

ARTICLE V

"The Congress, whenever two-thirds of both Houses shall deem it necessary, shall propose Amendments to this Constitution, or, on the application of the Legislatures of two-thirds of the several States, shall call a

---

[38] See the Thirteenth Amendment, which nullified this paragraph.

Convention for proposing Amendments, which, in either Case, shall be valid to all Intents and Purposes, as part of this Constitution, when ratified by the Legislatures of three-fourths of the several States, or by Conventions in three-fourths thereof, as the one or the other Mode of Ratification may be proposed by the Congress; Provided that no Amendment which may be made prior to the Year One thousand eight hundred and eight shall in any Manner affect the first and fourth Clauses in the Ninth Section of the first Article; and that no State, without its Consent, shall be deprived of it's equal Suffrage in the Senate."

ARTICLE VI

"All Debts contracted and Engagements entered into, before the Adoption of this Constitution, shall be as valid against the United States under this Constitution, as under the Confederation."

"This Constitution, and the Laws of the United States which shall be made in Pursuance thereof; and all Treaties made, or which shall be made, under the Authority of the United States, shall be the supreme Law of the Land; and the Judges in every State shall be bound thereby, any Thing in the Constitution or Laws of any State to the Contrary notwithstanding."

"The Senators and Representatives before mentioned, and the Members of the several State Legislatures, and all executive and judicial Officers, both of the United States and of the several States, shall be bound by Oath or Affirmation, to support this Constitution; but no religious Test shall ever be required as a Qualification to any Office or public Trust under the United States."

ARTICLE VII

"The Ratification of the Conventions of nine States shall be sufficient for the Establishment of this Constitution between the States so ratifying the Same.

> Done in Convention by the Unanimous Consent of the States present the Seventeenth Day of September in the Year of our Lord one thousand seven hundred and Eighty seven and of the Independence of the United States of America the Twelfth. In Witness whereof We have hereunto subscribed our Names.
>
> G° WASHINGTON
> *President and Deputy from Virginia*

NEW HAMPSHIRE
John Langdon   Nicholas Gilman

MASSACHUSETTS
Nathaniel Gorham   Rufus King

CONNECTICUT
Wm Saml Johnson   Roger Sherman

NEW YORK
Alexander Hamilton

NEW JERSEY
Wil: Livingston   Wm Paterson
David Brearley   Jona: Dayton

PENNSYLVANIA
B. Franklin   Thomas Mifflin
Robt. Morris   Geo. Clymer
Thos. Fitzsimons   Jared Ingersoll
James Wilson   Gouv Morris

DELAWARE
Geo: Read   Gunning Bedford Jun
John Dickinson   Richard Bassett
Jaco: Broom

MARYLAND
James McHenry   Dan: of St Thos Jenifer
Danl Carroll

Virginia
John Blair— James Madison Jr.
North Carolina
Wm Blount
Hu Williamson   Richd Dobbs Spaight,
South Carolina
J. Rutledge   Charles Cotesworth Pinckney
Charles Pinckney   Pierce Butler
Georgia
William Few   Abr Baldwin

Attest: WILLIAM JACKSON, *Secretary.*"

It will be observed that the Constitution was signed by *States* through their representatives.

There was a "gentlemen's agreement" that if the Constitution were passed in the form submitted by the Constitutional Convention, a bill of rights would be passed shortly after to meet certain suggestions made by those who were chary of signing the Constitution without such guaranties. In pursuance of this agreement, amendments were passed to the number of ten at one time. The other amendments were passed at different times. They follow here in the order in which they were passed, together with the reasons for the passage of some of them.

"The various *State* Conventions which passed upon the Constitution suggested the amendments from which the first ten which were ratified were selected. Massachusetts had suggested nine, South Carolina, four; New York, thirty-two; New Hampshire, twelve; Virginia, twenty; North Carolina, twenty-six; Pennsylvania minority, fourteen; Maryland minority, twenty-eight. To quiet the opposition which had been raised by the adoption of the Constitution, Madison laid before the first Congress all these suggested amendments. The House reduced the whole number to seventeen, and the Senate, to twelve. When submitted to the *States,* ten of these twelve amendments were approved by the necessary three-fourths of the *States,* and two amendments were rejected." [39]

A *State* cannot first approve, and then rescind its action regarding an amendment, but it can first reject and afterwards ratify a proposed amendment. In addition to those (resolutions submitting) amendments passed by both Houses, nine have passed the Senate but did not pass the House, and nine have passed the House but did not pass the Senate." [40] Consequently they did not become law.

AMENDMENTS TO THE CONSTITUTION OF THE UNITED STATES

Amendments from I to X, inclusive, were proposed at the first session of the first Congress of the United States, which was held at the city of New York on the 4th day of March, 1789, and were adopted by the requisite number of *States* on the following dates: New Jersey, November 20th, 1789; Maryland, December 19th, 1789; North Carolina, December 22d, 1789; South Carolina, January 19th, 1790; New Hampshire, January 25th, 1790; Delaware, January 28th, 1790; Pennsylvania, March 10th, 1790; New York, March 27th, 1790; Rhode Island, June 15th, 1790; Vermont, November 3d, 1791, and Virginia, December 15th, 1791.

The following preamble and resolution preceded the original proposition of the amendments:

[39] Lee's *The Story of the American Constitution,* p. 101.
[40] *Ibid.,* pp. 124–25.

"CONGRESS OF THE UNITED STATES

Begun and held at the city of New York, on Wednesday, the 4th day of March, 1789.

The conventions of a number of the states having, at the time of their adopting the Constitution, expressed a desire, in order to prevent misconstruction or abuse of its powers, that further declaratory and restrictive clauses should be added, and as extending the ground of public confidence in the government will best insure the beneficent ends of its institution:

"*Resolved,* By the Senate and House of Representatives of the United States of America, in congress assembled, two-thirds of both houses concurring, that the following articles be proposed to the legislatures of the several states, as amendments to the constitution of the United States; all or any of which articles, when ratified by three-fourths of the said legislatures, to be valid to all intents and purposes, as part of the said constitution, namely:"[41]

ARTICLE I

"Congress shall make no law respecting an establishment of religion, or prohibiting the free exercise thereof; or abridging the freedom of speech, or of the press; or the right of the people peaceably to assemble, and to petition the Government for a redress of grievances."

The *State* of New York has similar provisions in its Constitution.[42]

---

[41] The first ten amendments were declared in force December 15th, 1791.
[42] Article I, sections 1, 8, 9.

ARTICLE II

"A well regulated Militia, being necessary to the security of a free State, the right of the people to keep and bear Arms, shall not be infringed."

This was to protect against interference by the Federal Government from carrying arms, and to allow the *States* to arm their militia.

ARTICLE III

"No Soldier shall, in time of peace be quartered in any house, without the consent of the Owner, nor in time of war, but in a manner to be prescribed by law."

The expression "in a manner to be prescribed by law" practically detooths the article.

ARTICLE IV

"The right of the people to be secure in their persons, houses, papers, and effects, against unreasonable searches and seizures, shall not be violated, and no Warrants shall issue, but upon probable cause, supported by Oath or affirmation, and particularly describing the place to be searched, and the persons or things to be seized."

ARTICLE V

"No person shall be held to answer for a capital, or otherwise infamous crime, unless on a presentment or indictment of a Grand Jury, except in cases arising in the land or naval forces, or in the Militia, when in actual service in time of War or public danger; nor shall any person be subject for the same offence to be twice put in jeopardy of life or limb; nor shall be compelled in any criminal case to be a witness against himself, nor be deprived of life, liberty, or property, without due process of law; nor shall private property be taken for public use, without just compensation."

(Cooley says:

"Due process in each particular case means such an exercise of the powers of government as the settled maxims of law permit and sanction, and under such safeguards for the protection of individual rights as those maxims prescribe for the class of cases to which the one in question belongs." [43]

The "just compensation" part of this amendment is intended to limit the powers of the *States,* all of whom have similar constitutional clauses.

This amendment is a check on the Federal Government, as the fourteenth is on the *State* Governments.

The Grand Jury must not have less than sixteen nor over twenty-three, and there must be twelve votes to indict.)

ARTICLE VI

"In all criminal prosecutions, the accused shall enjoy the right to a speedy and public trial, by an impartial jury of the State and district wherein the crime shall have been committed, which district shall have been previously ascertained by law, and to be informed of the nature and cause of the accusation; to be confronted with the witnesses against him; to have compulsory process for obtaining witnesses in his favor, and to have the Assistance of Counsel for his defence."

(If the accused is poor, free counsel will be assigned him by the Court.)

ARTICLE VII

"In suits at common law, where the value in controversy shall exceed twenty dollars, the right of trial

[43] Cooley's *Constitutional Limitations.*

by jury shall be preserved, and no fact tried by a jury, shall be otherwise re-examined in any Court of the United States, than according to the rules of the common law."

(A court can set aside a verdict of guilty, but cannot direct a "guilty" verdict. "The *People*" have no appeal from a "not guilty" verdict.)

ARTICLE VIII

"Excessive bail shall not be required, nor excessive fines imposed, nor cruel and unusual punishments inflicted."

ARTICLE IX

"The enumeration in the Constitution, of certain rights, shall not be construed to deny or disparage others retained by the people."

ARTICLE X

"The powers not delegated to the United States by the Constitution, nor prohibited by it to the States, are reserved to the States respectively, or to the people."

(There are those who contend that some of the sections at least of the ten amendments known as the Bill of Rights were unnecessary. Congress had been given no power respecting "an establishment of religion, abridging the freedom of speech, or of the press, or the right of the *people* peaceably to assemble and petition," so why was Article I, forbidding these things, necessary? The same observation may be made regarding Article II. And as to Article III, it hardly seems necessary, because it does permit the soldiers "to be quartered in any house, without the consent of the owner," provided it is done "in a manner to be prescribed by law." The common law provided all the guaranties contained in Article IV. Article V was a necessary amendment, and it may be that part of Article VI was necessary. It is difficult to see why it was necessary to declare that "no fact tried by a jury shall be otherwise re-examined in any court of the *United States* than according to the common law." The Constitution itself, in its Judiciary Article, had given the Federal Government the power to re-examine a fact tried by jury otherwise than as the common law provided. Article VIII was but a restatement of the common law. Article IX is difficult to fathom. No thinker could have seriously contended that the enumeration of certain rights in the Constitution could deny other rights retained by the *people*. The two thoughts are unrelated. The fact that the *States* had ceded rights to the Federal Government has nothing to do with the rights not ceded, which, of course, remained in the *people*. The article was unnecessary.)

ARTICLE XI [44]

"The judicial power of the United States shall not be construed to extend to any suit in law or equity, commenced or prosecuted against one of the United States by Citizens of another State, or by Citizens or Subjects of any Foreign State."

ARTICLE XII

"The Electors shall meet in their respective states and vote by ballot for President and Vice-President, one of whom, at least, shall not be an inhabitant of the

[44] The Eleventh Amendment was proposed to the legislatures of the several *States* by the Third Congress on March 5th, 1794, and was declared in force January 8th, 1798.

same state with themselves; they shall name in their ballots the person voted for as President, and in distinct ballots the person voted for as Vice-President, and they shall make distinct lists of all persons voted for as President, and of all persons voted for as Vice-President, and of the number of votes for each, which lists they shall sign and certify, and transmit sealed to the seat of the government of the United States, directed to the President of the Senate;—The President of the Senate shall, in the presence of the Senate and House of Representatives, open all the certificates and the votes shall then be counted;—The person having the greatest number of votes for President, shall be the President, if such number be a majority of the whole number of electors appointed; and if no person have such majority, then from the persons having the highest numbers not exceeding three on the list of those voted for as President, the House of Representatives shall choose immediately, by ballot, the President. But in choosing the President, the votes shall be taken by states, the representation from each State having one vote; a quorum for this purpose shall consist of a member or members from two-thirds of the states, and a majority of all the states shall be necessary to a choice. And if the House of Representatives shall not choose a President whenever the right of choice shall devolve upon them, before the fourth day of March next following, then the Vice-President shall act as President, as in the case of the death or other constitutional disability of the President. The person having the greatest number of votes as Vice-President, shall be the Vice-President, if such number be a majority of the whole number of electors appointed, and if no person have a majority, then from the two highest numbers on the list, the Senate shall choose the Vice-President; a quorum for the purpose shall consist of two-thirds of the whole number of Senators, and a majority of the whole number shall be necessary to a choice. But no person constitutionally ineligible to the office of President shall be eligible to that of Vice-President of the United States."

Proposed December 12th, 1803; declared in force September 25th, 1804. (This has been amended by the Twentieth Amendment, sections 3 and 4.) See page 198.

ARTICLE XIII

Section 1

"Neither slavery nor involuntary servitude, except as a punishment for crime whereof the party shall have been duly convicted, shall exist within the United States, or any place subject to their jurisdiction."

Section 2

"Congress shall have power to enforce this article by appropriate legislation."

This section was offered in Congress in February, 1865, after President Lincoln had emancipated the slaves by a proclamation of January 1st, 1863. It was declared in force December 18th, 1865.

ARTICLE XIV

Section 1

"All persons born or naturalized in the United States, and subject to the jurisdiction thereof, are citizens of the United States and of the State wherein they reside. No State shall make or enforce any law which shall abridge the privileges or immunities of citizens of the United States; nor shall any State deprive any person of life, liberty, or property, without due process of law; nor deny to any person within its jurisdiction the equal protection of the laws."

(A citizen owes allegiance not only to his *State*, but to his nation.)

Section 2

"Representatives shall be apportioned among the several States according to their respective numbers, counting the whole number of persons in each State, excluding Indians not taxed. But when the right to vote at any election for the choice of electors for President and Vice-President of the United States, Representatives in Congress, the Executive and Judicial officers of a State, or the members of the Legislature thereof, is denied to any of the male inhabitants of such State, being twenty-one years of age, and citizens of the United States, or in any way abridged, except for participation in rebellion, or other crime, the basis of representation therein shall be reduced in the proportion which the number of such male citizens shall bear to the whole number of male citizens twenty-one years of age in such State."

Section 3

"No person shall be a Senator or Representative in Congress, or elector of President and Vice-President, or hold any office, civil or military, under the United States, or under any State, who, having previously taken an oath, as a member of Congress, or as an officer of the United States, or as a member of any State legislature, or as an executive or judicial officer of any State, to support the Constitution of the United States, shall have engaged in insurrection or rebellion against the same, or given aid or comfort to the enemies thereof. But Congress may by a vote of two-thirds of each House, remove such disability."

Section 4

"The validity of the public debt of the United States, authorized by law, including debts incurred for payment of pensions and bounties for services in suppressing insurrection or rebellion, shall not be questioned. But neither the United States nor any State shall assume or pay any debt or obligation incurred in aid of insurrection or rebellion against the United States, or any claim for the loss or emancipation of any slave; but all such debts, obligations and claims shall be held illegal and void."

Section 5

"The Congress shall have power to enforce, by appropriate legislation, the provisions of this article."

The Fourteenth Amendment was proposed in June, 1866, and adopted July 21st, 1868. Georgia, South Carolina, Delaware, Maryland, Kentucky, Texas, and North Carolina voted against it.

ARTICLE XV

Section 1

"The right of citizens of the United States to vote shall not be denied or abridged by the United States or by any State, on account of race, color, or previous condition of servitude."

Section 2

"The Congress shall have power to enforce this article by appropriate legislation."

Proposed in February, 1869. Adopted March 30th, 1870. Tennessee, California, Delaware, Maryland, and Kentucky voted against it.

ARTICLE XVI

"The Congress shall have power to lay and collect taxes on incomes, from whatever source derived, without apportionment among the several States, and without regard to any census or enumeration."

The Sixteenth Amendment was proposed to Legislatures July 12th, 1909, and declared in force February 25th, 1913.

Professor Lee says:

"In 1894 Congress imposed an income tax of 2 per cent on incomes over $4000 received from any source. In the case of Pollock *vs.* Farmers Loan & Trust Co., 157 U. S. 429, a majority of the Court held that the tax on income derived from real estate is a direct tax, which Congress was forbidden to lay, and that a tax on income from *State* and municipal bonds was invalid, since it was a tax on the necessary instruments of government. Judge Jackson not sitting, the Court divided on whether a tax on income from corporate stocks and bonds or personal property was a direct tax, and whether the entire act was invalid. On a re-argument Justice Shires changed his views, and the whole act was held unconstitutional by five to four. To meet this situation, the Sixteenth Amendment was proposed by Congress July 31st, 1909. It was before the *States* three years, six months, and twenty-four days, the longest time any amendment has been considered before ratification. It was proclaimed adopted February 25th, 1913. The amendment was rejected by Connecticut, Rhode Island, and Utah. It gave Congress the power to lay and collect taxes on incomes, from whatever source derived, regardless of census or enumeration. Under section 1,

Article III of the Constitution the salaries of all Federal Judges are exempted from this amendment. John Marshall said this provision was to render the Judge 'perfectly and completely independent, with nothing to influence or control him but God and his conscience.' "[45]

ARTICLE XVII

"1. The Senate of the United States shall be composed of two Senators from each State, elected by the people thereof, for six years; and each Senator shall have one vote. The electors in each State shall have the qualifications requisite for electors of the most numerous branch of the State legislatures."

"2. When vacancies happen in the representation of any State in the Senate, the executive authority of such State shall issue writs of election to fill such vacancies: Provided, that the legislature of any State may empower the executive thereof to make temporary appointment until the people fill the vacancies by election as the legislature may direct."

"3. This amendment shall not be so construed as to affect the election or term of any Senator chosen before it becomes valid as part of the Constitution."

(First introduced during John Quincy Adams' administration, recommended by President Johnson in 1869, endorsed by Populists in 1892, and by Democrats in 1900. Passed in 1894, and afterwards by House, but voted down by Senate; approved by Senate in 1911, adopted May 14th, 1913.)

ARTICLE XVIII

"1. After one year from the ratification of this article the manufacture, sale, or transportation of intoxi-

[45] Lee's *The Story of the American Constitution*, p. 111.

cating liquors within, the importation thereof into, or the exportation thereof from the United States and all territory subject to the jurisdiction thereof for beverage purposes is hereby prohibited."

"2. The Congress and the several States shall have concurrent power to enforce this article by appropriate legislation."

"3. This article shall be inoperative unless it shall have been ratified as an amendment to the Constitution by the legislatures of the several States, as provided in the Constitution, within seven years from the date of the submission hereof to the States by the Congress."

(Submitted December 19th, 1917; ratified January 16th, 1919, and declared in full force and effect January 16th, 1920. Maryland passed no *State* enforcement act, and Rhode Island and Connecticut voted against its adoption.)

ARTICLE XIX

"The right of citizens of the United States to vote shall not be denied or abridged by the United States or by any State on account of sex."

"Congress shall have power to enforce this article by appropriate legislation."

First introduced in 1868; proposed by Congress May 19th, 1919, after President Wilson recommended it. Adopted August 26th, 1920. It was rejected by Maryland, Virginia, and Alabama.

ARTICLE XX

Section 1

"The terms of the President and Vice President shall end at noon on the 20th day of January, and the terms of Senators and Representatives at noon on the 3d day of January, of the years in which such terms would have ended if this article had not been ratified; and the terms of their successors shall then begin."

Section 2

"The Congress shall assemble at least once in every year, and such meeting shall begin at noon on the 3d day of January, unless they shall by law appoint a different day."

Section 3

"If, at the time fixed for the beginning of the term of the President, the President elect shall have died, the Vice President elect shall become President. If a President shall not have been chosen before the time fixed for the beginning of his term, or if the President elect shall have failed to qualify, then the Vice President elect shall act as President until a President shall have qualified; and the Congress may by law provide for the case wherein neither a President elect nor a Vice President elect shall have qualified, declaring who shall then act as President, or the manner in which one who is to act shall be selected, and such person shall act accordingly until a President or Vice President shall have qualified."

Section 4

"The Congress may by law provide for the case of the death of any of the persons from whom the House of Representatives may choose a President whenever the right of choice shall have devolved upon them, and for the case of the death of any of the persons from whom the Senate may choose a Vice President whenever the right of choice shall have devolved upon them."

Section 5

"Sections 1 and 2 shall take effect on the 15th day of October following the ratification of this article."

Section 6

"This article shall be inoperative unless it shall have been ratified as an amendment to the Constitution by the legislatures of three-fourths of the several States within seven years from the date of its submission."

(Submitted by Congress to the States March 3rd, 1932. Ratified January 23rd, 1933. Sections 1 and 2 of the Amendment became effective October 15th, 1933.)

(Professor Lee says:

"A Vice President is also provided, who is elected in the same manner as the President, and assumes the office of President upon the death, resignation, or inability of that officer to discharge the duties of his office. The President's duties are designated as Commander-in-chief of the Army and Navy; granting reprieves and pardons (except in cases of impeachment) for offenses against the United States; appointing and commissioning Ambassadors, Ministers, Judges, and all other officers of the *United States;* furnishing Congress with information concerning the state of the *Union;* convening Congress in special session on extraordinary occasions." [46])

ARTICLE XXI

Section 1

"The Eighteenth Article of Amendment to the Constitution of the United States is hereby repealed."

[46] *Ibid.,* p. 31.

Section 2

"The transportation or importation into any State, Territory, or possession of the United States for delivery or use therein of intoxicating liquors, in violation of the laws thereof, is hereby prohibited."

Section 3

"This article shall be inoperative unless it shall have been ratified as an amendment to the Constitution by Conventions in the several States, as provided in the Constitution, within seven years from the date of the submission hereof to the States by the Congress."

(The resolution was adopted by Congress February 16th, 1933, and submitted to the *States;* it has been ratified by 36 states.)

(Professor Lee says:

"Congress should fix a time limit for ratification or rejection by the *States.* There are now five proposed amendments pending before the *States,* without a time limit. Two of these were submitted by Congress in 1789—one fixing the compensation of members of Congress, and the other apportioning the representation in the House of Representatives. The third proposed amendment was submitted in 1810, and needed the approval of but one more *State* to make it effective. It would deprive a person of citizenship if he accepted a present from royalty. The fourth proposed amendment was submitted to the *States* by Congress in 1861, permitting slavery without constitutional interference. It was ratified by three *States.* The fifth proposed amendment, without a time limit for ratification, the so-called 'Child Labor Amendment,' was submitted by Congress in 1924. Although thirteen *States* have rejected it, it may still become part of the Constitution, because any of these *States* may later change their vote and ratify the amendment, joining the thirty-six *States* necessary for ratification." [47])

[47] *Ibid.,* p. 100.

CHAPTER XV

AMENDING THE CONSTITUTION

AFTER the people of the *States* of the *United States* had had time to digest the Constitution they had ratified, they realized that it was not a completed instrument, and that it did not contain all it should. The framers of it knew this when they submitted it, but they wanted the best Constitution they could persuade the *States* to accept, and they knew that if they put too much in it, it would be rejected by the *State* Conventions. Many of the *State* Conventions did suggest the inadequacies that they perceived in it. So there was the tacit or "gentlemen's agreement" that the Constitution should be amended as soon as possible, to cover some of the important things that had been left out. This understanding was carried out, and the first ten amendments, now known as the "Bill of Rights," were acted on by Congress in 1790. By ratification of the requisite number of *State* Legislatures they became, in 1791, part of the Constitution. The amendments are set out on pages 187 to 202.

Thus, while the Constitution itself was ratified by "assemblies" or conventions of the *people,* because the *States* composing the *Confederation* had asked that it be ratified by conventions, in adopting the first ten amendments, which constitute the "Bill of Rights," and in adopting the next ten amendments, the framers of the amendments departed from that plan, and ratified them by *State* Legislatures.

The Eighteenth (Prohibition) Amendment, if repealed, will be the first one ever repealed. In fact, the sections of the Constitution, even after they are repealed, are always retained in the instrument.

"James Madison said, in the First Congress, on proposing the first ten amendments to the Constitution, that the omission of a bill of rights was one of the chief causes of the opposition: 'I believe the great mass of the *people* who proposed it disliked it because it did not contain effectual provisions against the encroachment on particular rights and those safeguards which they have long been accustomed to have interposed between them and the magistrate who exercises the sovereign power.'" [1]

In this time of demand for an immediate change in a law that some citizens find unsatisfactory, it is interesting to read the following:

"No change (in the Constitution) can be hastily made. . . . Acts of Parliament can at any time alter the 'Constitution' of England; no similar power is delegated to the Congress of the *United States,* which, like Parliament, may be swayed by the shifting majorities of party. . . . The Legislatures of the *States* or of the *United States* are alone allowed to open 'the constitutional door to amendments,' and these can be made valid only through the combined intervention of all the Legislatures elected expressly for the purpose by the *people* of the several *States*. In this way no change in the Constitution can be made in haste or by stealth, but only by consent of three-fourths of

[1] Warren's *The Making of the Constitution,* p. 769.

the *States,* after full and free and oft-repeated discussion." [2]

Every thinker wants the intelligent majority to rule. But the basic instrument of every proper organization must be studied to find out how it started; second, how the laws adopted for its government provide that it can be amended. If there is no provision in the instrument for amending it, it can only be amended by a majority vote. If some other method of amending it is provided, that method must be strictly followed.

The Constitution of the *United States* of America provides in Article V how amendments to the Constitution may be made. It reads:

"The Congress, whenever two-thirds of both Houses shall deem it necessary, shall propose amendments to this Constitution; or, on the application of the Legislatures of two-thirds of the several *States,* shall call a convention for proposing amendments which, in either case, shall be valid to all intents and purposes, as part of this Constitution, when ratified by the Legislatures of three-fourths of the several *States,* or by Conventions in three-fourths thereof, as one or the other mode of ratification may be proposed by the Congress; provided, that no amendment which may be made prior to the year one thousand eight hundred and eight shall in any manner affect the first and fourth clauses in the ninth section of the first article; and that no *State,* without its consent, shall be deprived of its equal suffrage in the Senate."

First, we must consider of what the organization known as the *United States* of America is composed.

[2] Bancroft's *History of the Constitution of the United States,* Vol. II, p. 329.

The reader may by this time have made up his mind whether the united Government was at the start made up of the *people,* or of *Colonies* or *States* composed of the *people.* If he has concluded with the great Lincoln, that it is a government of the *people,* for the *people,* and by the *people,* the inquiry has probably already arisen in his mind as to how the *people* as such can amend the Constitution. He may have probably concluded that there is no (exclusive) constitutional way provided by which the mass of the *people* as such can amend the Constitution, and that the only ways to amend it are the ways provided under Article V of the Constitution itself. In that article he will also discover that the most definite way to get popular opinion on any proposed amendment is to refer it for ratification to Conventions of the *States,* specifically called for the exclusive purpose of considering such amendments. He will find that one of the two methods provided for ratification in Article V.

It may also occur to him that the Constitution provides no direct means by which the *people* may suggest such amendments to the *States* for ratification, but under Article V such amendments have to be proposed by two-thirds of both Houses of Congress, or Congress on the application of the Legislatures of two-thirds of the *States* shall call a convention to propose amendments.

Perhaps it was arranged this way because ours is not, technically speaking, a government of, for, and by the *people* (direct), but a representative government, where the *people* of each *State* act through their *State* legislators or their chosen (*State*) representatives in Congress.

Thus it will be seen that there are two methods of

proposing amendments: One, when two-thirds of both Houses of Congress shall deem it necessary, Congress shall propose them to *State* Legislatures or Conventions for ratification; the other, when the Legislatures of two-thirds of the several *States* apply for it, Congress shall "call a convention for proposing amendments."

The first method of securing amendments is the only one that has ever been employed. No Constitutional Convention has ever been called by Congress upon the application of the Legislatures of two-thirds of the several *States* to propose amendments to the Constitution. Although many attempts have been made to thus secure a national convention for the purpose of proposing amendments to the Constitution, this method has never been adopted. And after it has been proposed by Congress, the only way an amendment has ever been adopted (except the Twenty-first [Prohibition Repeal] Amendment) has been by the Legislatures of three-fourths of the several *States*.

These amendments so proposed, by either method, shall be "valid to all intents and purposes as part of this Constitution, when ratified by the Legislatures of three-fourths of the several *States*, or by Conventions in three-fourths thereof, as the one or the other mode of ratification may be proposed by the Congress."

It is not necessary to go into the reasons for this preference for the method of ratification by the Legislatures of three-fourths of the *States* over the ratifications by Conventions of three-fourths of the several *States*. Sometimes some Legislatures have petitioned for a convention, but enough Legislatures have never petitioned Congress to call a convention for proposing amendments to make up the required "Legislatures of two-thirds of the several *States*."

Up to 1899 there were efforts by resolutions introduced in Congress to have a national Constitutional Convention called to amend the Constitution, but all of these efforts were unsuccessful.

The only way ever employed to suggest constitutional amendments has been by Congress, but up to 1899 "nearly two hundred Constitutional Conventions to revise *State* Constitutions had been called, and many attempts made to summon a Convention for the purpose of amending the *United States* Constitution." Representatives from Virginia, New York, the Legislatures of Virginia, Kentucky, Ohio, New Jersey, Indiana, Illinois, South Carolina, Alabama, and Georgia unsuccessfully attempted to secure a convention to propose a constitutional amendment. A general Constitutional Convention was requested in a resolution which had been adopted by the Legislature of Indiana and presented by the Vice President in the Senate in 1861. The same proposition adopted by the General Assembly of Ohio was presented to Congress.

A peace convention of twenty-one *States* which met at Virginia's invitation proposed a Constitutional Convention. Constitutional Conventions were proposed by two Representatives in 1861. There were three other similar efforts in Congress before 1890. In 1876 Senator Ingalls, "as a result of the disputed presidential election, introduced a resolution recommending to the Legislatures of the different *States* that they apply to Congress for a convention to consider amendments to the Constitution and for the submission of the proposed amendments to a Convention in each

State chosen by the *people.*" There were many other similar unsuccessful attempts.

There has never been a decision as to "whether Congress with the consent of both Houses could call a Constitutional Convention.

"In only one other case has a *State* called a convention to act upon an amendment proposed. This was when the Corwin Amendment of 1861 was ratified by an Illinois Convention in 1862.

"Opponents to proposed amendments to the Federal Constitution have at times proposed ratification by Conventions in order to make it easier to defeat the amendment in the *States;* this was done by Mr. Pendleton, of Ohio, in 1864, when the Thirteenth Amendment was proposed, and when Senator Dixon made the same attempt with regard to the Fifteenth Amendment in 1869. There have been several efforts made to change the majorities required by Article V of the Constitution. One proposition was to require only two-thirds of the State Legislatures or Conventions, instead of three-fourths, as section 5 provides. A similar effort was made to change the required majority to three-fifths.

"The two-thirds vote required has been held to mean two-thirds of a quorum present.

"The signature of the President to constitutional amendments has been held not to be essential to their validity.

"Six different attempts have been made in Congress so to change the Constitution that all future amendments should be submitted to the vote of the *people* of each *State,* and that a majority of the *people* entitled to vote in three-fourths of the several *States* should be necessary for its ratification" ... "but all failed of passage."[3]

The twenty-one amendments have all been proposed by *Congress,* which body has in every case (except the Twenty-first [Prohibition Repeal] Amendment) provided for *ratification by the State Legislatures.*[4] The repeal of the Eighteenth Amendment was ratified, by the adoption of the Twenty-first Amendment, by *State* Conventions of the *people* themselves.

"The President's approval of a proposed amendment is not required. In Hollingsworth *vs.* Virginia (3 Dall. 378; 1 L. ed. 644) the Court without argument said: 'The negative of the President applies only to the ordinary cases of legislation; he has nothing to do with the proposition or adoption of amendments to the Constitution.' In 1865 a proposed amendment having been inadvertently sent to the President, the Senate adopted the following resolution:

" 'Resolved, That the article of amendment proposed by Congress to be added to the Constitution of the United States respecting the extinction of slavery

[3] Lowell W. Raymond in *Case and Comment,* January-February-March, 1930.

[4] Willoughby's *The Constitutional Law of the United States,* Vol. I, p. 591.

The *States* in ratifying amendments have acted through the power vested in them by the Federal Constitution. (Hawke *vs.* Smith, 253 U. S. 221; Rhode Island *vs.* Palmer, 253 U. S. 350; Leser *vs.* Garnett, 258 U. S. 130; National Prohibition Cases, 253 U. S. 350.)

Two-thirds of a quorum of Congress is enough to submit amendments, and not two-thirds of the entire membership. (Missouri Pacific Ry. Co. *vs.* Kansas, 248 U. S. 276.) A quorum is "the House." A majority is one-half or more of a quorum. The First Congress had about sixty-five members. The First Amendment was voted for by thirty-seven, "obviously not two-thirds of the entire House." (Willoughby's *The Constitutional Law of the United States,* Vol. I, p. 592. First Session, First Congress, *Journal,* p. 121, Gales and Seaton Edition.)

therein having been inadvertently presented to the President for his approval, it is hereby declared that such approval was unnecessary to give effect to the action of Congress in proposing said amendment, inconsistent with the former practice in reference to all amendments to the Constitution heretofore adopted, and being inadvertently done, should not constitute a precedent for the future; and the Secretary is hereby instructed not to communicate the notice of the approval of said proposed amendment by the President to the House of Representatives.'"[5]

A *State* Legislature which has rejected an amendment proposed by Congress, may later reconsider its action and give its approval.

The highest court in Maine said that in Article V of the Constitution "the *people* divested themselves of all authority, and conferred the power of *proposal* (of a constitutional amendment) upon Congress, or upon a national Constitutional Convention (called by Congress upon request of the Legislatures of two-thirds of the several *States*), and the *ratification* upon the *State* Legislatures, or upon *State* Constitutional Conventions." This view has the sanction not only of reason, but of authority. Mr. Iredell, in the North Carolina Convention which ratified the Federal Constitution, in discussing this ratifying clause, said: "By referring this business to the Legislatures, expense would be saved, and in general, it may be presumed, they would speak the general sense of the *people*. It may, however, on some occasions, be better to consult an immediate delegation for that purpose. That is, therefore, left discretionary."[6]

[5] *Ibid.*, p. 593.
[6] Elliott's *Debates on the Federal Constitution,* Vol. IV, p. 177.

The reader would find, if he investigated the subject thoroughly, that when the Congress has suggested amendments the *people* of the *States* have never been directed by Congress (except for the Twenty-first [Prohibition Repeal] Amendment) to pass upon them in specifically called Conventions of the *States* to consider the amendments, but that in all other cases the *States* have been directed by Congress to pass upon the amendments by their *Legislatures,* and that this has been done.

The reader may probably conclude that up to this time the *people* of the *States,* acting through their representatives in Congress, preferred to have constitutional amendments considered only by the trained *State* legislators they have delegated to act for them as *States.* If he reaches this conclusion, he will not necessarily conclude, however, that at this time the *people* may not have had a change of heart, because now Congress has called Conventions to vote on a prohibition repeal amendment to the Constitution.

The Congress has seen fit to have the *people* of the *States* consider this amendment to the Constitution in conventions officially called to pass on that particular amendment. It has ample authority for so doing under Article V of the Constitution.

Many who believe in majority rule by the *people* complain that the will of a majority of the *people* is thwarted under the Constitution by the provision in Article V that one *State* over one-fourth of the forty-eight *States* can defeat any amendment. This is a logical complaint, and it must have a logical answer. The answer is that the *people* acting by *States,* as the Constitution provides, can amend the method of amending the Constitution as soon as they get the necessary three-fourths of the *States* to vote for it.

It will be remembered in considering this proposition, that to form governments to carry out common purposes, men agree in their compact of government to give up certain natural rights that they cherish, so that others composing the government will also relinquish certain natural rights that they cherish, in order that out of this mutual sacrifice of natural rights by each member of the government, the sum of power ceded by all may form the government they seek. One of the powers always transferred to governments is the right to forbid every member from doing the things a majority of its members think would be injurious to the interests of the majority.

At the start, every government has only the powers given over to it by its members. It has no more powers unless it votes itself additional powers. And these can only be voted in the manner provided by the instrument it adopted when it organized. But the *States,* having ceded certain powers to the national Government, can only withdraw them in the manner the Constitution provides.

Those who contended that the Eighteenth Amendment was unconstitutional gave as one of the reasons that it was not an amendment of any existing subject in the Constitution, and therefore instead of being an amendment, introduces entirely new matter. The Courts have been uniform in deciding that this made no difference. Under the court decisions there is no limit to the amendability of the Constitution of the *United States*. No court has ever decided that there is any such limit. Those who contend that there is no limit to the amendability of the Constitution point to the fact that slavery was not only forbidden by the

Constitution, but it was provided that slavery should exist undisturbed until 1808, and yet it was abolished almost eighty years after the Constitution was adopted.

"In scope the amending power is now expressly limited as to but one subject, namely, as to the equal representation of the *States* in the Senate. It has, however, been argued that even this limitation may be evaded by adopting a constitutional amendment eliminating this limitation upon the amending power, and thus opening the way to subsequent amendments providing for unequal representation of the *States* in the Senate.

"It has, however, been strenuously argued by reputable writers that, although not expressly declared, there are limitations as to what may be accomplished by constitutional amendments to the Federal Constitution—limitations which are implied by the very nature of that instrument which, these writers declare, was intended to perpetuate a form of political union in which the *States* should have control over their own citizen composition and play a distinctive and definitely determined part in the general scheme of government that was to exist. Thus, it has been argued that the Fifteenth Amendment is unconstitutional, because it attempts, against the wills of the *States* that did not ratify it, to fix the composition of their several electorates. As to this contention, it is sufficient to say that it was disposed of by the case of Texas *vs.* White, in which, speaking of the *State* of Texas, which, at the time of the decision, had not ratified either the Thirteenth or the Fourteenth Amendment, Chief Justice Chase pointed out that by the Thirteenth Amendment the freed negroes, living in the *State*, necessarily became a part of its *people,* that the *people* still constituted the *State*, and that it was the *State*, as thus constituted and as a member of the *Union*, which was entitled to the constitutional guaranty of a government republican in form." [7]

"It will be noted that no restriction whatever was expressed in Madison's motion (providing the method of amending the Constitution) as to the kind or extent of the amendment which might be proposed. Unless some implied restriction was to be read into it, amendments might take away or restrict powers granted to Congress by the Constitution; or might enlarge or add to them; or might contain additional restrictions on the powers of the *States*, or remove those already imposed, or deny to the *States* powers which they now retained and reserved under the Constitution; amendments might even alter or upset the great compromise which formed the basis of agreement on a draft of Constitution." [8]

"Nothing in the debates of the Convention, or in the *State* Conventions of 1788, or in the decisions of the Supreme Court, would seem to afford any basis for discriminating between the various parts or sections of the Constitution, with respect to its amendability." [9]

"There is no legal road to the amendment of the Constitution but through the consent of the *people* given in the form prescribed by law. America, being charged with the preservation of liberty, has the most

---

[7] Willoughby's *The Constitutional Law of the United States*, Vol. I, pp. 598, 599.

The Fifteenth Amendment reads as follows: "The right of citizens of the *United States* shall not be denied or abridged by the *United States* or by any *State* on account of race, color, or previous condition of servitude."

[8] Warren's *The Making of the Constitution*, p. 678.

[9] *Ibid.*, p. 681.

conservative polity in the world, both in its government and in its *people*." [10]

"The *Union* without self-existent *States* is a harp without strings; the *States* without *union* are as chords that are unstrung. But for *States' Rights* the *Union* would perish from the paralysis of its limbs. The *States*, as they gave life to the *Union*, are necessary to the continuance of that life. . . . But *States' Rights* are to be defended inside of the *Union;* not from an outside citadel from which the *Union* may be struck at or defied. The *States* and the *United States* are not antagonists; the *States* in union form the *Federal* Republic; and the system can have life and health and strength and beauty only by their harmonious action. In short, the Constitution knows nothing of the *United States* alone, or *States* alone; it adjusts the parts harmoniously in an organized unity." [11]

"Is it asked, who is the sovereign of the *United States?* The words 'sovereign' and 'subjects' are unknown to the Constitution." [12]

"Is it asked, who are the *people* of the *United States* that instituted the 'general government'? The Federal Government and the Constitution answer, that it is the concurring *people* of the several *States*. The Constitution is constantly on its guard against permitting the action of the aggregate mass as a unit, lest the whole *people*, once accustomed to acting together as an individual, might forget the existence of the *States*, and the *States* now in union succumb to centralization and absolutism. The *people* of the *States* demanded

---

[10] Bancroft's *History of the Constitution of the United States,* Vol. II, p. 330.
[11] *Ibid.*, p. 332.
[12] *Ibid.*, p. 333.

a Federal Convention to form the Constitution; the Congress of the *Confederation,* voting by *States,* authorized the Federal Convention; the Federal Convention, voting likewise by *States,* made the Constitution; at the advice of the Federal Convention the Federal Congress referred that Constitution severally to the *people* of each *State;* and by their united voice taken severally it was made the binding form of government." [13]

[13] *Ibid.,* pp. 334, 335.

CHAPTER XVI

SHALL CONGRESS REFER PROPOSED AMENDMENTS TO THE CONSTITUTION, FOR ADOPTION OR REJECTION BY THE STATES, TO STATE LEGISLATURES OR TO CONVENTIONS CHOSEN BY THE PEOPLE OF EACH STATE?

THE reader must decide whether he thinks it is better for Congress to submit proposed amendments to the Legislatures of the *States,* or to *State* Conventions especially elected by direct vote of the *people* of the *States* to pass upon an amendment. Some writers claim it is a fairer method to let *State* Conventions pass on amendments that Congress submits to the *States,* because, they say, the *people* can more definitely vote on a precise amendment which the delegates are exclusively elected to vote upon. This is a weighty argument. To it the reply is that a Legislator is presumed to represent his constituents on all questions, and that to disregard them means such legislator's political death, because having once found him unfaithful, his constituents will never return him to office. These writers also say that it advantages the *people* to have men of legislative experience to pass upon laws. Their objection to special conventions of the *States* passing upon amendments is that the *people* have to pay the expense of them, and they say that a legislator chosen to represent the people of a county or a district is generally less apt to be swayed by passing political passion than a delegate elected to a Convention after a heated campaign in which but one question has been discussed. Also, these authorities point out that no objection has been made that the Legislatures have under Article V of the Constitution frequently suggested that Congress submit certain amendments to the *States* (Legislatures or Conventions) for ratification, and they say that there is no difference in principle between *State* Legislatures suggesting proposed amendments to Congress for submission to the *States,* and having the *State* Legislatures (if Congress adopts that alternative method) vote for ratification or rejection, after amendments have been submitted to the *States.*

Article V of the Constitution provides that either method may be used by Congress for having the *States* determine whether they will adopt or reject a proposed amendment, and the *United States* Supreme Court has said that Congress under the fifth article of the Constitution had the right to refer the Eighteenth Amendment to the Legislatures of the *States,* and that the Legislatures of three-fourths of the *States* having adopted the amendment, that amendment is constitutional. But there has been so much discussion about this, that in this chapter I set out the following history of the adoption of the fifth (the amending) article of the Constitution by the Constitutional Convention, so that the reader may see just what happened there.

It will be recalled that in the Constitutional Convention after Mr. Randolph, of Virginia, had on May 29th, 1787, offered his fifteen resolutions, which became the basis for the discussions of the Constitution, they were referred to a Committee of the Whole, and that on June 13th, 1787, and June 19th, 1787, that Committee had reported nineteen resolutions to the Constitutional Convention.

On July 23rd, 1787, "On the question to agree to the nineteenth resolution, as reported from the Committee of the Whole House, namely, '*Resolved,* That the amendments which shall be offered to the *Confederation* by the Convention ought, at a proper time or times after the approbation of Congress, to be submitted to an assembly or assemblies of representatives, *recommended* by the several Legislatures, to be expressly *chosen* by the *people* to consider and decide thereon,' it passed in the affirmative."[1]

This resolution was passed by a vote of nine *States* to one *State,* Delaware alone voting against it. As I have already pointed out, it was passed in response to the requests which had been made by some of the several *States* that they should, through *State* Conventions, vote upon the Constitution to be proposed by the Constitutional Convention to the *Confederation.* I refer to this specially because after the original Constitution as a whole was referred by Congress to Conventions of the *States,* that method was never again adopted, until the vote on the Twenty-first Amendment, probably because a sufficient number of *States* never again requested it.

In the Convention on July 23rd, 1787, it was

"XIX. *Resolved,* That provision ought to be made for the amendment of the Articles of Union whensoever it shall seem necessary.

* * * * * * *

"XXI. *Resolved,* That the amendments which shall

[1] Elliot's *Debates on the Federal Constitution,* Vol. I, p. 215. Farrand's *The Records of the Federal Constitution of 1787,* Vol. II, p. 132.

be offered to the *Confederation* by the Convention ought, at a proper time or times after the approbation of Congress, to be submitted to an assembly or assemblies of representatives, recommended by the several Legislatures, to be expressly chosen by the *people*, to consider and decide thereon." [2]

These three resolutions were part of the twenty-three resolutions which the Convention on July 26th, 1787, referred to a "Committee of Detail" for the purpose of reporting a constitution.

In the draft of the Constitution reported on August 6th, 1787, by the Committee of Five on Detail, the foregoing Article XXI became Article XXII, which then read as follows:

"Article XXII. This Constitution shall be laid before the *United States* in Congress assembled, for their approbation; and it is the opinion of this Convention that it should be afterwards submitted to a Convention chosen in each *State*, under the recommendation of its Legislature, in order to receive the ratification of such Convention." [3]

On August 7th, 1787, five *States* voted to refer it to a Committee of the Whole, four voting in the negative.

On August 31st, 1787 (on motion of Mr. Gouverneur Morris and Mr. Pinckney, in the Constitutional Convention), it was moved and seconded to agree to the following amendment of the twenty-second article:

"This Constitution shall be laid before the *United States* in Congress assembled. And it is the opinion of this Convention that it (the whole Constitution) should afterwards be submitted to a Convention chosen

[2] Elliot's *Debates on the Federal Constitution*, Vol. I, p. 223.
[3] *Ibid.*, p. 230.

in each *State,* in order to receive the ratification of such Convention: to which end the several Legislatures ought to provide for the calling Conventions within their respective *States* as speedily as circumstances will permit";[4]

But this motion was lost, four *States* voting for it and seven against it. After the Convention had refused by a vote of eight *States* to three *States* to postpone consideration of Article XXII, the article as amended by the Committee on Detail was passed by the vote of ten *States,* only Maryland voting against it.

On September 10th, 1787, the Convention reconsidered, and it was moved to amend the (twenty-second) article by adding: "or the Legislature may propose amendments to the several *States* for their approbation, but no amendment shall be binding until consented to by the several *States."*

Then a motion to insert "two-thirds of" before the words "the several *States"* was lost by six to five *States.* It may be argued that some members of the Convention were in favor of a ratification by all the "several *States"* and therefore voted against it, and it may be argued that others thought that two-thirds of the *States* were too many to require for ratification or rejection.

But the doubt is more easily resolved, because almost immediately there was a motion to insert before the words "the several *States"* the words "three-fourths of," and it passed unanimously. The amendment was postponed to take up the following: "The Legislature (Congress) of the *United States,* whenever two-thirds of both Houses shall deem necessary, or on the application of two-thirds of the Legislatures of the

[4] *Ibid.,* p. 278.

several *States,* shall propose amendments to this Constitution, which shall be valid to all intents and purposes as parts thereof, when the same shall have been ratified by three-fourths at least, of the Legislatures of the several *States,* or by Conventions in three-fourths thereof, as one or the other mode of ratification may be proposed by the Legislature (Congress) of the *United States;* provided, that no amendments which may be made prior to the year 1808 shall in any manner affect the fourth and fifth sections of Article VII," [5] which was passed by nine *States,* Delaware voting in the negative and New Hampshire being divided.

On the same day the Convention resolved to reconsider by a vote of seven *States* to three *States,* with New Hampshire's vote again divided. There was a motion to postpone consideration in order to take up the following resolution:

"*Resolved,* That the foregoing plan of the Constitution be transmitted to the *United States,* in Congress assembled, in order that, if the same shall be agreed to by them, it may be communicated to the Legislatures of the several *States,* to the end that they may provide for its final ratification, by referring the same to the consideration of a Convention of deputies in each *State,* to be chosen by the *people* thereof; and that it be recommended to the said *Legislatures, in their respective acts for organizing such Conventions,* to declare that, if the said Convention shall approve of the said Constitution, such approbation shall be binding and conclusive upon the *State;* and further, that if the said Convention should be of opinion that the same, upon the assent of any new *States* thereto, ought to take effect between the *States* so assenting,

[5] *Ibid.,* p. 296.

such opinion shall thereupon be also binding upon each *State;* and the said Constitution shall take effect between the *States* assenting thereto."

But that resolution to postpone was lost by a vote of ten *States* to one, only Connecticut voting to postpone. It was then moved to restore the words "for their (Congress's) approbation" in Article XXII of the draft of the Constitution, but that motion was lost. Evidently the Convention did not think the approbation of Congress was at all necessary before the proposed Constitution should be communicated by them to the several *States* for adoption or rejection. The revised draft of the Constitution, submitted by the Committee of Revision, reported Article V of the Constitution as follows:

"The Congress, whenever two-thirds of both Houses shall deem necessary, or on the application of two-thirds of the Legislatures of the several *States,* shall propose amendments to this Constitution, which shall be valid to all intents and purposes, as part hereof, when the same shall have been ratified by three-fourths at least of the Legislatures of the several *States,* or by Conventions in three-fourths thereof, as the one or the other mode of ratification may be proposed by the Congress; provided, that no amendment which may be made prior to the year 1808 shall in any manner affect the first and fourth clauses in ninth section of Article I." [6]

On September 13th, 1787, "the Hon. Mr. Johnson, from the Committee of Revision, reported the following as a substitute for Article XXII:

"*Resolved,* That the preceding Constitution be laid before the *United States* in Congress assembled; and

[6] *Ibid.,* pp. 279–97.

that it is the opinion of this Convention that it should afterwards be submitted to a Convention of delegates chosen in each *State* by the *people* thereof, under the recommendation of the Legislature, for their assent and ratification; and that each Convention, assenting to and ratifying the same, should give notice thereof to the *United States* in Congress assembled." [7]

It was then moved and seconded to postpone consideration of the report of the Committee respecting Article XXII, which was carried by nine *States,* Connecticut alone voting against it.

"On September 13th, 1787, Dr. Johnson had reported from the Committee of Style a draft of a resolution recommending that the Constitution when adopted should be laid before Congress, and expressing 'the opinion of this Convention' that it should be submitted to a Convention of delegates chosen in each *State* under the recommendation of its Legislature 'for their assent and ratification'; that Congress, as soon as the Conventions of nine *States* should have ratified, should fix a date for the election of the new Government; and that after such election 'the Congress, together with the President, should, without delay, proceed to execute the Constitution.'" "This resolution was now voted 'by the unanimous order of the Convention.'" [8]

As already pointed out previously, the *States* then had religious and property qualifications for voters. The Colonists evidently did not want the vote on the Constitution restricted to the qualified voters in the Legislatures, so they insisted on Conventions. This for the additional reason, too, that there was no re-

[7] *Ibid.,* pp. 306, 307.
[8] Warren's *The Making of the Constitution,* p. 717.

striction on the size of the Conventions. Now that there is universal manhood (and womanhood) suffrage, one of the objections to legislative ratification has disappeared. This may account in some degree for the reference of the (subsequent) amendments (except the Twenty-first, or Prohibition Repeal Amendment) to the Legislatures for ratification. Conventions, it may be remarked, also avoided the difficulties that action by two branches of the Legislatures might present.

September 15th, 1787, it was moved: "that amendments to the plan might be offered by the Conventions, which should be submitted to, and finally decided on, by another General Convention"; which was "passed in the negative"—all the *States* concurring.

It was moved and seconded, on the same day, "that amendments to the plan might be offered by the *State* Conventions, which should be submitted to, and finally decided on, by another General Convention," which "passed unanimously in the *negative.*"

The blanks in the fifth article of the revised draft on the same day were filled up; and it was otherwise amended to read as follows:

"The Congress, whenever two-thirds of both Houses shall deem it necessary, shall propose amendments to this Constitution, or, on the application of the Legislatures of two-thirds of the several *States,* shall call a convention for proposing amendments, which, in either case, shall be valid to all intents and purposes, as part of this Constitution, when ratified by the Legislatures of three-fourths of the several *States,* or by Conventions in three-fourths thereof, as the one or the other mode of ratification may be proposed by the Congress: Provided, that no amendment which may be made prior to the year 1808 shall in any manner affect the first and fourth clauses in the ninth section of the first article; and that no *State,* without its consent, shall be deprived of its equal suffrage in the Senate."

On the question to agree to the Constitution as amended, it passed in the affirmative—ALL THE STATES CONCURRING.

Ordered, That the Constitution be engrossed. The House adjourned.[9]

On September 28th, 1787, Congress, having received *the report of the Convention* lately assembled in Philadelphia, *"Resolved, unanimously,* That the said report, with the resolutions and letter accompanying the same, be transmitted to the several *Legislatures,* in order to be submitted to a *Convention of delegates chosen in each State,* by the *people* thereof, in conformity to the resolves of the Convention made and provided in that case." [10]

[9] Elliot's *Debates on the Federal Constitution,* Vol. I, p. 317.
[10] *Ibid.,* p. 319.

CHAPTER XVII

THE NINTH, TENTH, AND EIGHTEENTH AMENDMENTS

THE important constitutional amendments to consider in this book are the Ninth and Tenth. Amendment IX reads: "The enumeration, in the Constitution, of certain rights shall not be construed to deny or disparage others retained by the *people*."

Amendment X reads as follows: "The powers not delegated to the *United States* by the Constitution, nor prohibited by it to the *States,* are reserved to the *States,* respectively, or to the *people*" (of the *United States*).

This referred to the delegation of powers that had been made to the *United States* by the separate *States*. Of course, if subsequent powers were delegated by the *States,* such powers would no longer be "reserved" to them.

The adoption of this amendment was evidently intended to scotch the contention that "an affirmation in particular cases implies a negation in all others" or that "a negation in particular cases implies an affirmation in all others." These maxims are "perfectly sound and safe; but have often been strangely forced from their natural meaning into the support of the most dangerous political heresies." "The amendment was undoubtedly suggested by the reasoning of

The Federalist[1] on the subject of a general bill of rights."[2]

"The latter part of the Tenth Amendment 'or to the *people*' would seem to leave the subject just where it was before any amendment of the Constitution was adopted. A power not ceded resides somewhere. It either resides in the *State* as a *State*, or it resides in the *people*. If the amendment had said 'or to the *people* of a *State*' or 'the *people* of the *States*,' as opposed to the collective mass of the *people* of the whole *nation* (the *United States*), there would be no difficulty in construing this amendment. If the power is reserved to the *people* of the *United States* as a whole, they can register their will through their Congressmen; if the power is reserved to the *States* as *States*, they can, if enough of them agree, propose amendments to their Congress, and can afterwards ratify or reject them, as provided in Article V. It was proposed in Congress "to insert the word 'expressly' before the words 'delegated to the *United States* by the Constitution, etc.,' but after it had been

---

[1] Letters written for the newspapers by Madison, Hamilton, and John Jay, under the pseudonym of "Publius," in 1787 and 1788, and collected in book form in *The Federalist*. Warren's *The Making of the Constitution*, p. 788.

[2] Story's *Commentaries on the Constitution*, Vol. II, p. 651. *The Federalist*, No. 84, ante 1852 to 1857. Lloyd's *Debates*, 433, 437–1 Tuck. Blackstone's Comm. App. 307–308.

"By the Fourteenth Amendment the *people* wrote into the Constitution that 'all persons born or naturalized in the *United States*, and subject to the jurisdiction thereof, are citizens of the *United States* and the *State* wherein they reside,' thus forever destroying the doctrine that the citizen owed allegiance to his *State* only." (Lee's *The Story of the American Constitution*, p. 72.)

"Sherman said that 'the *State* Declarations of Rights are not repealed by this Constitution; and being in force are sufficient.'" (*Ibid.*, p. 59.)

remarked that 'it is impossible to confine a government to the exercise of express powers' and that 'there must necessarily be admitted powers, by implication, unless the Constitution descended to the most minute details,' the motion was rejected. Indeed, one of the greatest defects of the *Confederation* . . . was that it contained a clause prohibiting the exercise of any power, jurisdiction or right not *expressly* delegated. The consequence was that Congress was crippled at every step of their progress, and were often compelled by the very necessities of the times to usurp powers which they did not constitutionally possess, and thus in effect to break down all the barriers against tyranny and oppression." [3]

"A doctrine of construction radically different from that which has just been stated (strict construction a corollary of the *States' Rights* doctrine), and which has never been accepted by the Supreme Court, is one which has been ascribed to James Wilson, of Pennsylvania, and in later years urged by Theodore Roosevelt.

"This doctrine is, that when a subject has neither been expressly excluded from the regulating power of the Federal Government, nor necessarily left within the exclusive control of the *States*, it may be regulated by Congress if it be, or become, a matter the regulation of which is of general importance to the whole nation, and at the same time a matter over which the *States* are, in practical fact, unable to exercise the

---

[3] This referred to the delegation of powers that had been made to the *United States* by the *States*. Of course, if separate powers were delegated by the *States,* such powers would no longer be "reserved to them." Story's *Commentaries on the Constitution,* Vol. II, p. 652. *The Federalist,* Nos. 33, 38, 43, 44.

necessary controlling power. According, then, to this doctrine, the Ninth and Tenth Amendments which declare that: 'The enumeration in the Constitution of certain rights shall not be construed to deny or disparage others retained by the *people*,' and that 'The powers not delegated to the *United States* by the Constitution, nor prohibited by it to the *States*, are reserved to the *States*, respectively, or to the *people*,' are not to be interpreted as reserving to the *States*, or to the *people*, those powers which, though not granted to the Federal Government, are, in fact, such as are of Federal importance and which the *States* are unable effectively to exercise.

"The argument of James Wilson, made in 1785, when the *United States* was under the Articles of Confederation but applicable, *a fortiori*, to the present Constitution, is in the following language: 'Though the *United States* in Congress assembled derive from the particular *States* no power, jurisdiction, or right which is not expressly delegated by the *Confederation*, it does not then follow that the *United States* in Congress have no other powers, jurisdiction, or rights, than those delegated by the particular *States*. The *United States* have general rights, general powers, and general obligations, not derived from any particular *States*, nor from all the particular *States* taken separately; but resulting from the union of the whole. . . . To many purposes the *United States* are to be considered as one undivided, independent nation; and as possessed of all the rights, powers, and properties by the law of nations incident to such. Whenever an object occurs, to the direction of which no particular *State* is competent, the management of it must, of necessity, belong to the *United States* in Congress assembled. There are many objects of this extended nature.'

"President Roosevelt expressly adopted the foregoing doctrine as sound. He said: 'I cannot do better than base my theory of governmental action upon the words and deeds of one of Pennsylvania's greatest sons, Justice James Wilson.' Interpreting this theory, President Roosevelt said: 'He developed even before Marshall the doctrine (absolutely essential not merely to the efficiency but to the existence of this nation) that an inherent power rested in the nation, outside of the enumerated powers conferred upon it by the Constitution, in all cases where the object involved was beyond the power of the several *States* and was a power ordinarily exercised by sovereign nations. In a remarkable letter in which he advocated setting forth in orderly and clear fashion the powers of the national Government, he laid down the proposition that it should be made clear that there were neither vacancies nor interferences between the limits of *State* and national jurisdictions, and that both jurisdictions together composed only one uniform and comprehensive system of government and laws; that is, whenever the *States* cannot act, because the need to be met is not one merely of single locality, then the national Government, representing all the *people*, should have complete power to act. . . . Certain judicial decisions have done just what Wilson feared: they have, as a matter of fact, left vacancies, left blanks between the limits of actual national jurisdiction over the control of the great business corporations. . . . The legislative or judicial actions and decisions of which I complain, be it remembered, do not really leave to the *States* power to deal with corporate wealth in business. Actual experience has shown that the *States* are wholly powerless to deal with this subject; and any action or decision that deprives the nation of the power to deal with it, simply results in leaving the corporations absolutely free to work without any effective supervision whatever; and such a course is fraught with untold danger to the future of our whole system of government, and, indeed, to our whole civilization.'" [4]

The Preamble [5] has already been referred to as containing the expression, "the general welfare."

"The phrase 'general welfare' is also used in the body of the Constitution, namely, in Article I, section 8, which provides that Congress shall have the power 'to lay and collect taxes, duties, imposts, and excises, to pay the debts and provide for the common defense and general welfare of the *United States.*' Determined and repeated efforts have been made by those anxious to magnify the powers of the Federal Government, or to support the constitutionality of specific proposed or enacted measures of Congress, to have this provision construed as a comprehensive grant of power to the *United States* to take any action which, conceivably, may aid in the common defense or promote the general welfare of the *people* of the *United States.* The

[4] Willoughby's *The Constitutional Law of the United States,* Vol. I, pp. 80, 81. President Roosevelt's speech at the dedication of the Pennsylvania capitol at Harrisburg.

[5] "As Story says: 'The preamble of a statute is a key to open the mind of the makers as to the mischiefs which are to be remedied, and the objects which are to be accomplished by the provisions of the statute.'" (Willoughby's *The Constitutional Law of the United States,* Vol. I, p. 62.)

adoption of such a construction by the Supreme Court has been repeatedly urged upon it, although it is evident that, were it accepted, the general Government would at once become one whose powers would be without any effective limit.

"Story says (Section 919): 'A power to lay taxes for any purposes whatsoever is a general power; a power to lay taxes for certain specified purposes is a limited power. A power to lay taxes for the common defense and general welfare of the *United States* is not in common sense a general power. It is limited to those objects. It cannot constitutionally transcend them." [6]

In deciding upon the constitutionality of a law, "the ultimate question is not what is the true meaning of the Constitution, but whether legislation is sustainable or not (under the Constitution)." ... The courts "can only disregard the act when those who have the right to make the laws have not merely made a mistake, but have made a very clear one—so clear that it is not open to rational question. That is the standard of duty to which courts bring legislative acts; that is the test which they apply—not merely their own judgment as to constitutionality, but their conclusion as to what judgment is permissible to another department

---

[6] *Ibid.*, pp. 97, 98. (In a note on pp. 97, 98, Vol I, Willoughby says: "Gouverneur Morris, when preparing the final report of the Committee on Style, in the Constitutional Convention of 1787, put these words ['general welfare'] in the form of a distinct and separate grant. Upon objection, however, of Roger Sherman, they were again placed in their present position in the Constitution. For a full discussion of the circumstances under which these words became embodied in the Constitution, see the long letter of James Madison to Andrew Stevenson, of November 17th, 1830, and reprinted in Farrand's *The Records of the Federal Convention of 1787*, Vol. III, pp. 483ff.)

which the Constitution has charged with the duty of making it."[7]

"Professor Cushman says: 'The most workable theory in regard to the matter is this: the doctrine of reasonable doubt means that a statute should not be declared unconstitutional so long as a reasonable doubt as to its invalidity remains *in the minds of those to whom is entrusted the power to decide the question of constitutionality*—and under the present rule this means a majority of the Court. In other words, so long as the rule exists that five members of the Court decide questions for the Court, all the doctrine can be reasonably said to mean is that five of the nine members of the Supreme Court must be sure in their minds that a law is invalid. This being true, the fact that four other judges disagree is entirely irrelevant.'"[8]

"If the question at issue is as to whether a given power resides in the Federal Government or in the *States*, the fact that a *State* Legislature in its enactment has asserted that it is invested in the *States*, is no presumption in favor of the validity of the decision. The Supreme Court in passing finally upon this point is not, then, called upon to review the act of a coordinate department, but has to decide between the conflicting claims of two governments, and quite properly feels itself at liberty to decide the point as an original proposition; namely, upon the basis of its own judgment as to what is the most reasonable construction of the constitutional provisions involved."[9]

There have been some who have argued that the

---

[7] Willoughby's *The Constitutional Law of the United States*, Vol. I, p. 45.
[8] *Ibid.*, p. 46.
[9] *Ibid.*, p. 47.

adoption of the Eighteenth Amendment was an unconstitutional exercise of the amending power, since it sought to bring within Federal control a matter which, under the Constitution as originally drawn and adopted, it was intended should never be withdrawn from *State* control. So distinctively different, it is argued by writers taking this ground, is the matter of the regulation of the manufacture, sale, transportation, and exportation and importation of intoxicating liquors from all other matters subjected by the Constitution to Federal regulation, that the amendment constitutes an addition to the Constitution rather than an amendment of it, and furthermore, such an addition or draft upon it, as to disturb, if not to destroy, its essential character. And, it is declared, this brings the change outside the amending power, since, it is asserted, it could not have been the intention of the framers of the Constitution, or of those who originally adopted it, that, under the amending power, a way should be opened to defeat the essential purpose of the Constitution and thus, as it were, to destroy it.

"Space cannot be spared for a full discussion of the points thus raised. It is sufficient to say that, whatever be their merits—which the author believes to be very slight—the Supreme Court has, in cases too numerous to cite, recognized the validity of the Eighteenth Amendment, and in Leser *vs.* Garnett has deemed the contention as to the invalidity of the Nineteenth Amendment worth only a very summary discussion. The Court in that case said: 'The first contention is that the power of amendment conferred by the Federal Constitution and sought to be exercised does not extend to this amendment because of its character. The argument is that so great an addition to the electorate, if made without the *State's* consent, destroys its autonomy as a political body. This amendment is in character and phraseology precisely similar to the Fifteenth. For each the same method of adoption was pursued. One cannot be valid and the other invalid. That the Fifteenth Amendment is valid, although rejected by six *States* . . . has been recognized and acted on for half a century. The contention that the Fifteenth was incorporated in the Constitution, not in accordance with the law, but practically as a war measure which has been validated by acquiescence, cannot be entertained.'

"To the author of the present treatise, the fundamental error of all those who have sought to place inherent limitations upon the amending power as provided for in the Federal Constitution is that they necessarily start with the assumption that the Constitution is in the nature of an agreement or compact between the *States,* or that it implies an understanding between them, or between them and the national Government, that the allocation of powers as provided for in the original instrument shall not be changed in any of its more important or essential features. It is surprising to the writer that this theory which, since the Civil War, has been so decisively rejected by the American *people* and by the courts, should be again brought forward to support a constitutional argument."[10]

"Sometimes confused with, but quite distinct from the doctrine which ascribes to the Federal Government plenary authority in matters international, and quite different also from the doctrine of resulting powers,

---

[10] *Ibid.,* pp. 599, 600. Leser *vs.* Garnett, Vol. 258 U. S. Reports, p. 130.

is that theory which argues the possession generally by the *United States* of 'inherent' sovereign powers; that is, powers regarded not as implied in express grants of authority whether singly or collectively considered, but as flowing directly from the simple fact of national *sovereignty*. The two former doctrines are fairly deducible from the doctrine of implied powers. The latter doctrine, upon the contrary, would derive Federal authority not from powers expressly granted, but from an abstraction, and would, at a stroke, equip the Federal Government with every power possessed by any other sovereign *State*." [11]

"The Constitution is a legal instrument distributing governmental powers between the Federal and *State* Governments, according to the general principle that the powers granted the Federal Government are specified, expressly or by implication, and that the remainder of the possible governmental powers 'not delegated to the *United States* by the Constitution, nor prohibited by it to the *States*,' are reserved to the *States* respectively, or to the *people*." [12]

"The *States* have never been treated upon a basis of equality with the *United States*, such as would have resulted from a division of *sovereignty*—had such a thing been juristically possible—but, in every instance, whether with reference to the use of the socalled concurrent powers, or to the many instances in which *State* and Federal powers have, in their exercise, come into conflict with each other, the *States* have been obliged to yield to the *United States*. This supremacy of Federal authority over that of the *States*

---

[11] Willoughby's *The Constitutional Law of the United States*, Vol. I, pp. 91, 92.
[12] *Ibid.*, p. 76.

has resulted from, and its continued enforcement has demonstrated, the *sovereignty* of the *United States.*" [13]

"Without in any way questioning the validity of the rule (that Federal powers are to be liberally construed) . . . it is to be observed that its propriety is absolutely dependent upon the prior assumption that the Federal Government exists as the agent of the *people,* and not, as declared by the *States' Rights* theory, as the agent of the *States.* Had the theory which conceives the *United States* to be a confederacy of sovereign *States,* and its government as the agent of these creating component units, been accepted, it would have logically followed that a doctrine of strict construction of Federal powers would have been appropriate, for then these powers would have been in direct derogation of the rights reserved by the *States that* granted them. Strict construction while thus a logical corollary of the *States' Rights* theory, is not required by the nationalistic theory." [14]

[13] *Ibid.,* p. 130.
[14] *Ibid.,* pp. 79, 80.

"If the validity of a Federal action is questioned, the authority for it must be shown in the Federal Constitution, but if the question is as to the validity of *State* action, it is not the justification, but the prohibition of it which must be pointed out. That is, *State* action is presumed to be well-warranted until the objector has been able to point out the specific provision of either the Federal Constitution or the *State* statute with which it is incompatible."

" . . . A certain measure of power has been entrusted to the national Government, and the remainder is reserved to be exercised by the several *States,* or to remain in abeyance until the *people* shall see fit to delegate it to one or the other Government." (Black's *American Constitutional Law,* p. 35.)

"Supreme *sovereignty* resides in the *people* of the *United States,* not in the Government. But it is to be borne in mind at the same time that the *people* of the *United States* intended to vest the general Government with all the powers necessary for managing the affairs of a great nation. And this legitimate resort is only

"The Ninth Amendment, providing that 'the enumeration in the Constitution of certain rights shall not be construed to deny or disparage others retained by the *people*,' was manifestly introduced to prevent any perverse or ingenious misapplication of the well-known maxim that an affirmation in particular cases implies a negation in all others, and, *e converso*, that a negative in particular cases implies an affirmative in all others.

"The maxim properly understood is perfectly sound and safe, but it has often been strangely forced from its natural meaning into the support of the most dangerous political heresies. The Ninth Amendment was undoubtedly suggested by the reasoning of *The Federalist* on the subject of a general Bill of Rights."

The Tenth Amendment to the Constitution provides that "the powers not delegated to the *United States by* the Constitution, nor prohibited *by it* to the *States,* are reserved to the *States,* respectively, or to the

to be recurred to for the purpose of enlarging or altering the powers of the Government when necessary. The *people* do not in any other way interfere with its operations. When the *States* and the Government come into contact, the general good requires, and the *people* have declared, that the general Government must prevail. Except in the cases authorized in the Constitution, neither has the power to interfere with the other." (Bayard's *Brief Exposition of the Constitution*.)

"Thus leaving the question whether this (any) particular power which may become the subject of contest has been delegated to the one Government or prohibited to the other to depend on a fair construction of the instrument." (McCulloch *vs.* Maryland, 4 Wheaton, pp. 316–406.)

"James Wilson, of Pennsylvania, was opposed to the election by the State Legislatures. After explaining his reasons, it was necessary to observe the twofold relations in which the *people* would stand, first as citizens of the general Government, and secondly as citizens of their particular *State.* The general Government was meant for them in the first capacity, the *State* Governments in the second. Both Governments were derived from the *people,* both *people.*" This short clause has caused more discussion than any sentence with the same number of words that was ever written.

The Tenth Amendment reads as follows:

"The powers not delegated to the *United States* by the Constitution, nor prohibited by it to the *States,* are reserved to the *States* respectively, or to the *people.*"

It is so laconically expressed that it becomes necessary for the purpose of considering it to interpolate some words to see what it really means. The sentence cannot have been intended to mean "the powers not delegated to the *United States by* the Constitution," but it must have been intended to mean the powers not delegated to the *United States in* the Constitution. The Constitution was merely the instrument which enumerated the powers delegated to the *United States.* By whom were these powers delegated?

If we recall the history of the adoption of the Articles of Confederation, we realize that they covered a situation where the *States* not only voted *as States,* but where it was impossible to amend them without the unanimous consent of *all the States.* Of course, always back of these *States* loomed that intangible entity, "the *people*"—two words that politicians and even statesmen like to roll under their tongues. Concretely and individually applied, it means to every ear that hears it and every eye that sees it in print: YOU. Nothing so flatters mankind as to

meant for the *people,* both therefore ought to be regulated on the same principle. The general Government is not an assemblage of *States,* but of individuals for certain political purposes. It is not meant for the *States* or the individuals composing them. The individuals therefore, not the *States,* ought to be represented in it. (*James Wilson, Patriot, and the Wilson Doctrine,* p. 7.)

hear that we are at once the source and end of all power—the court of last resort. But each of us knows that alone he is powerless to do anything. Discounting, therefore, the universal flattery of "I, the *people*" (a flattery common alike to the tailors of Tooley Street when they said, "we, the *people* of London," and to Louis the Fourteenth, when he said, "I am the state") and forgetting for the moment that no very great importance was attached by those who framed the Constitution to the words, "We, the *people* of the *United States*," in the preamble of the Constitution, and getting down to a practical construction of this most comprehensive clause in the Tenth Amendment, our first inquiry is, who did delegate certain powers to the *United States?*

It is a fair answer to say that the Legislatures (composed of representatives of "the *people*"), acting first in a *State* capacity, asked the other *States* represented in similar Legislatures for a gathering of "commissioners" of *States* to meet, *not as States,* but as the representatives of those *States* tired of the loose confederacy of *States* that was called the *Confederation,* for the purpose of proposing to these same *States* an instrument to be called a constitution, which should only become effective as a constitution when it should be ratified by *State* Conventions of "the *people*," chosen upon call of the *Legislatures* of nine *States* out of the thirteen. And it may be added that it was only at the end of the Convention that adopted the Constitution that the question came up as to how the representatives of these nine *States* should ratify the Constitution that was proposed to the *States.* And it may also be added that one, at least, of the reasons why the Constitution was referred for ratification to Conventions (chosen at the call of the *Legislatures of the States*) to be composed of "the *people*," was because a great many of "the *people*" were at that time prevented from being members of the Legislatures on account of the educational and property qualifications that prevailed. We thus find the anomaly that "the *people*" who voted in the *State* Conventions that were called to pass on the new Constitution were not the same "the *people*" who proceeded to enjoy its benefits after it was adopted. As soon as the Constitution was ratified, some of them found they were still disqualified from holding certain offices, and in some of the *States* from voting at all, because they did not possess the educational or property qualifications made necessary by the laws of the *States* in which they lived. If we assume that "the *people*" meant every man who voted for delegates to the *State* Conventions, that term in most of the *States* included all the male citizens of the *States* that made up the *United States*. If "the *people*" meant "the *people*" who enjoyed the Constitution afterwards, their number was very much smaller. But this feature is not as important as it is to determine whether the framers of the Constitution meant that the powers were delegated to the *United States* by the mass of "the *people*" of the nation or by the *State* composed of "the *people*" of the *States*. If the powers were delegated by the *States,* no more powers could be delegated by the *States* than they *as States* possessed. If, on the other hand, the powers were delegated by "the *people*" as a mass, they could delegate to the national Government any powers not already possessed by the *States*. All powers not already possessed by the *States*, in order to secure the advantages of citizenship in the *States*, were reserved to them, and they could either retain them or cede them to the national Government.

It might be more exact to say that the powers delegated to the *United States* in the Constitution were delegated by the *States* to the extent that they represented "the *people*" of the *States*, and by the mass of "the *people*" to the extent that they could delegate powers not already possessed by the *States* in which they lived. This is the limit of construction, because the Courts have held that a *State* acting through its citizens in voting on a national constitutional amendment was exercising a Federal function, conducted by and under the auspices of a *State*. And they have likewise ruled in regard to the function of citizens of a *State* voting in a congressional election.

Starting, therefore, with the proposition that the powers were delegated to the nation partly by the *States* acting as far as they were authorized for the citizens of those *States*, it is easy to see why the Tenth Amendment uses the expression that "the powers not delegated to the *United States* . . . are reserved to the *States*." But there is great difficulty deciding what the other words, "reserved to the *people*," mean. Do they mean that the powers not delegated to the *United States* are reserved to "the *people*" of the *States?* It would have been easy to say "to the *people* of the *States*," if that was what was meant, which would have made it very clear. Or, did the framers mean, when they said that the powers not delegated to the *United States* were reserved to the *States*, that only the powers the *States* had not delegated to the nation were reserved to the *States*, and that the powers not delegated to the nation by the mass of "the *people*" were reserved to that mass unless they were powers which had belonged to the *States,* or could not belong to them under the Constitution?

The amendment would have been much clearer if it had read: "The powers not delegated to the *United States* by the Constitution nor prohibited by it to the *States,* are reserved to the *people* or to the *States,* respectively." That would have been a more orderly, consecutive statement, if we assume that the powers were delegated by "the *people*" of the nation, or by the *States* representing the *people* of the *States.*

There are three ways of construing this amendment. First, that the powers not delegated by the *States* are reserved to the *States,* or to "the *people*" of the *States;* second, that the powers not delegated by the mass of "the *people*" (a larger number than the then voting population of all the *States*) or not delegated by the *States* as *States,* were reserved to the mass of "the *people*" as *people* of the nation, and to the *States* as *States;* third, that the powers not delegated by the *States* as representatives of "the *people*" of the *States,* and the mass of "the *people*" as *people* of the nation, were reserved in each instance to the source which had not parted with them. That is, that on national matters these rights were reserved to "the *people*" of the nation, and on *State* matters to "the *people*" of the *States.*

The words "nor prohibited by it (the Constitution) to the *States*" are really unnecessary, because the Constitution could only prohibit to the *States* the powers which the *States* had already delegated to the *United States.*

I am inclined to think that the second construction is the correct one, and I believe that the reason the expression "reserved to the *people*" was placed last in the sentence is that the framers of the amendment preferred to keep together the two expressions, "nor prohibited by it to the *States*" and "are reserved to the *States*," and I believe that they preferred to balance the first part of the sentence, "the powers not delegated (from the *people*) to the *United States* by the Constitution" with the expression, "are reserved to the *people*." I believe the clause should be construed to mean that "the powers not delegated to the *United States* (by the *States* acting for 'the *people*' of the *States,* and not delegated by the mass of 'the *people*' as citizens of the *United States*) nor prohibited by it (the Constitution) to the *States,* are reserved to the *States,* respectively (that is to say, not as a confederation of *States*), or to the *people*" (that is, to "the *people*" as citizens of the *United States*).

The clause could not have meant that any powers not ceded to the *United States* were reserved to "the *people*" of the *States,* because the words just preceding said to the *"States respectively,"* which meant *States as States.* If the clause had been intended to mean reserved to "the *people*" of the *States,* it would have been easy to have added after the word *"people"* the short word "thereof." But that was not what they meant, and there is, so far as I know, no prevailing opinion of the Supreme Court of the *United States* that goes that far.

The reasoning of the earlier judges and authors is better than anything that has been written since, so I proceed to quote what some of them said on this subject of the Ninth and Tenth Amendments to the Constitution.

" . . . The powers not delegated to the *United*

States by the Constitution, nor prohibited by it to the *States*, are reserved to the *States* respectively, or to the *people*. This amendment is a mere affirmation of what, upon just reasoning, is a necessary rule of interpreting the Constitution; being an instrument of limitation and enumerated powers, it follows, irresistibly, that what is not conferred is withheld, and belongs to the *State* authorities if invested by their constitutions of government respectively in them; and if not so invested, it is retained by the *people,* as part of their residuary *sovereignty*." [15]

"When this Tenth Amendment was before Congress, a proposition was moved to insert the word 'expressly' before 'delegated,' so as to read, 'the powers not expressly delegated to the *United States,*' etc. On that occasion it was remarked that it is impossible to confine a government to the exercise of express powers. There must necessarily be admitted powers by implication, unless the Constitution descended to the most minute details."

"Mr. Madison added that the word 'expressly' had been moved in the Virginia Convention by the opponents to the ratification, and after a full and fair

---

[15] Story's *Commentaries on the Constitution,* pp. 651–52.

"By the sovereign power is meant the making of laws. And wherever that power resides, all others must conform to and be directed by it, whatever appearance and outward form an administration of justice may put on. It being at any time in the option of the Legislature to alter that form and administration by a new edict or rule, and to put the execution of the laws into whatever hands it pleases, and all the other powers of the *State* must obey the legislative power in the execution of their several functions or laws, the Constitution is at an end." (I Tucker's *Blackstone's Commentaries,* Appendix, pp. 307, 308. Blackstone's *Compendium,* p. 49.)

discussion, was given up by them, and the system allowed to retain its present form." . . .[16]

"It is a general principle that all corporate bodies possess all powers to a corporate capacity, without being absolutely expressed. The motion was accordingly negatived. Indeed, one of the great defects in the *Confederation* was, as we have already seen, that it contained a clause prohibiting the exercise of any jurisdiction or power not expressly delegated. The consequence was that Congress were crippled at every stage of their progress, and were also compelled by the very necessities of the times to usurp powers they did not constitutionally possess, and thus in effect to break down all the great barriers against tyranny and oppression; . . . it could not have been the intention . . . to give this (Tenth Amendment) effect as an abridgment of any of the powers granted under the Constitution, whether . . . express or implied, direct or incidental. Its sole design is to exclude any interpretation by which other powers should be assumed beyond those which are granted. All that are granted in the original instrument, whether express or implied, whether direct or incidental, are left in their original state. All powers not delegated (not all powers not *expressly* delegated) and not prohibited are reserved. The attempts, then, which have been made from time to time to force upon this language an abridging or restrictive influence, are utterly unfounded in any just rules of interpreting the words or the sense of the instrument." [17]

"Stripped of the ingenious disguises in which they

---

[16] Lee's *The Story of the American Constitution*, p. 65. Lloyd's *Debates*, p. 234.
[17] McCulloch *vs.* Maryland, 4 Wheaton 406, 407.

are clothed, they are neither more nor less than attempts to foist into the text the word "expressly," to qualify what is general and obscure what is clear and defined. They make the sense of the passage bend to the wishes and prejudices of the interpreter, and employ criticism to support a theory, and not to guide it. One should suppose, if the history of the human mind did not furnish abundant proof to the contrary, that no reasonable man would contend for an interpretation founded neither in the letter nor in the spirit of an instrument. Where is controversy to end if we desert both the letter and the spirit? What is to become of constitutions of government if they are to rest, not upon the plain import of their words, but upon conjectural enlargements and restrictions, to suit the temporary passions and interests of the day? Let us never forget that our constitutions of government are solemn instruments, addressed to the common sense of the *people*, and designed to fix and perpetuate their rights and their liberties. They are not to be frittered away to please the demagogues of the day. They are not to be violated to gratify the ambition of poiltical leaders. They are to speak in the same voice now and forever. They are of no man's private interpretation. They are ordained by the will of the *people;* and can be changed only by the sovereign command of the *people*." [18]

It is a gratifying reflection that President Franklin D. Roosevelt has not exercised any of the great powers he wields without having first secured Congressional authority.

[18] Story's *Commentaries on the Constitution*, Vol. II, p. 653.

SUMMARY

THROUGH all the maze of discussions in the Convention, in Congress, and in the *State* Conventions, and through all the opinions of the great writers who have commented on the Constitution, there stands out one thing, and that is that ours is a *nation* hogtied by the veto power of *States,* as provided for by the amending article (the fifth) of the Constitution.

The situation of the nation and the *States* is much the same as if a prolific parent had said to a family of thirteen children: "I am your ruler, under rules I have laid down for you, on everything that you can't do for yourselves, but I can never change the manner or form of my rules unless two-thirds of you ask me to change my rules, and unless, after you have asked me to change them, I submit the proposition back to you and get the consent of three-fourths of you. And I not only make this compact with you thirteen, but with any other children that may be born to me, or that I may adopt."

Thirteen *States* adopted the Constitution. It takes just thirteen now to keep it from being changed.

APPENDIX A

PARALLEL COMPARISON OF THE ARTICLES OF THE VIRGINIA PLAN AND OF THE NEW JERSEY PLAN

THE VIRGINIA PLAN	THE NEW JERSEY PLAN

1. Resolved, that the Articles of Confederation ought to be so corrected and enlarged as to accomplish the objects proposed by their institution; namely,
    common defense,
    security of liberty,
    and general welfare.
	1. Resolved, that the Articles of Confederation ought to be so revised, corrected, and enlarged, as to render the Federal Constitution adequate to the exigencies of government, and
	the preservation of the Union.

2. Resolved, therefore, that the rights of suffrage in the National Legislature ought to be proportioned to the quotas of contribution, or to the number of free inhabitants, as the one or the other rule may seem best in different cases.	
3. Resolved, that the National Legislature ought to consist of two branches.	
4. Resolved, that the members of the first branch of the National Legislature ought to be elected by the people of the several States every ——— for the term of ———; to be of the age of ——— years at least; to receive liberal sti-	

The Virginia Plan

pends by which they may be compensated for the devotion of their time to public service; to be ineligible to any office established by a particular State, or under the authority of the United States, except those peculiarly belonging to the functions of the first branch, during the term of service, and for the space of ―――― after its expiration; to be incapable of re-election for the space of ―――― after the expiration of their term of service, and be subject to recall.

5. Resolved, that the members of the second branch of the National Legislature ought to be elected by those of the first, out of a proper number of persons nominated by the individual legislatures; to be of the age of ―――― years at least; to hold their offices for a term sufficient to ensure their independency; to receive liberal stipends, by which they may be compensated for the devotion of their time to public service; and to be ineligible to any office established by a particular State, or under the authority of the United States, except those peculiarly belonging to the functions of the second branch, during the term of service; and for the space

The New Jersey Plan

The Virginia Plan

of ———— after the expiration thereof.

6. Resolved, that each branch ought to possess the right of originating acts; that the National Legislature ought to be empowered to enjoy the legislative rights vested in Congress by the Confederation, and moreover to legislate in all cases to which the separate States are incompetent, or in which the harmony of the United States may be interrupted by the exercise of individual legislation; to negative all laws passed by the several States contravening, in the opinion of the National Legislature, the Articles of Union; and to call forth the force of the Union against any member

The New Jersey Plan

Mr. Wilson first stated the difference between the two plans.

Virginia plan proposes two branches in the Legislature; Jersey, a single legislative body.

Virginia, the legislative powers derived from the *people;* Jersey, from the *States.*

Virginia, a single executive; Jersey, more than one.

Virginia, a majority of the Legislature can act; Jersey, a small majority can control.

Virginia, the Legislature can legislate on all national concerns; Jersey, only on limited objects.

Virginia, Legislature to negative all *State* laws; Jersey, giving power to the executive to compel obedience by force.

Virginia, to remove the executive by impeachment; Jersey, on application of a majority of the *States.*

Virginia, for the establishment of inferior judiciary tribunals; Jersey, no provision.

Yates' Minutes in Elliot's *Debates on the Federal Constitution,* Vol. I, p. 414.

The Virginia Plan	The New Jersey Plan
of the Union failing to fulfill its duty under the Articles thereof. 7. Resolved, that a National Executive be instituted; to be chosen by the National Legislature for the term of ———— years; to receive punctually, at stated times, a fixed compensation for the services rendered, in which no increase or diminution shall be made, so as to affect the magistracy, existing at the time of increase or diminution, and to be ineligible for a second time; and that besides a general authority to execute the national laws, it ought to enjoy the executive rights vested in Congress by the Confederation.	4. Resolved, that the United States in Congress be authorized to elect a Federal Executive, to consist of ———— persons, to continue in office for the term of ———— years, to receive punctually at stated times a fixed compensation for their services, in which no increase or diminution shall be made so as to affect the persons composing the Executive at the time of such increase or diminution, to be paid out of the Federal treasury, to be incapable of holding any other office or appointment during their time of service and for ———— years thereafter; to be ineligible a second time, and removable by Congress on application by a majority of the Executives of the several States; that the Executives besides their general authority to execute the Federal acts, ought to appoint all Federal officers not otherwise provided for, and to direct all military operations; provided, that none of the persons composing the Federal Executive shall on any occasion take command of any troops, so as personally to conduct any military enter-

The Virginia Plan	The New Jersey Plan
	prise as General or in any other capacity.
8. Resolved, that the Executive and a convenient number of the national Judiciary, ought to compose a Council of Revision, with authority to examine every act of the National Legislature before it shall operate, and every act of a particular Legislature before a negative thereon shall be final; and that the dissent of the said Council shall amount to a rejection, unless the act of the National Legislature be again passed, or that of a particular Legislature be again negatived by ——— of the members of each branch.	
9. Resolved, that a National Judiciary be established to consist of one or more supreme tribunals, and of inferior tribunals to be chosen by the National Legislature, to hold their offices during good behavior, and to receive punctually, at stated times, fixed compensation for their services, in which no increase or diminution shall be made so as to affect the persons actually in office at the time of such increase or diminution. That the jurisdiction of the inferior tribunals shall be to hear and determine in the first instance,	5. Resolved, that a Federal Judiciary be established, to consist of a supreme tribunal, the Judges of which to be appointed by the Executive, and to hold their offices during good behavior; to receive punctually at stated times a fixed compensation for the services, in which no increase or diminution shall be made, so as to affect the persons actually in office at the time of such increase or diminution. That the Judiciary so established shall have authority to hear and determine in the first instance on all impeachments

The Virginia Plan	The New Jersey Plan
and of the supreme tribunal to hear and determine, in the dernier resort, all piracies, and felonies on the high seas, captures from an enemy; cases in which foreigners, or citizens of other States, applying to such jurisdictions, may be interested, or which respect the collection of the national revenue; impeachments of any national officers, and questions which may involve the national peace and harmony.	of Federal officers; and by way of appeal, in the dernier resort in all cases touching the rights of ambassadors, in all cases of captures from an enemy; in all cases of piracies and felonies on the high seas; in all cases in which foreigners may be interested, in the construction of any treaty or treaties, or which may arise on any of the acts for regulation of trade, or the collection of the Federal revenue; that none of the Judiciary shall, during the time they remain in office, be capable of receiving or holding any other office or appointment during their time of service, or for ——— thereafter.
10. Resolved, that provision ought to be made for the admission of States lawfully arising within the limits of the United States, whether from a voluntary junction of government and territory, or otherwise, with the consent of a number of voices in the National Legislature less than the whole.	7. Resolved, that provision be made for the admission of new States into the Union.
11. Resolved, that a republican government, and the territory of each State, except in the instance of a voluntary junction of government and	

The Virginia Plan

territory, ought to be guaranteed by the United States to each State.

12. Resolved, that provision ought to be made for the continuance of Congress and their authorities and privileges, until a given day after the reform of the Articles of Union shall be adopted, and for the completion of all their engagements.

13. Resolved, that provision ought to be made for the amendment of the Articles of Union whensoever it shall seem necessary, and that the assent of the National Legislature ought not to be required thereto.

14. Resolved, that the legislative, executive, and judiciary powers, within the several States, ought to be bound by oath to support the Articles of Union.

The New Jersey Plan

6. Resolved, that all acts of the United States in Congress made by virtue and in pursuance of such powers hereby and by the Articles of Confederation vested in them, and all treaties, made and ratified under the authority of the United States, shall be the supreme law of the respective States, so far forth as those acts or treaties shall relate to the said States or their citizens, and that the Judiciary of the several States shall be bound thereby in their decisions, anything in the respective laws of the individual States to the

The Virginia Plan

The New Jersey Plan

contrary notwithstanding; and that if any State, or any body of men in any State, shall oppose or prevent the carrying into execution such acts or treaties, the Federal Executive shall be authorized to call forth the power of the Confederated States, or so much thereof as may be necessary to enforce and compel an obedience to such acts, or an observance of such treaties.

15. Resolved, that the amendments which shall be offered to the Confederation, by the Convention, ought at a proper time, or times, after the approbation of Congress to be submitted to an assembly or assemblies of representatives, recommended by the several Legislatures to be expressly chosen by the people, to consider and decide thereon.

2. Resolved, that in addition to the powers vested in the United States in Congress, by the present existing Articles of Confederation, it shall levy duties on all goods or merchandise, of foreign growth or manufacture, imported into any part of the United States, by stamps on paper, vellum, or parchment; and by a postage on all letters or packages passing through the general

The Virginia Plan	The New Jersey Plan
	post office, to be applied to such Federal purposes as they shall deem proper and expedient; to make rules and regulations for the collection thereof; and the same from time to time, to alter and amend in such manner as they shall think proper; to pass acts for the regulation of trade and commerce as well with foreign nations as with each other; provided, that all punishments, fines, forfeitures, and penalties to be incurred for contravening such acts, rules, and regulations, shall be judged by the common law Judiciaries of the State in which any offense contrary to the true intent and meaning of such acts, rules, and regulations shall have been committed or perpetrated, with liberty of commencing in the first instance all suits and prosecutions for that purpose in the superior common law Judiciary in such States, subject, nevertheless, for the correction of all errors, both in law and fact, in rendering judgment, to an appeal to the Judiciary of the United States. 3. Resolved, that whenever requisition shall be necessary, instead of the rule for making requisitions mentioned in the Articles of Confederation, the United States in Congress be

The Virginia Plan	The New Jersey Plan
	authorized to make such requisitions in proportion to the whole number of white and other free citizens and inhabitants of every age, sex, and condition, including those bound to servitude for a term of years, and three-fifths of all other persons not comprehended in the foregoing description, except Indians not paying taxes; that if such requisitions be not complied with, in the time specified therein, to direct the collection thereof in the noncomplying States, and for that purpose to devise and pass acts directing and authorizing the same; provided, that none of the powers hereby vested in the United States in Congress shall be exercised without the consent of at least ——— States, and in that proportion if the number of confederated States should hereafter be increased or diminished.

8. Resolved, that the rule for naturalization ought to be the same in every State.

9. Resolved, that a citizen of one State committing an offense in another State of the Union, shall be deemed guilty of the same offense as if it had been committed by a citizen of the State in which the offense was committed. |

APPENDIX B

PARALLEL COMPARISON OF THE ARTICLES OF CONFEDERATION AND THE CONSTITUTION

ARTICLES OF CONFEDERATION

Article 1. The style of this confederacy shall be "The United States of America."

Article 2. Each State retains its sovereignty, freedom, and independence, and every power, jurisdiction, and right which is not by this confederation expressly delegated to the United States in Congress assembled.

Article 3. The said States hereby severally enter into a firm league of friendship with each other for their common defense, the security of their liberties, and their mutual and general welfare, binding themselves to assist each other against all force offered to or attacks made upon them, or any of them, on account of religion, sovereignty, trade, or any other pretense whatever.

Article 4. The better to secure and perpetuate mutual friendship and intercourse among the people of the dif-

THE CONSTITUTION

Preamble:
We . . . do ordain and establish this constitution for the United States of America.

Article X. The powers not delegated to the United States by the Constitution, nor prohibited by it to the States, are reserved to the States respectively, or to the people.

Preamble. We, the people of the United States, in order to form a more perfect Union, establish justice, insure domestic tranquillity, provide for the common defense, promote the general welfare, and secure the blessings of liberty to ourselves and our posterity, do ordain and establish this Constitution for the United States of America.

Article IV, Section 2, Subdivision 1. The citizens of each State shall be entitled to all privileges and immunities of

Articles of Confederation	The Constitution
ferent States in this Union, the free inhabitants of each of these States, paupers, vagabonds, and fugitives from justice excepted, shall be entitled to all privileges and immunities of free citizens in the several States; and the people of each State shall have free ingress and regress to and from any other State, and shall enjoy therein the privileges of trade and commerce, subject to the same duties, impositions, and restrictions as the inhabitants thereof respectively, provided, that such restrictions shall not extend so far as to prevent the removal of property imported into any State to any other State, of which the owner is an inhabitant; provided also, that no imposition, duties, or restriction, shall be laid by any State on the property of the United States or either of them.	citizens in the several States.
If any person guilty of or charged with treason, felony, or other high misdemeanor, in any State, shall flee from justice, and be found in any of the United States, he shall, upon demand of the governor or executive power, be delivered up, and removed to the State having jurisdiction of his offense.	*Article IV, Section 2, Subdivision 2.* A person charged in any State with treason, felony, or other crime, who shall flee from justice, and be found in another State, shall, on demand of the Executive authority of the State from which he fled, be delivered up, to be removed to the State having jurisdiction of the crime.

Articles of Confederation

Full faith and credit shall be given in each of these States to the records, acts, and judicial proceedings of the courts and magistrates of every other State.

Article 5. For the more convenient management of the general interests of the United States, delegates shall be annually appointed in such manner as the legislature of each State shall direct, to meet in Congress on the first Monday in November, in every year, with a power reserved to each State to recall its delegates or any of them, at any time within the year, and to send others in their stead for the remainder of the year.

No State shall be represented in Congress by less than two nor by more than seven members; and no person shall be capable of being a delegate for more than three years in any term of six years; nor shall any person being a delegate, be capable of holding any office under the United States, for which he, or another for his benefit, receives any salary, fees, or emolument of any kind.

The Constitution

Article IV, Section 1. Full faith and credit shall be given in each State to the public acts, records, and judicial proceedings of every other State. And the Congress may by general laws, prescribe the manner in which such acts, records, and proceedings shall be proved, and the effect thereof.

Article I, Section 2, Subdivision 2. The House of Representatives shall be composed of members chosen every second year by the people of the several States . . .

Article I, Section 4, Subdivision 2. The Congress shall assemble at least once in every year, and such meeting shall be on the first Monday in December, unless they shall by law appoint a different day.

Article I, Section 3, Subdivision 1. The Senate of the United States shall be composed of two Senators from each State . . . for six years; and each Senator shall have one vote.

Article I, Section 6, Subdivision 2. No Senator or Representative shall, during the time for which he was elected, be appointed to any civil office under the authority of the United States, which shall have been created, or the emoluments whereof shall have

Articles of Confederation	The Constitution
	been increased during such time; and no person holding any office under the United States, shall be a member of either House during his continuance in office.
Each State shall maintain its own delegates in a meeting of the States, and while they act as members of the committee of the States.	*Article I, Section 6, Subdivision 1.* The Senators and Representatives shall receive a compensation for their services, to be ascertained by law, and paid out of the Treasury of the United States.
In determining questions in the United States in Congress assembled, each State shall have one vote.	. . . . .
Freedom of speech and debate in Congress shall not be impeached or questioned in any court or place out of Congress; and the members of Congress shall be protected in their persons from arrests and imprisonments, during the time of their going to and from and attendance on Congress, except for treason, felony, or breach of the peace.	*Article I, Section 6, Subdivision 1.* The Senators and Representatives . . . shall in all cases except treason, felony, and breach of the peace, be privileged from arrest during their attendance at the session of their respective Houses, and in going to and returning from the same; and for any speech or debate in either House, they shall not be questioned in any other place.
Article 6. No State, without the consent of the United States in Congress assembled, shall send any embassy to, or receive any embassy from, or enter into any conference, agreement, alliance, or treaty, with any king, prince, or state;	*Article I, Section 9, Subdivision 7.* No title of nobility shall be granted by the United States; and no person holding any office of profit or trust under them, shall, without the consent of Congress, accept of any present, emolument, office,

Articles of Confederation	The Constitution
nor shall any person holding any office of profit or trust under the United States, or any of them, accept of any present, emolument, office, or title of any kind whatever, from any king, prince, or foreign state; nor shall the United States in Congress assembled, or any of them, grant any title of nobility.	or title, of any kind whatever, from any king, prince, or foreign state. *Article I, Section 10, Subdivision 1.* No State shall enter into any treaty, alliance, or confederation; . . . or grant any title of nobility.
No two or more States shall enter into any treaty, confederation, or alliance whatever between them, without the consent of the United States in Congress assembled, specifying accurately the purposes for which the same is to be entered into, and how long it shall continue.	*Article I, Section 10, Subdivision 3.* No State shall, without the consent of Congress, . . . enter into any agreement or compact with another State.
No State shall lay any imposts or duties, which may interfere with any stipulations in treaties entered into by the United States in Congress assembled, with any king, prince, or state, in pursuance of any treaties already proposed by Congress to the courts of France and Spain.	*Article I, Section 10, Subdivision 2.* No State shall, without the consent of the Congress, lay any imposts or duties on imports or exports, except what may be absolutely necessary for executing its inspection laws; and the net produce of all duties and imposts, laid by any State on imports or exports, shall be for the use of the Treasury of the United States; and all such laws shall be subject to the revision and control of the Congress.
No vessels of war shall be	*Article I, Section 10, Subdi-*

Articles of Confederation	The Constitution
kept up in time of peace by any State, except such number only as shall be deemed necessary by the United States in Congress assembled for the defense of such State or its trade; nor shall any body of forces be kept up by any State in time of peace, except such number only as, in the judgment of the United States in Congress assembled, shall be deemed requisite to garrison the forts necessary for the defense of such state; but every State shall always keep up a well regulated and disciplined militia, sufficiently armed and accoutred, and shall provide and have constantly ready for use, in public stores, a due number of field pieces and tents, and a proper quantity of arms, ammunition, and camp equipage.	vision 2. No State shall, without the consent of Congress, . . . keep troops, or ships of war in time of peace . . . *Article (Amendment) II.* A well-regulated militia being necessary to the security of a free State, the right of the people to keep and bear arms shall not be infringed.
No State shall engage in any war without the consent of the United States in Congress assembled, unless such State be actually invaded by enemies, or shall have received certain advice of a resolution being formed by some nation of Indians to invade such State, and the danger is so imminent as not to admit of delay till the United States in Congress assembled can be consulted; nor shall any State grant commis-	*Article I, Section 10, Subdivision 2.* No State shall without the consent of Congress . . . engage in war unless actually invaded or in such imminent danger as will not admit of delay.

Articles of Confederation

sions to any ships or vessels of war, nor letters of marque or reprisal, except it be after a declaration of war by the United States in Congress assembled, and then only against the kingdom or state, and the subjects thereof, against which war has been so declared, and under such regulations as shall be established by the United States in Congress assembled, unless such State be infested by pirates, in which case vessels of war may be fitted out for that occasion, and kept so long as the danger shall continue, or until the United States in Congress assembled shall determine otherwise.

Article 7. When land forces are raised by any State for the common defense, all officers of or under the rank of colonel, shall be appointed by the legislature of each State, respectively, by whom such forces shall be raised, or in such manner as such State shall direct; and all vacancies shall be filled up by the State which first made the appointment.

Article 8. All charges of war, and all other expenses that shall be incurred for the common defense or general welfare, and allowed by the

The Constitution

Article I, Section 10, Subdivision 1. . . . No State shall grant letters of marque and reprisal . . .

Article I, Section 8, Subdivision 1. The Congress shall have power to lay and collect taxes, duties, imposts, and excises; to pay the debts and

Articles of Confederation

United States in Congress assembled, shall be defrayed out of a common treasury, which shall be supplied by the several States in proportion to the value of all land within each granted to or surveyed for any person, as such land and the buildings and improvements thereon shall be estimated, according to such mode as the United States in Congress assembled shall from time to time direct and appoint.

The taxes for paying that proportion shall be laid and levied by the authority and direction of the legislatures of the several States, within the time agreed upon by the United States in Congress assembled.

Article 9. The United States in Congress assembled shall have the sole and exclusive right and power of determining on peace and war, except in the cases mentioned in the sixth article;

of sending and receiving ambassadors;

The Constitution

provide for the common defense and general welfare of the United States; but all duties, imposts and excises shall be uniform throughout the United States.

Article I, Section 9, Subdivision 4. No capitation or other direct tax shall be laid, unless in proportion to the census or enumeration hereinbefore directed to be taken.

Article (Amendment) XVI. The Congress shall have power to lay and collect taxes on incomes, from whatever sources derived, without apportionment among the several States, and without regard to any census or enumeration.

Article I, Section 8, Subdivision 11. Congress shall have the power to declare war.

Article II, Section 2, Subdivision 2. The President shall have the power to nominate, and by and with the advice and consent of the Senate, appoint ambassadors, other public ministers, and consuls.

Articles of Confederation	The Constitution
entering into treaties and alliances;	*Article II, Section 2, Subdivision 2.* The President shall have power, by and with the advice and consent of the Senate, to make treaties, provided two-thirds of the Senators present concur;
of establishing rules for deciding in all cases, what captures on land or water shall be legal, and in what manner prizes taken by land or naval forces in the service of the United States shall be divided or appropriated;	*Article I, Section 8, Subdivision 11.* The Congress shall have power . . . to make rules concerning captures on land and water.
of granting letters of marque and reprisal;	*Article I, Section 8, Subdivision 11.* The Congress shall have power to grant letters of marque and reprisal.
appointing courts for the trial of piracies and felonies committed on the high seas; and establishing courts for receiving and determining finally appeals in all cases of captures; provided that no member of Congress shall be appointed a judge of any of the said courts.	*Article I, Section 8, Subdivision 10.* The Congress shall have the power to define and punish piracies and felonies committed on the high seas, and offenses against the law of nations.
The United States in Congress assembled shall also be the last resort on appeal in all disputes and differences now subsisting or that hereafter may arise between two or more States concerning boundary, jurisdiction, or any other cause	*Article III, Section 2, Subdivision 1.* The judicial power (of the Supreme Court of the United States) shall extend to . . . all controversies between two or more States, between a State and citizens of another State, between citizens of dif-

Articles of Confederation	The Constitution
whatever; which authority shall always be exercised in the manner following; whenever the legislative or executive authority or lawful agent of any State in controversy with another shall present a petition to Congress, stating the matter in question, and praying for a hearing, notice thereof shall be given by order of Congress to the legislative or executive authority of the other State in controversy, and a day assigned for the appearance of the parties, by their lawful agents, who shall then be directed to appoint by joint consent commissioners or judges to constitute a court for hearing and determining the matter in question; but if they cannot agree Congress shall name three persons out of each of the United States, and from the list of such persons each party shall alternately strike out one, the petitioners beginning, until the number shall be reduced to thirteen; and from that number not less than seven nor more than nine names, as Congress shall direct, shall, in the presence of Congress, be drawn out by lot; and the persons whose names shall be so drawn, or any five of them, shall be commissioners or judges, to	ferent States, between citizens of the same State claiming lands under grants of different States, and between a State, or the citizens thereof, and foreign States, citizens, or subjects.

Articles of Confederation	The Constitution
hear and finally determine the controversy, so always as a major part of the judges, who shall hear the cause, shall agree in the determination; and if either party shall neglect to attend at the day appointed, without showing reasons which Congress shall judge sufficient, or being present shall refuse to strike, the Congress shall proceed to nominate three persons out of each State, and the secretary of Congress shall strike in behalf of such party absent or refusing; and the judgment and sentence of the court to be appointed in the manner before prescribed, shall be final and conclusive; and if any of the parties shall refuse to submit to the authority of such court, or to appear, or defend their claim or cause, the court shall nevertheless proceed to pronounce sentence or judgment, which shall in like manner be final and decisive, the judgment or sentence and other proceedings, being in either case transmitted to Congress for the security of the parties concerned; provided, that every commissioner, before he sits in judgment, shall take an oath, to be administered by one of the judges of the supreme or superior court of the State, where the	

Articles of Confederation	The Constitution
cause shall be tried, "well and truly to hear and determine the matter in question, according to the best of his judgment, without favor, affection, or hope of reward"; provided also, that no State shall be deprived of territory for the benefit of the United States.	
All controversies concerning the private right of soil, claimed under different grants of two or more States, whose jurisdiction as they may respect such lands and the States which passed such grants are adjusted, the said grants or either of them being at the same time claimed to have originated antecedent to such settlement of jurisdiction, shall, on the petition of either party to the Congress of the United States, be finally determined, as near as may be, in the same manner as is before prescribed for deciding disputes respecting territorial jurisdiction between different States.	
The United States in Congress assembled shall also have the sole and exclusive right and power of regulating the alloy and value of coin struck by their own authority, or by that of the respective States; fixing the standard of weights and	*Article I, Section 8, Subdivision 5.* The Congress shall have power to coin money, regulate the value thereof, and of foreign coin, and fix the standard of weights and measures.

Articles of Confederation	The Constitution
measures throughout the United States;	
regulating the trade and managing all affairs with the Indians not members of any of the States; provided, that the legislative right of any State within its own limits shall not be infringed or violated;	*Article I, Section 8, Subdivision 3.* The Congress shall have the power to regulate commerce . . . with the Indian tribes.
establishing and regulating post offices from one State to another throughout all the United States, and exacting such postage on the papers passing through the same as may be requisite to defray the expenses of the said office;	*Article I, Section 8, Subdivision 7.* The Congress shall have power to establish post offices and post roads.
appointing all officers of the land forces in the service of the United States, excepting regimental officers; appointing all the officers of the naval forces, and commissioning all officers whatever in the service of the United States; making rules for the government and regulation of the said land and naval forces, and directing their operations;	*Article I, Section 8, Subdivision 14.* The Congress shall have power to make rules for the government and regulation of the land and naval forces. *Article II, Section 2, Subdivision 1.* The President shall be Commander-in-chief of the Army and Navy of the United States.
The United States in Congress assembled shall have authority to appoint a committee to sit in the recess of Congress, to be denominated "a committee of the States"; and to consist of one delegate from each State, and to appoint such	

Articles of Confederation	The Constitution
other committees and civil officers as may be necessary for managing the general affairs of the United States, under their direction; to appoint one of their number to preside, provided that no person be allowed to serve in the office of president more than one year in any term of three years;	
to ascertain the necessary sums of money to be raised for the service of the United States, and to appropriate and apply the same for defraying the public expenses;	*Article I, Section 7, Subdivision 1.* All bills for raising revenue shall originate in the House of Representatives. *Article I, Section 9, Subdivision 7.* No money shall be drawn from the Treasury but in consequence of appropriations made by law; and a regular statement and account of the receipts and expenditures of all public money shall be published from time to time. *Article I, Section 8, Subdivision 1.* The Congress shall have power to collect taxes, duties, imposts, and excises, to pay the debts and provide for the common defense and general welfare of the United States . . .
to borrow money or emit bills on the credit of the United States, transmitting every half year to the respective States an account of the sums of	*Article I, Section 8, Subdivision 2.* The Congress shall have the power to borrow money on the credit of the United States.

ARTICLES OF CONFEDERATION	THE CONSTITUTION
money so borrowed or emitted; to build and equip a navy;	*Article I, Section 8, Subdivision 13.* Congress shall have the power to provide and maintain a navy.
to agree upon the number of land forces, and to make requisitions from each State for its quota, in proportion to the number of white inhabitants in such State; which requisition shall be binding, and thereupon the legislature of each State shall appoint the regimental officers, raise the men, and clothe, arm, and equip them in a soldierlike manner, at the expense of the United States; and the officers and men so clothed and equipped, shall march to the place appointed, and within the time agreed on by the United States in Congress assembled; but if the United States in Congress assembled, shall, on consideration of circumstances, judge proper that any State should not raise men or raise a smaller number than its quota, and that any other State should raise a greater number of men than the quota thereof, such extra number shall be raised, officered, clothed, armed, and equipped, in the same manner as the quota of such State, unless the Legislature of such State shall judge	*Article I, Section 8, Subdivision 12.* The Congress shall have the power to raise and support armies, but no appropriation of money to that use shall be for a longer term than two years.

ARTICLES OF CONFEDERATION | THE CONSTITUTION

ARTICLES OF CONFEDERATION

that such extra number cannot be safely spared out of the same; in which case they shall raise, officer, clothe, arm, and equip, as many of such extra number as they judge can be safely spared. And the officers and men so clothed, armed, and equipped, shall march to the place appointed, and within the time agreed on by the United States in Congress assembled.

The United States in Congress assembled shall never engage in war, nor grant letters of marque and reprisal in time of peace, nor enter into any treaties or alliances, nor coin money, nor regulate the value thereof, nor ascertain the sums and expenses necessary for the defense and welfare of the United States or any of them, nor emit bills, or borrow money on the credit of the United States, nor appropriate any money, nor agree upon the number of vessels of war to be built or purchased, or the number of land or sea forces to be raised, nor appoint a commander-in-chief of the army or navy unless nine States assent to the same; nor shall a question on any other point, except for adjourning from day to day, be determined, unless by the votes of a

Articles of Confederation	The Constitution
majority of the United States in Congress assembled. The Congress of the United States shall have power to adjourn to any time within the year, and to any place within the United States, so that no period of adjournment be for a longer duration than the space of six months; and shall publish the journal of their proceedings monthly, except that such parts thereof relating to treaties, alliances, or military operations, as in their judgment require secrecy; and the yeas and nays of the delegates of each State on any question shall be entered on the journal, when it is desired by any delegate; and the delegates of a State, or any of them, at his or their request, shall be furnished with a transcript of said journal, except such parts as are above excepted, to lay before the Legislatures of the several States. *Article 10.* The Committee of the States, or any nine of them, shall be authorized to execute in the recess of Congress, such of the powers of Congress as the United States in Congress assembled, by the consent of nine States, shall,	*Article I, Section 5, Subdivision 4.* Neither House, during the session of Congress shall, without the consent of the other, adjourn for more than three days, nor to any other place than that in which the two Houses shall be sitting. *Article I, Section 5, Subdivision 3.* Each House shall keep a journal of its proceedings, and from time to time publish the same, excepting such parts as may in their judgment require secrecy; and the yeas and nays of the members of either House on any question shall, at the desire of one-fifth of those present, be entered on the journal.

Articles of Confederation

from time to time, think expedient to vest them with; provided, that no power be delegated to the said Committee, for the exercise of which, by the Articles of Confederation, the voice of nine States in the Congress of the United States assembled is requisite.

Article 11. Canada acceding to this Confederation, and joining in the measures of the United States, shall be admitted into, and entitled to, all the advantages of this union; but no other colony shall be admitted into the same unless such admission be agreed to by nine States.

Article 12. All bills of credit emitted, moneys borrowed, and debts contracted, by or under the authority of Congress, before the assembling of the United States, in pursuance of the present Confederation, shall be deemed and considered as a charge against the United States, for payment and satisfaction whereof the said United States and the public faith are hereby solemnly pledged.

Article 13. Every State shall abide by the determina-

The Constitution

Article IV, Section 3, Subdivision 1. New States may be admitted by the Congress into this Union; but no new State shall be formed or erected within the jurisdiction of any other State, nor any State be formed by the junction of two or more States, or parts of States, without the consent of the Legislatures of the States concerned, as well as of the Congress.

Article VI, Section 1. All debts contracted and engagements entered into before the adoption of this Constitution, shall be as valid against the United States under this Constitution as under the Confederation.

Article VI, Section 2. This Constitution and the laws of

Articles of Confederation	The Constitution
tion of the United States in Congress assembled, on all questions which, by this Confederation, are submitted to them. And the Articles of this Confederation shall be inviolably observed by every State, and the Union shall be perpetual;	the United States which shall be made in pursuance thereof and all treaties made, or which shall be made, under the authority of the United States, shall be the supreme law of the land, and the judges in every State shall be bound thereby, anything in the Constitution or laws of any State to the contrary notwithstanding.
nor shall any alteration at any time hereafter be made in any of them, unless such alteration be agreed to in a Congress of the United States, and be afterwards confirmed by the Legislature of every State.	*Article V.* The Congress, whenever two-thirds of both Houses shall deem it necessary, shall propose amendments to this Constitution, or, on the application of the Legislatures of two-thirds of the several States, shall call a convention for proposing amendments, which, in either case, shall be valid to all intents and purposes, as part of this Constitution, when ratified by the legislatures of three-fourths of the several States, or by conventions in three-fourths thereof, as the one or the other mode of ratification may be proposed by the Congress; provided, that no amendment which may be made prior to the year one thousand eight hundred and eight shall in any manner affect the first and fourth clauses in the ninth section of the First Article; and

ARTICLES OF CONFEDERATION

THE CONSTITUTION

that no State, without its consent, shall be deprived of its equal suffrage in the Senate.

And whereas it has pleased the Great Governor of the world to incline the hearts of the Legislatures we respectfully represent in Congress, to approve of and to authorize us to ratify the said articles of confederation and perpetual union: *Know Ye,* That we, the undersigned delegates, by virtue of the power and authority to us given for that purpose, do, by these presents, in the name and in behalf of our respective constituents, fully and entirely ratify and confirm each and every of the said articles of confederation and perpetual union, and all and singular the matters and things therein contained; and we do further solemnly plight and engage the faith of our respective constituents, that they shall abide by the determinations of the United States in Congress assembled, on all questions which, by the said confederation, are submitted to them; and that the articles thereof shall be inviolably observed by the States we respectively represent; and that the union shall be perpetual.

APPENDIX C

SUMPTUARY LAWS

THE following are extracts from the early references in the records of the Constitutional Convention to "sumptuary laws":

In the Continental Congress on August 20th, 1787, "it was moved and seconded to insert the following clause in the first section, seventh article: 'to make sumptuary laws'; which was passed in the negative.

"*Yeas:* Delaware, Maryland, Georgia, three. *Nays:* New Hampshire, Massachusetts, Connecticut, New Jersey, Pennsylvania, Virginia, North Carolina, South Carolina, eight." [1]

August 20th, 1787, "Mr. Mason moved to enable Congress 'to enact sumptuary laws.' No government can be maintained unless the manners be made consonant to it. Such a discretionary power may do good and can do no harm. A proper regulation of excises and of trade may do a great deal, but it is best to have an express provision. It was objected to sumptuary laws that they were contrary to nature. This was a vulgar error. The love of distinction, it is true, is natural; but the object of sumptuary laws is not to extinguish this principle, but to give it a proper direction.

"Mr. Ellsworth said the best remedy is to enforce taxes and debts. As far as the regulation of eating

---

[1] Elliot's *Debates on the Federal Constitution*, Vol. I, p. 251.

and drinking can be reasonable, it is provided for in the power of taxation.

"Mr. Gouverneur Morris argued that sumptuary laws tended to create a landed nobility, by fixing in the great landholders and their posterity their present possessions.

"Mr. Gerry said the law of necessity is the best sumptuary law.

"On motion of Mr. Mason 'as to sumptuary laws'

"Delaware, Maryland, Georgia, ay, three; New Hampshire, Massachusetts, Connecticut, New Jersey, Pennsylvania, Virginia, North Carolina, South Carolina, no, eight."[2]

September 13th, 1787, in Convention, "Colonel Mason had moved, without success, for a power to make sumptuary regulations. He had not yet lost sight of his object. After descanting on the extravagance of our manners, the excessive consumption of foreign superfluities, and the necessity of restricting it, as well with economical as republican views, he moved that a Committee be appointed, to report articles of association for encouraging, by the advice, the influence, and the example of the members of the Convention, economy, frugality, and American manufactures. Dr. Johnson seconded the motion, which was, without debate, agreed to, *nem con.*,[3] and a Committee appointed, consisting of Colonel Mason, Dr. Franklin, Mr. Dickinson, Dr. Johnson, and Mr. Livingston."[4]

[2] Elliot, Vol. V, p. 447.
[3] "Nem con." means "No one to the contrary."
[4] Elliott, Vol. V, p. 539. (This motion, and appointment of the Committee, do not appear in the printed *Journal*. No report was made by the Committee.)

APPENDIX D

HOW RHODE ISLAND RATIFIED THE CONSTITUTION

SEPTEMBER 22nd, 1787,[1] the Governor called a special session of the General Assembly at Newport . . . to prepare a letter to the President of Congress assigning the reasons why Rhode Island was not represented in the Philadelphia Convention. . . . The letter stated that the Assembly had not power to appoint delegates, as this right could only belong to the *people* at large. It set forth the doctrine of popular *sovereignty,* and of the entire subserviency of the Legislature to the public will—in singular contrast with the despotic authority which its authors had exercised within the past few months.

October 20th, 1787, the question (of ratification) came up before the General Assembly upon a motion for printing and distributing to the towns copies of the report of the Convention (at Philadelphia), and recommending the appointment of delegates as therein provided. This was voted down by a large majority, but a vote to print and circulate a thousand copies was afterwards passed.

February 29th, 1788, in the lower House, a long debate ensued upon a motion to call a *State* Convention to consider the Constitution in the manner proposed

[1] Samuel Greene Arnold's *History of Rhode Island and Providence Plantations,* Vol. 2, pp. 539–62.

in the report of its framers. The *States' Rights* party desired to refer the subject directly to the *people* in their town meetings, and it was so decided by a vote of fifteen to 42. The National party opposed a reference that was certain to defeat the Constitution. "Better have no action at all," said the Nationalists, "than one which is not recognized by the instrument itself, and which, by depriving the *people* of the power to suggest alterations, must result in defeat." The National party, hopeless of success, and disapproving the action of the Assembly, resolved not to vote upon the Constitution. . . . The *State* contained more than 6000 freemen, less than half of whom voted upon the question. . . . In Newport eleven votes were cast, ten against and one in favor of the Constitution. In Warwick and East Greenwich, the minority (Nationalists) protested against the whole proceeding as illegal, but in most of the towns the question was "carried in the negative" by acclamation.

March 24th, 1787, in Providence, where the friends of the Constitution were in the majority, a Committee was appointed at the town meeting to draft a petition to the General Assembly, in which it pointed out the objections to the mode of decision prescribed by the Assembly (to vote on the question of ratification at town meetings); it prevented the country and seaport towns from hearing and discussing each other's views; that the information essential to a just decision could not easily be conveyed to all the freemen; that many persons would be excluded from voting at all, who might desire to offer amendments, which could not be done in a town meeting; that Congress required a Convention to be held, and would receive propositions for amendments only through that source; and that such a Convention must ultimately be called, as the *State* could not exist out of the *Union;* they therefore prayed that some action might be taken by the Assembly to accomplish this object. Similar petitions were presented from Newport and other towns.

The Assembly at first refused to receive these petitions, but finally did so. No reply was made to the arguments offered in their behalf. The majority refused to discuss the subject, and the petitions were dismissed.

June 9th, 1788, the General Assembly again convened at Newport, but nothing was done about the Constitution.

When New Hampshire ratified the Constitution, there were demonstrations of joy when the news reached Providence. . . . There could be no mistaking the national sentiments of the *people* of Providence.

July 3rd, 1788, a town meeting was called at Providence to arrange a joint celebration of the anniversary of independence and of the completion of the national *Union.* The Federal proclivities of Providence gave great offense to the *people* of the country towns, who assembled in arms to prevent the proposed celebration. The *States' Rights* party viewed this as an indignity offered to themselves, and an insult to the *State,* where, they said, four-fifths of the *people* were inimical to the Constitution.

A similar rejoicing occurred in Providence when, on July 25th, 1788, New York ratified the Constitution.

The Assembly convened at Providence, October 27th to November 1st, 1788, where a proposal to call a Convention was voted down by a decided majority.

December 6th, 1788, the *people* of Providence instructed their deputies to move at the approaching session of the Assembly for a Convention to adopt the Constitution and propose amendments.

December 29th, 1788, the General Assembly again refused to call a State Convention, and adjourned January 3rd, 1789.

May 6th, 1789, a petition from the freemen of Newport and Providence was presented to the General Assembly, praying them to call a State Convention.

September 15th, 1789, the Governor called a special meeting of the Assembly at Newport. It ordered town meetings to be held in October to instruct the deputies on the subject of calling a Convention to consider the Constitution. . . . A letter was prepared by the Assembly to the President and Congress of the eleven *States*. This address assigned the reasons that influenced the majority to oppose the Constitution. It set forth the attachment of the *people* to their democratic charter, and the fear that this would in some degree be limited by the new Federal system, and for this cause they had waited to observe its operation, and to see if the proposed amendments would be adopted before yielding their assent to the new Government.

October 12th, 1789, at an adjourned session of the Assembly, held at Greenwich, the amendments to the Constitution recently adopted by Congress were ordered to be printed for the use of freemen at their town meetings.

October 19th, 1789, the House rejected by 17 to 39 the proposition of calling a *State* Convention to consider ratification of the Constitution.

January 11th, 1790, the General Assembly convened at Providence. (The population of Providence at this time was 6380, and of the *State* of Rhode Island, 68,825.)

January 15th, 1790, a bill was introduced into the lower House of Assembly by Benjamin Bourn, of Providence, to call a Convention to meet on the 22nd of February, 1790, to decide upon the Constitution. After a long debate it was carried by a majority of five, thirty-four in favor and twenty-nine against the measure.

The next day (January 16th, 1790) the Senate nonconcurred. There were eight Senators, who were equally divided on the question, and the vote of Deputy Governor Owen was cast in the negative. By the same vote the Senate passed a bill to call town meetings for the purpose of instructing the deputies whether to call a Convention or not.

The bill was sent down to the House, where, after a long debate, it was voted late in the evening of January 16, 1790, by a majority of fourteen to nonconcur.

Both Houses then adjourned until the next morning, which was Sunday (January 17th, 1790), when Henry Marchant, of Newport, offered a substitute for Mr. Bourn's bill, altering the time for holding the Convention to the 1st of March, 1790, and directing that a copy of the act be sent to Congress.

This was passed in the lower House by a majority of twenty-one—thirty-two yeas and eleven nays.

A bill then came down from the Senate, similar to the one that passed that body the day before, with the addition of a preamble.

This was rejected in the House, and Marchant's bill was sent up to the Senate for concurrence.

Meanwhile, one of the anti-Federal Senators, who was a minister and opposed to legislation on the Sabbath, left town. This made a tie in the Senate, and threw the casting vote on Governor Collins, who, after a speech in which he assigned the distresses of the *State* resulting from disconnection with the *Union* as the reason for his vote, decided for concurrence, and the (Marchant's) bill passed the Senate.

January 17th, 1790, the Assembly adjourned, after voting that a copy of the act should be forwarded to Congress with the request that the indulgence granted to Rhode Island's commerce might be continued. This was conceded, and the act extended to the 1st of April, 1790.

February 8th, 1790, town meetings were held throughout the *State* to choose delegates to the Convention. Each town was to send the same number as it had of deputies in the Assembly.

When the important day (March 1st, 1790) arrived, every member was present at South Kingstown. It soon appeared that a majority were opposed to the Constitution.

On March 2nd, 1790, rules were adopted to govern the proceedings, the Constitution was read, and a discussion arose which continued through the two following days, when a Committee of two from each county was appointed to prepare amendments. The next day it reported a bill of rights in sixteen articles, resembling that proposed by New York, and eighteen amendments to the Constitution.

The debate on these points continued the greater part of two days, when, on March 6th, 1790, Marchant moved that the Constitution be ratified. A motion to adjourn was made, to prevent a vote. Upon this a debate arose on a point of order involving the power of the Convention to adjourn without deciding the question which they were appointed to determine. An adjournment to the fourth Monday in May, 1790, then to meet at Newport, was carried by forty-one to twenty-eight, a majority of thirteen.

The feeling in Congress was embittered against Rhode Island by the repeated delays in adopting the Constitution. The extension of privilege to vessels of this *State* had already expired. A bill was brought into the Senate (of the *United States*) to prohibit all commercial intercourse with Rhode Island, and to require the payment of $27,000 in specie due upon the old Continental requisitions.

On May 24th, 1790, the day appointed for the Convention to reassemble at Newport, a large meeting of the freemen of Providence instructed their delegates in case of the rejection of the Constitution, or further postponement of the question, "to enter a solemn and spirited protest against such rejection or adjournment," and resolved in that event to unite with Newport and such other towns as might join them, in an application to Congress for protection, and to be received into the *Union*.

No business was done until Wednesday, May 26th, 1790, when the instructions from the several towns were read. A test question was presented by a motion to adjourn, which was defeated by a majority of nine votes.

The motion to adopt the Constitution was then taken up, and the instrument was read. The Statehouse could not contain the crowd of people assembled to witness the momentous proceedings. For more ample accommodations the Convention on May 27th, 1790, moved to the Second Baptist Church, where for three days the great debate continued.

On Saturday afternoon, May 29th, 1790, the final vote was taken. Thirty-four members voted to adopt the Constitution, and thirty-two voted in the negative. A majority of two votes saved the *people* of Rhode Island from anarchy and from dismemberment.

Many of the delegates were bound by instructions to vote against the adoption, and there was no time to obtain from their constituents a revision of these instructions, as had been done in the case of New Hampshire. Had it been so, the majority would have been greater.

The news reached Providence before midnight, and was announced by ringing of bells and the booming of cannon.

The news was forwarded by the President of the Convention to the President of the *United States*, in a letter of which Colonel William Barton was the bearer, and was communicated in a special message to both Houses of Congress. The further consideration of the bill to prevent commercial intercourse with Rhode Island was dismissed, and bills for extending the laws of the *United States* over the new *State* were introduced.

Governor Fenner convened a special session of the General Assembly, at which all the members of the Government took the oath or affirmation of fealty to the Constitution.

Two Senators were chosen, and at a subsequent election Benjamin Bourn was chosen to be the Representative in Congress.

Soon after adjournment of the Assembly President Washington visited Rhode Island, and was received with great enthusiasm throughout the *State*.

INDEX

Adams, John Quincy, 22, 71, 130, 136, 155, 197
Samuel, n. 146
Allegheny Mountains, 11
Amending the Constitution, 62, 63, 138, 185, 186, 202, 204, 205, 206, 207, 209, 210, 214, 215, 220, 222, 223, 224, 228
Amendments to be referred to Legislatures or Conventions, 218, 219
Ames, Fisher, 153
Amherst, Mass., 49
Annapolis, 14, 47, 51, 71, 152
Convention, 46, 47, 48, 51, 72
Anti-Federalists, n. 152
Armis (North Carolina trader), 45
Army disbanded, 1783, 69
of Revolution, 64, 66, 67, 68
Article V, 60, 62, 63, 205, 206, 209, 211, 212, 219 (history of adoption), 224
XXI, Sections 1, 2, and 3, 200, 201
Articles of Confederation, vi, vii, 24, 25, 26, 27, 28, 29, 30, 31, 32, 33, 35, 40, 41, 42, 43, 44, 48, 52, 55, 86, 89, 103, 119, 134, 149, 161, 220, 231, 261 (compared with Constitution)
of Union, 103
"Assemblies," 203, 204

Baldwin, Abraham, 73, 122, 184
Baltimore, Lord, 10

Barton, Col. William, 290
Bassett, Richard, 73, 81, 184
Beckley, John, 47
Bedford, Gunning, Jr., 73, 131, n. 131, 184
Berkeley, Lord, 9
Bill of Rights (Virginia), 20
(in U. S. Constitution), 139, 185, 202, 203, 204, 240
Blair, John, 73, 76, 82, 184
Blount, William, 75, 142, 184
Board of War and Ordnance, 22
of Trade, British, 13, n. 13
Boston, 14, 17, 19, 22
Massacre, 14
"Boston Tea Party," 14, 15
Bourn, Benjamin, 287, 290
Brearly, David, 74, 81, 184
Brooke, H., 47
Brooks, Colonel, 64
Broom, Jacob, 73, 81, 184
Bryce, James, x
Burgesses, Virginia House of, 15
Burgoyne, 32
Butler, Pierce, 75, 82, 83, 128, 184

Cabot, John, 6
Canada, 11, 18
Carpenters Hall, 15
Carrington, Edward, n. 102
Carroll, Daniel, 73, 184
Carteret, Sir George, 9
Philip, 9
Caswell, Richard, 73
Catholics, 20
Cayuga Indians, n. 12
Census, 124

Charles I, 10
Charles II, 8, 9, 10
Charleston, S. C., 14
Charlestown, Mass., 22
Chase, Chief Justice, 214
Chesapeake Bay, n. 6, 46
Chester, Pa., 77
Civil War, American, 59, 237
Clark, Abraham, 73
Clinton, Governor George, 158
Clymer, George, 75, 152, 184
Coffee illustration by Washington, 101
Collins, Governor, 288
Colonial Legislatures, 13
Colonies, American, 11, 12, 16, 20, 22, 24, 25, 206
  cost of war to, 69
  people of, 134
Colony, each one vote, 15
Columbia University, 72
"Commissioners" at Annapolis, 48
Committee of Correspondence, 16
  of Detail, 134
  of Style, 55, 139, 234
  of the States, 29, 39
"Common Sense" (Paine's), 21
Compact between the States, 237
Concord, Mass., 18, 68
Confederacy, 12, 83, 91, 203, 217, 220, 221
  of States, 59, 66
Confederation, 44, 78, 87, 105
  Congress, 72, 158
  defects, 85
Congress, 13, 15, 16, 17, 20, 21, 23, 24, 25, 26, 29, 30, 31, 32, 33, 36, 37, 41, 42, 44, 48, 50, 51, 64, 68, 69, 70, 208, 221
  debates in, not considered, 2
  Fifth, 44
  powers of, 67

Seventh, 51
submits Constitution, ix
Connecticut compromise, n. 86, 104
  plan, 104
  ratifies, 153
Constitution:
  Article I
    Section 1, 162
    Section 2, 162–164
    Section 3, 164–165
    Section 4, 165–166
    Section 5, 166
    Section 6, 166–167
    Section 7, 167–168
    Section 8, 168–170
    Section 9, 170–172
    Section 10, 172–173
  Article II
    Section 1, 174–177
    Section 2, 177–178
    Section 3, 178
    Section 4, 178
  Article III
    Section 1, 179
    Section 2, 179–180
    Section 3, 180–181
  Article IV
    Section 1, 181
    Section 2, 181–182
    Section 3, 182
    Section 4, 182
  Article V, 182–183
  Article VI, 183
  Article VII, 184
Amendments:
  Article I, 187
  Article II, 188
  Article III, 188
  Article IV, 188
  Article V, 188–189
  Article VI, 189
  Article VII, 189–190
  Article VIII, 190
  Article IX, 190

INDEX

Article X, 190
Article XI, 191
Article XII, 191–193
Article XIII
  Section 1, 193
  Section 2, 193
Article XIV
  Section 1, 193–194
  Section 2, 194
  Section 3, 194
  Section 4, 195
  Section 5, 195
Article XV
  Section 1, 195
  Section 2, 195
Article XVI, 196
Article XVII
  Sections 1, 2, 3, 197
Article XVIII
  Sections, 1, 2, 3, 197
Article XIX, 198
Article XX
  Section 1, 198–199
  Sections 2, 3, 4, 199
  Sections 5, 6, 200
Article XXI
  Section 1, 200
  Section 2, 201
  Section 3, 201
Constitution, a central, vii
  adopted, 141, 227
  amendability of, is unlimited, 213
  compared with Articles of Confederation, 261
  England's, 54
  laid before State Conventions, 143
  of Confederacy, 94
  spirit of, 1
  how amendable, 212
Constitutional Convention (Philadelphia), 20, 48, 51, 52, 72, 77, 83, 219
Constitutionalist, 37

Constitutionality, 234
Constitutions, 36
Continental Army, 19
  Conference, 21
  Congress, 15, 18, 25, 281
    First, 15, 70
    Second, 18
  troops, 25
Continentalist, The, 37
Convention adjournment, 145
  proposed, 42
Conventions, Constitutional, 52, 61, 76, 124, 208, 209
  of States, 38, 203, 206, 207, 208, 210, 218, 219, 222, 223, 224, 225
Cornwallis, Lord, 35
Cost of Revolutionary War, 69

Dana, Francis, 73
Davie, William R., 74, 75, 82
Dayton, Jonathan, 74
Declaration of Independence, vi, vii, viii, 19, 23, 24, 25, 35, 72, 77
  of Rights, 14
Delaware ratifies, 152
  River, 9, 46
Delftshoven, 8
Democratic principle, 92
  vote, 137, 138
Dickinson, John, 43, 73, 96, n. 96, 100, 107, 184, 282
Douglas, Stephen A., 59
Draft plan of Constitution, 88
Dred Scott case, 60
Duane, James, n. 32, 33
Dutch loan, 40, 66

East Greenwich, R. I., 284
Eighteenth Amendment, ix, 61, 204, 210, 213, 219, 236
Elizabeth, Queen, 7, 71
Ellsworth, Oliver, 72, 73, 74, 118, 134, 135, 138, 281

INDEX

Emancipation Proclamation, 60
England, 6, 11, 37, 44, 70, 71, 204
  American treaty with, 38
Equality between States and United States, 239
Erie Canal, 45
Executive, one, 139
Express powers, 229
"Expressly delegated" powers, 230

Federal compact, 67
  Convention, 77
  Government, 48, 85, 89, 91, 235, 236
  judiciary, 94
  system, n. 50
Federalist, The, n. 229
Fenner, Governor, 290
Few, William, 73, 82, 184
Fitzsimons, Thomas, 75, 81, 184
Five Nations, 12
Florida, 11
Fourteenth Amendment, 125, 229
France, 11
  treaty of alliance with (U. S.), 38
Franklin, Benjamin, 14, 20, 22, 25, 68, 71, 74, 75, 77, 92, 123, 141, 142, 152, 184, 282
Free inhabitants, 125
French loan, 66

Gadsden, Christopher, 154
Gage, General, 14, 16
Gardoqui, 44
Gates, Sir Thomas, 6
General Council of Massachusetts, 43
  welfare, 131
    clause, 233
"Gentlemen's agreement," 185
George, King, 71

George II, 10
George III, 14
Georgia ratifies, 153
Gerry, Elbridge, 42, 73, 74, 75, 76, 93, 97, 101, 103, n. 105, 124, 134, 139, 141, 148, 153, 282
Gilman, Nicholas, 74, 184
Gorham, Nathaniel, 67, 74, 104, 134, 135, 184
Grand Committee of Congress, 65, 66, 124
Grayson, William, 156
Great Britain's national debt, 69
Great Lakes, 11
Greene, General, 35
Greenwich, R. I., 286

Hamilton, Alexander, xi, 33, 34, 38, 47, 48, 66, 70, 73, 74, 75, 80, 81, 91, 107, 110, 111, 114, 116, 139, 141, 147, 148, 158, n. 161, 168, 184, n. 229
Hamilton's plan, 107, 108, 109, 110
Hancock, John, 25, 153
Harrigan, Cape, n. 6
Harrisburg, Pa., n. 233
Harrison, Benjamin, 32, 156
  Governor, 40, 67
Hartford, Conn., 9, 33, 41
  Convention, 33
Harvard University, 72
Hatteras, Cape, n. 6
Henrietta Maria, Queen, 10
Henry, Patrick, 20, 40, 72, 74, 76, n. 146, 156, 157, 160
Henry VII, 6
Holland, 11
Houston, William C., 74, 81
Houstoun, William, 73
Hudson River, 9
Hutchinson, Anne, 8

INDEX

Independent States, 118
Indians, 6, 12, 13
Ingersoll, Jared, 75, 184
Inherent sovereign powers, 238
Ingalls, Senator, 208
Iredell, Justice, 211
Ireland, 16, 20

Jackson, William, 82, 184
James I, 6, 7
James II, 10, 13
James River, 45
Jay, John, 38, 41, 44, 45, 71, 158, n. 161, n. 229
Jay's treaty, 38, 39
Jefferson, Thomas, 20, 22, 23, 32, 39, 44, 68, 69, 101, 130, 136
Jenifer, Daniel of St. Thomas, 73, 184
Johnson, Andrew, 197
  Thomas, 151
Johnson, William Samuel, 72, 110, 118, 121, 140, 148, 184, 224, 225, 282
Jones, Joseph, 68
  Walter, 47
  Willie, 73

King, Rufus, 42, 44, 51, 52, 74, 84, 114, 115, 127, 134, 148, 159, 184
Kings County, New York, 158

Lafayette, General, 40
Langdon, John, 74, 184
Lansing, John, 41, 74, 105
"Large State" plan, n. 86
"League of Friendship," 24, 30
Lee, General (Light Horse Harry), 155
  Richard Henry, n. 20, 21, 40, 41, 76, n. 146, 149
  Robert E., 156
Legislature of New York, 37

Legislatures, State, 25, 27, 31, 42, 51, 57, 92, 94, 96, 97, 133, 140, 204, 207, 210, 211, 218, 219, 222, 223, 224, 225
Lexington, Mass., 18
Liberty, 22, 124
Lincoln, Abraham, 59, 193, 206
  James, 154
Livingston, Robert R., 22, 41, 136, 158
  William, 74, 184, 282
Locke, John, 13
London, England, 242
Long Island Sound, 9
Louis XIV, 242

MacDougall, Major General, 64, 66
Madison, James, vi, n. 1, 36, 40, 44, 46, 47, 50, 52, 59, 67, 68, 73, 74, 76, 78, 80, 82, 84, 89, 91, 92, 101, 104, 121, 122, 126, 129, 134, 136, n. 146, 155, 156, 157, 160, n. 161, 185, 204, 215, n. 229, n. 234, 247
Magna Charta, 54
Manhattan Island, 158
Marchant, Henry, 287, 288
Marshall, John, 155, 197
Martin, Alexander, 75, 82
  Luther, 73, n. 105, 117, n. 117, 121, 122
Maryland Assembly, 151
  Convention (1776), 24
  ratifies, 154
Mason, George, 32, 47, 73, 76, 82, 95, n. 95, 99, 101, n. 105, 119, 126, 133, 134, 138, 139, 141, 156, 281, 282
Massachusetts Bay Company, 8
  General Court of, 43
  Legislature, 43

296 INDEX

ratification convention, 153
Mayflower, 8
McClurg, J., 74, 76, 82
McHenry, James, xi, 73, 75, 184
Mecklenburg Declaration of Independence, 19
Mercer, John Francis, 67, 73, 74
Merrimac River, 9
Mexico, Gulf of, 6
Mifflin, Thomas, 74, 75, 184
Mississippi River, 11, 33, 38, 44, 45
Mohawk Indians, n. 12
Valley, 45
Monroe, James, 43, 44, 156
Morris, Gouverneur, 74, 75, 76, 79, 81, 90, 91, 124, 127, 142, 147, 148, 221, n. 234, 282
Robert, 34, 39, 75, 81, 82, 84, 184
Mount Vernon, Va., 46

Narragansett Bay, 8
Natchez, Miss., 45
Nation, 100
of people, 59
National Government, 90, 116
judiciary, 94
legislation, 92, 106
Legislature, n. 87
"National plan" of Virginia, 86
Neilson, John, 73
Nelson, Thomas, 32, 76
Newark, N. J., 9
Newburgh, N. Y., 67
New England, 12
New Hampshire ratifies, 154
New Haven, Conn., 9
New Jersey plan, n. 86, 105, 110, 112, 117, 250–260 (compared with Virginia plan) ratifies, 152
Newport, R. I., 284, 285, 286, 287, 289

New York evacuated by British, 70
ratifies, 158
City, 14, 41, 62, 70, 71, 186
New Orleans, La., 45
Nicholas, 32
Ninth Amendment, 228
North Carolina rejects, 158, 159
trader, 44
North, Lord, motion of, 20, 37, 67
Northwestern Territory, 33, 51

Ogden, Colonel, 64
Oglethorpe, James, 10
Ohio River, 11, 46
Oneida Indians, n. 12
Onondaga Indians, n. 12
Ordinance of 1787, 51
Oswald's Commission, 38
Oxford University, 72
Owen, Deputy Governor, 287

Paine, Thomas, 21
Paterson, William, xi, 73, 74, 75, 81, n. 88, 90, 100, 102, 103, 104, 105, 106, 117, 184
Paulus Hook, 71
Peace between England and United States, 68
Pendleton, Edmund, 155
Nathaniel, 32, 73, 157
Penn, William, 9, 13
Pennsylvania Assembly, 43
Council of, 43
ratifies, 152
University, 72
People, 50, 54, 55, 56, 57, 58, 59, 87, 89, 92, 94, 95, 96, 97, 98, 99, 104, 105, 111, 119, 134, 137, 138, 149, 154, 157, 169, 203, 206, 209, 212, 216, 218, 225, 228,

INDEX

229, 241, 283, 284, 285, 286
Personnel of delegates, 72
Philadelphia, 14, 15, 24, 48, 70, 77, 156, 283
Pickering, John, 73
Pierce, William, xi, 73, 96, n. 96
Pilgrim Fathers, 8
Pinckney, Charles, 20, 49, 74, 75, 80, 82, n. 88, 90, 94, 120, 159, 184
 Charles C., 75, 82, 123, 154, 184, 221
Pitt, William, 14, 45, 67, 68, 71
Plan of Constitution, 88
Plymouth, 8
Popular sovereignty, 283
Portsmouth, N. H., 8
Potomac River, 45, 46
 Valley, 45
Poughkeepsie, N. Y., 158
Powers, expressly delegated, 230
 reserved, 239
Preamble of Constitution, 54, 55, 56, 58, 136, 233
Presbyterians, 9
Princeton, N. J., 70
Prohibition Amendment, ix, 60, 61, 204, 210, 213, 219, 236
Providence, R. I., 8, 284, 285, 286, 287, 289, 290
Puritans, 9

Quakers, English, 9
Quebec, 17, 18
 Act (1774), 11

Raleigh, Sir Walter, 7
Randolph, Edmund, 37, 47, 73, 74, 76, 78, 82, 83, 85, 86, 90, 93, 100, 106, 117, 124, 133, 135, 141, 155, 156, 219
 Peyton, 15

Ratification, 55, 134, 148
 of Constitution, tardy, by Rhode Island, 283
Read, George, 73, 75, 81, 184
Religious freedom, 20
Repealing Amendments or Articles, 62
Representation, equitable, 92
Representative government, 206
Republican principle, 86
Reserved powers of States, 228, 239
Resolutions:
 The Fifteen, 88
 The Nineteen, 88
 The Twenty-three, 88, 221
Revolution, American, 20, 24, 36, 70 (end of)
Revolutionary soldiers, 33, 39
Rhode Island ratifies, 159
Richmond, Virginia, 40
"Rising sun," Franklin's remark about, 142
Rockingham, Lord, 38
Ronald, William, 47
Roosevelt, Franklin Delano, 249
 Theodore, 230, 232, n. 233
Ross, David, 47
Rules of Constitutional Convention, 80, 83
Ruskin, John, 74
Rutledge, Edward, 136
 John, 73, 75, 82, 97, 134, 135, 154, 184

St. John Islands, 6
Savannah, Ga., 20
Schuyler, Philip, 34
Seneca Indians, n. 12
Senate, 63, 100, n. 101, 122, 130, 140
 representation in, 214
Shays, Daniel, 49
Shelburne, Lord, 67
Shepard, General, 49

INDEX

Sherman, Roger, 22, 75, 95, n. 95, 98, 118, 184, n. 234
Signing of Constitution, 141
Single legislative body, 92
Slavery, 42, 51, 59, 60, 126, 130, 213, 214
Slaves, n. 30, 125, 127, 128, 129, 130
Smaller States, 129
Smith, Meriwether, 47
Sole end of government, 128
South, the, 59
South Carolina ratifies, 154
South Kingstown, R. I., 288
Southern States, 59, 127, 128
Southampton, England, 8
Sovereign, 23, 216
  power, definition of, 248
"Sovereign State," 238
Sovereignty, 29, 30, 34, 35, 42, 60, 89, 90, 106, 110, 112, 115, 116, 138, 144, 149
  supreme, 239
Spaight, Richard D., 75, 82, 184
Spain, 11
Spanish possessions, 38
Speedwell, 8
Springfield, Mass., 49
Stairs, Lord, 13
Stamp Act, 14
  Congress, 14
State, 59, 61, 87, 89, 97, 119, 120, 121, 122, 123, 124, 130, 137, 138, 149
  Constitutions, 20, 56, 83
  Governments, 97, 99, 103
  names not inserted, 147
States, 20, 49, 51, 58, 59, 60, 62, 63, 65, 69, 70, n. 72, 77, 79, 83, 84, 85, 86, 89, 90, 92, 93, 95, 96, 100, 102, 103, 104, 105, 114, 115, 120, 121, 122, 123, 132, 133, 134, 140, 141, 144, 149, 151, 154, 157, 202, 205, 228, 229, 235
  equality between, and United States, 239
States' Rights, x, 46, 60, 104, 216, 229, 283
  group, 104
Stevenson, Andrew, n. 234
Story, Justice, xi, 56
Strong, Caleb, 74, 134
Subterfuge, a patriotic, 4
Suffrage, 91, 92
  (Madison's compromise), 126
Sullivan, John, 34
Summary, 249
Sumptuary laws, 281
Supreme Court of United States, 60, 132, 246
Sweden, King of, 37

Taxation, 14
Tenth Amendment, 228
Thompson, Charles, 146
Thornton, Matthew, 24
Townshend Act, 14
Treaty different from Constitution, 136
  of Paris (1782), 38
  of 1763, 10
  with England, 70
Trenton, N. J., 41
Tucker, St. George, 47
Tuscarora Indians, n. 12
Tyler, John, 46, 156

Unconstitutionality, 234
Union, 32, 43, 47, 50, 51, 57, 59, 90, 92, 151, 159, 216
United States, 51, 59, n. 87, 61, 120, 132, 138
  Constitution, 228, 229

Varnum, James M., 37, 115
Varnum's letter to Washington, n. 115

INDEX

Veto, 93
  power of States, 63
Vincennes, Ind., 45
Virginia Convention, 155, 156
  Legislature, 45, 46, 52
  plan, 78, 86, 89, 92, 93, 97, 104, 105, 110, 112, 116, 117, 122
    and New Jersey plan compared, 251
  ratifies, 160
  resolution (1786), 47
    (1787), 92
Voting, 91

Walton, George, 73
War of 1812, American, 68
Warwick, R. I., 284
Washington, George, 19, n. 20, 22, 32, n. 32, 33, 34, 40, 44, 45, 52, 67, 68, 69, 71, 72, 73, 74, 75, 76, 82, 101, 115, 134, 143, 145, 151, 154, 155, 159, 184, 240

Webster, Noah, 41
  Pelatiah, 36
West, Benjamin, 73
Westchester County, New York, 158
Wethersfeld, Conn., 9
William and Mary University, 72, 76
Williams, Roger, 8
Williamson, Hugh, 75, 82, 184
Wilmington, N. C., n. 6
Wilson, James, 74, 75, 76, 93, 97, 100, 103, 118, 128, 134, 135, 136, 150, 152, 184, 230, 231, 232, n. 240
Windsor, Conn., 9
Wythe, George, 32, 75, 76, 80, 82, 83, 155, n. 157

Yates, Robert, xi, 74, n. 81, n. 105, 125
Yazoo, 54
York, Duke of, 9
Yorktown, Va., 27